Vera

To my darling
Irène

Vera

The amazing autobiography of
VERA CHESNO
written at the age of 94

With contributions from
Irène Noah and Aubrey Rose

Lennard Publishing

First published in 2001 by
Lennard Publishing
a division of
Lennard Associates Ltd
Mackerye End, Harpenden
Herts AL5 5DR

A version of this book was published as *The Long Road*
in 1990 by The Book Guild

A catalogue entry is available from the British Library.

ISBN 1 85291 147 6

Editor for Lennard Publishing: Michael Leitch
Jacket design: Paul Cooper Design

Printed and bound in Great Britain
by Biddles

CONTENTS

FOREWORD

This is a rare tale, encompassing extremes of wealth and poverty, safety and terror, glowing health and despairing illness, played out against the sombre background of the 1917 Russian Revolution and the grim era of Nazi madness.

What a century it was! Against its turbulent background we can observe the life of Vera Chesno, born in 1891 into an opulent family of Latvian Jews, a wealthy handful of people living amidst widespread Jewish misery, an elegant young woman whose life was thrown into turmoil by the Bolshevik menace and whose escape reads like some figment of a thriller-writer's imagination. But, for her, it was truth, not fiction.

France between the two world wars, with its blinkered gaiety, became the next station on her journey, a world of pampered illusion, blown apart by the Panzers in 1940. Again escape, Vichy France, partner in crime with its German overseers, episode after heart-stopping episode to avoid capture, relief at the Allied victory, only to be plunged, post-war, into a battle against illness, that of Irène, her precious daughter and only child.

For years the two of them battled, and the two of them overcame. Switzerland was the scene of this encounter, the sickly enclosed world of the TB clinic.

Emerging yet again into daylight, the long road they traversed together brought them to England, where, resolute to the end, Vera Chesno passed on to happier fields in 1985 at the ripe age of 94.

Meanwhile Irène, a victim of Nazism, the endless perils of near-capture and perpetual malnutrition, fell prey to a further illness, a marked sensitivity to all chemicals, yet, before that, she was able to make her mark in the world in unusual forms, reflecting the determination of her mother not to be beaten by soulless fate.

Throughout this remarkable story runs the golden thread of modern Jewish history. Vera's family was not only rich but also learned. We read of business correspondence carried on in Hebrew and Yiddish. The story embraces a host of Jewish luminaries: Nahum Sokolov, Chaim Weizmann and Shalom Aleichem (of *Fiddler on the Roof* fame).

Out of this accomplished multilingual family came the celebrated historian Sir Isaiah Berlin. Even the noted Bar-Ilan University in Israel took its name from Meir Berlin, another relative, whose surname was changed to Bar-Ilan.

We read of the Rothschilds, of Jabotinsky, names more widely known than the Hindin clan from which Vera emerged, though the Schneersons, founders of the Russian village of Lubavich, were also relatives, closely allied.

An even more illustrious ancestor was Rabbi Shneur Zalman of Lyady, the eighteenth-century founder of Habad Hassidism, one of the most fascinating religious movements of the modern era. It was inevitable that the Bolshevik Marxists would relentlessly and cruelly pursue those who had enjoyed wealth. It was just as inevitable that the race-crazed Nazis would hound Vera and her family for being born Jews. She lost, in the Holocaust, not only her husband, but also forty relatives.

All this she endured, survived, living life abundantly when permitted, escaping death breathtakingly, time after time. Even at the age of ninety, her daughter records with pride, she glowed. Her story, and Irène's, records the triumph of the human spirit over prosperity and adversity alike, and over a relentless catalogue of bitter experiences that would have felled and destroyed a lesser being.

Aubrey Rose, CBE, D Univ

THE FRONTIER

The Frontier consisted of a main road between two fields. There were two ways of crossing it, the peasant told us: either you crawled on your stomach till you reached the road and then made a dash for it, or else you crawled through a disused pipe which passed under the road. The danger above-ground was that the Germans hid in the long grass in the field and shot at any point where they saw grass moving. The danger below ground was that the Germans had discovered the existence of the pipe and would let the traveller inch his way almost to the end of it and then aim a machine gun into it and let go. We chose to go above ground. The possibility of being shot at in the open seemed less terrifying than being shot at in a pipe.

At two o'clock in the morning we began the perilous journey, crawling on our stomachs over fields and under hedges. The ground was full of thistles and Irène, who wore ankle socks and a short skirt, tore her skin as we crawled towards the frontier.

Suddenly the peasant motioned us into a ravine, urging us to lie quite still. To my horror I heard the barking of a dog. It was well known in France that that on the frontiers the Gestapo had fierce Alsatian police dogs who searched for refugees and tore them to pieces. There I was, holding the hand of my child, alone in a field except for the guide, near an Alsatian who would certainly maul us to death. I could not even pray, reproaching myself for bringing Irène here, for not finding a better way to save her young life. My mind a whirl, what did I not think of in these terrible few minutes as I listened to the barking of the dog, waiting for what I believed to be the end ....

My life flashed through my mind.

CHAPTER 1

Our Life in Riga

Our spacious apartment in Riga was in a corner house overlooking a magnificent park. At the entrance to the park was a wooden shield on which was elaborately written: 'FORBIDDEN TO DOGS AND JEWS'. We saw the park from our windows, but we never, never went into it.

As a small child I could never understand what dogs and Jews had in common to keep them out of a public garden. It was never explained to me, but even if it had been, I doubt whether I would have understood.

We had a grand apartment in Riga. The contents were magnificent. A special trip had been made to Venice to acquire the furniture. The chandeliers had been made in Murano. Mother was proud of her exquisite Savonnerie carpets of the palest green and pink, with hand-embroidered curtains to match.

Some years later, when the 1917 Revolution was at its height, we saw a soldier on the road wearing a funny pair of riding breeches – pale-green heavy silk, with pink roses on his behind. Mother at once recognised the Venetian curtains, which had been looted from our house. I said, 'So what's wrong with a couple of roses on his bottom?' Mother was not amused!

Despite the notice in the park, life was good for us in Riga, at least compared with that of our less fortunate Jewish brethren who lived in villages, especially in Russia. They toiled on the land from morning till night, or peddled their wares wherever they could to make ends meet. For them, life in Tsarist Russia, which then included Latvia, was hard, with harassment commonplace. Our lifestyle, by comparison, was sheltered. Education and wealth afforded a certain amount of protection, though the Bolshevik uprising was to shatter it – not because we were Jews, but because, in their eyes, we were too comfortable for the system! Until that time, however, life at home was beautiful and we enjoyed it to the full. Happy days indeed.

My mother's forebears, the brothers Isaiah and Schlomo Zalman Berlin, were among the best-known timber merchants and manufacturers in Riga. They owned large forests and many factories. The scale of their exports made them leading figures in the timber trade.

Isaiah Berlin (a later family luminary was to bear the same name) was married to the daughter of Menahem Nahum Schneerson of Niezin, a great-granddaughter of Rabbi Schneur Zalman of Lyady, the founder of Habad Hassidim, a movement famous in modern Judaism.

My maternal grandfather, Siskind Alexander Berlin, was a philosopher, a learned man, with silver-white hair and a long, silky, white beard. His eyes were a striking pale blue, his skin almost translucent white. He was tall and slim, with refined manners, always faintly smelling of Eau de Cologne. He passed his days in study and was a correspondent of the Russian Academy in St Petersburg, and famous professors made the journey to Riga to discuss philosophical matters with him. However, he was frail, lived frugally and almost never travelled.

As grandfather always felt cold, my grandmother had a special pair of trousers made for him to wear while he studied. These were so heavily quilted that they stood up on their own. I still remember my fright when, as a child, I passed my grandfather's open door one evening and saw the trousers standing by themselves. Grandfather had already gone to bed. The sight of those trousers standing upright in the moonlit room filled me with ghostly terror.

My paternal grandfather, Jacob Hindin, was the complete opposite. Though also tall, he was heavily built, with black eyes, black hair and a long black beard.

He owned many forests, and also an alcohol factory. His wealth was enormous. Through a second marriage, he became the brother-in-law of the famous Rabbi Schmuel Mohilever, a precursor of modern Zionism, who persuaded him to take an interest in the resettlement of Eretz Israel, the land of Israel. Grandfather Hindin purchased the Hedera lands there for his son-in-law Schneur Zvi Schneerson, one of the sons of the then Lubavicher Rebbe. Schneur was an early settler in Hedera, where his descendants continue to live.

When my grandfather Hindin visited us in Riga and learned that my sister, Raissa, was going to start school in the autumn, the scandal was terrible. He was furious that Raissa would sit next to children not of her own faith, and was certain that if she were influenced by the clergy she would end by rejecting her religion. He lost his temper, which was always short, and threatened to curse my mother and force father to divorce her. It needed all the love and tact of my parents to appease his wrath.

Raissa went to school on the strict understanding that she would not travel on Saturday, the Sabbath, but would be brought by the governess on foot. Nor would she write or carry her books on that day. Teachers had to be approached one by one, bribed, cajoled, and given to understand that Jewish law forbade work on the Sabbath, and that the child could not forsake her allegiance in any way. Some teachers were spiteful and would arrange for the most important written examinations to be held precisely on those days. On such occasions the child would have a 'zero' marked in her book.

When the time came for me to go to school, my parents, grandfather, and assorted uncles and aunts questioned me. They asked, for example, 'If a teacher ordered you to write on the Sabbath, would you do it?' I said I thought I probably would. So, as writing is strictly forbidden on the Jewish Sabbath, there was no school for me for another year.

The following year, the same question was put to me. This time I answered categorically that I would not do it. My school years began. I was eight years old. I had not fallen behind because teachers had coached me at home, but the year was lost all the same.

On the Sabbath there was no horse to take me to school. Instead, we often had to trudge through the snow and sleet, without umbrellas, as it was forbidden to carry anything on the Sabbath. Then, to have to sit with idle hands whilst the other pupils were busy writing was quite an ordeal for me.

Our French governess, Mlle Teillard de Querdrelle, was a fussy old maid with perfect manners and a good background. Her nails were exceedingly long, and she could do nothing with her fingers because of them. She was titled but poor, and considered Russia and all surrounding countries savage and of no interest whatsoever.

In the many years she lived with us she learned but one word of Russian. That word was *Swinia*. She never knew what it meant but thought it sounded nice. In fact, it means 'pig'. Her task was to teach us French and supervise our manners, and since we were all at school, this proved easy enough. She could relax and enjoy the good food, the comfort and her considerable salary.

My father, Zalman Hindin, was very wealthy. He owned forests, factories and seven ships, and these provided the only means of transport and freight along a vast territory on either side of the long River Dvina. There were, moreover, many towns and villages in this area. Railways were not built until many years later.

Father originally had four ships and a competitor three. Competition was fierce. At one stage, father gave everyone who boarded his ship a *bulka* – a small roll of bread. Upon hearing this, the competitor gave everyone who boarded his ship a *bulka* with sugar on top. It could not go on, and father eventually bought out his competitor.

The peasant women who travelled from their village to the next always tried very hard to avoid paying their fares. One in particular, a wizened old *babushka*, would sit on her little bundle of possessions and say: 'The guv'nor is so rich, surely one seat does not make a difference to him, especially as it is not a seat but my own little bundle.' The captain was a kind-hearted man and invariably let her travel free.

Father also owned a great number of forests, where timber suitable for pit props and the masts of ocean ships grew. Timber was the real family business, all kinds of softwood being shipped to England and Holland and many other countries. It was worked in factories in Riga and elsewhere in the Baltic, and would arrive by water, tied together by heavy ropes.

Father's many employees were devoted to him. Most of their forefathers had worked for his family for generations. Some lived in Riga. Many lived in the towns and villages along the river, but none lived in St Petersburg, which was out-of-bounds to Jews. Having to see a captain of a ship with his half-yearly report was, therefore, something of a problem, most of the captains being Jews. In Riga it was easier to get them a permit to stay a few days; in St Petersburg, it was almost impossible.

We lived in Riga until the First World War. An urgent request was then made by the military forces to transfer all the factories to St Petersburg. The Germans were getting nearer and everything important had to be saved. Several trains with platforms and wagons were brought as close as possible to the factory.

There was enough room too for those of our own belongings which mother would never leave behind, belongings which themselves represented quite a fortune. Our nine-roomed apartment in Riga, especially built to my mother's specification, contained the rarest furniture, including a grand salon equipped with antique Venetian furniture, *objets d'art* and armchairs with so much hand-carving that they were more pleasant to look at than to sit on. All these had to be packed by experts and sent to St Petersburg.

Then there was the question of my grandfathers. Grandfather Hindin lived in the country, away from the path of the German advance, so, true to form, he stayed – against everybody's advice – while grandfather Berlin would not leave Riga and stayed in his own house to the end because his books and manuscripts were too fragile to be transported. But all this was much later, after my childhood in Riga..

CHAPTER 2

Summers in the Baltic

Our summer villas away from the city of Riga were built in the middle of pine woods. Father bought a whole estate of uncut pine trees. Enormous trees were felled, made into planks in father's factories, and brought back to the clearings. Wooden houses were then constructed upon brick foundations. By law, an architect had to be employed to sign the papers, but the real planning was always done by father himself. He had a genuine talent for architecture, and his buildings in town were well known and admired.

Father built three villas, a large one for us, another for my married sister, and a third with two storeys for grandfather Berlin and my mother's married sister, who lived there together in the summer. Our villa had spacious rooms and verandas. An open veranda led directly into the garden, while a covered one served as a dining-room, seating about thirty. With family, friends, and friends of friends, it was almost always full.

My two brothers, students at Riga University, would bring guests, more often boys though sometimes girls. The boys would stay overnight but the girls never did.

Our summer exodus from Riga to the seaside usually began in May. Trunks were brought in, enormous monsters in wickerwork on wooden platforms, weighing tons! They were filled with household goods, linen, personal effects, foodstuffs, indeed everything a large family expecting numerous visitors would need.

It is with great joy that I remember those days, and especially the time in Latvia when Sholem Aleichem, one of the world's greatest Jewish writers, stayed in our beautiful summer villa on the edge of the Baltic Sea.

Sholem Aleichem would gather all the children around him and tell us the most witty and fascinating stories. We would even collect our neighbours' children to join in the fun.

He always felt cold, and we children were quite astounded to see this rather thin, small man taking his walk wrapped in a warm coat and hat, a huge scarf dangling from his neck, not to mention his large galoshes with garish violet-coloured woollen linings. Had it been winter, perhaps we would not have giggled, but in the middle of summer!

Sholem Aleichem was to us a Jewish Hans Christian Andersen. Wherever he went, a crowd of children followed – they knew he told the most wonderful stories. I doubt if there are many left who can remember this witty, whimsical character, who enchanted us with his stories – some sad, some delightfully funny. One, *The Enchanted Tailor*, concerned a billy goat who could change into a nanny goat and then back again. These antics eventually drove the poor tailor mad.

Little did we know while listening to the tale of *Tevye der Milchiger* ('Tevye the Dairyman') that years later we would see Topol play that character in the famous stage show and film *Fiddler on the Roof*, based on Sholem Alecheim's story. Had he lived to see this, the author would have been a rich man indeed, and a very happy man.

As it was, he knew both extreme poverty and great wealth. In 1890, a year before I was born, he became bankrupt, but his mother-in-law came to the rescue a year later and paid off all his debts.

Sholem Aleichem's health was not good, which probably accounted for his peculiar clothes. He suffered from tuberculosis, which unfortunately was passed on to a member of my family, but, for all that, he was always a much-loved guest.

I confess I used to show off a little, trotting along holding Sholem Aleichem's hand as we gathered up the children to take them home to listen at our special story times. Of course the adults had their treats too. Sometimes he would stand in the middle of the room, his scarf still dangling around his neck, everyone seated around, enthralled. He was a great actor and made each tale come vividly to life. His visits were an unforgettable and treasured part of my childhood.

The villa on the Baltic was our fairytale summer palace. The inner salon was used to receive people on rainy days. There stood the piano, indispensable since we could all play. Sports were welcome, especially croquet, at which mother was outstanding. Tennis was, as yet, unknown, but croquet we played regularly in front of the house. The area was well looked after by the gardeners. In the event of rain, umbrellas would come out if the party was interesting. Father, who never took part in sports, not even croquet, noticed the umbrellas and wet feet and had a mobile roof built over the croquet pitch. He also installed electric light, thus enabling play to continue in the evening or in rainstorms.

Sea-bathing every morning was a ritual, although there were some difficulties to be overcome. Men and women were not allowed to bathe together. Instead there were special hours for males and females, with police on the beach to ensure good order. My nephew, very tall for his eleven years, came one day to fetch his mother during the women's hour. Pandemonium! 'A man is here, a man came.' The women were furious and called the police. When his mother asked him why he had come during women's hour, he replied candidly: 'Mother, how could I know whether they were men or women? They were all naked.' Sexual instruction in the schools was then unheard of. Children were innocent and unknowing. Bathing suits were never worn, so everybody was quite naked. In previous years, before the sexes were separated, when the resort was unknown and before father's villas were built, anybody could bathe at any time of the day, man, woman, child or dog.

Mother, always a most elegant woman, ordered a special bathing costume consisting of trousers down to the ankles, a long coat-like dress, and a hat and gloves – yes, gloves! Her brother joked that if she wore galoshes, not a drop of water would touch her body!

My mother's brother was a learned type, so gifted in languages that there was scarcely a major language which he did not quickly learn to speak. At home we spoke our native tongue as well as French, German and English, but this uncle also spoke Dutch, Swedish, Norwegian and who knows how many others. He was also very good at croquet, but his real interest was in gambling. We all played a kind of bridge, but, as children, were not allowed to participate in blackjack, twenty-one, or home roulette, games which my uncle played almost every evening. He had great talent as a comic and today could have been one of the best-known comedians. He was born ahead of his time.

A skeleton staff was left in town between May and September each year to prepare father's meals, while one of the governesses usually looked after the younger children who remained there with him. The children incidentally had not only a French governess and an English governess, but also a Hebrew teacher who lived in the house.

Father commuted every evening by train. The husbands' train arrived each evening at six o'clock and on Fridays, preparing early for the weekend, at twelve noon. Each husband would be laden with parcels brought from town by special order of their wives, and, towards autumn, with parcels going back for the winter. The chief difficulty lay in sending back to town the pounds and pounds of jam which, under mother's supervision, was made in the summer by our cooks. This jam was made in the garden in enormous copper cauldrons, family heirlooms passed from mother to daughter.

Father only ate strawberry jam, mother insisted on blackcurrant, I only ate wild strawberry, and Raissa only black cherry. Consequently, each had his or her favourite preserves made with their name pasted on the containers. Each earthenware container held twenty to thirty, sometimes forty, pounds. They had to be put on the train by servants, taken out on arrival and then put on the horse-drawn carriages which came to fetch the gentlemen at the station.

I shall never forget how a member of my family, having been given a huge container of jam, had the misfortune to have it placed on the luggage rack. In the process, the porter banged it on a metal strip and, very slowly, heavy red syrup, exactly the colour of blood, started to seep out of the container. The police were called. A crime had obviously been committed! A corpse was travelling in an earthenware container! The police could not find the owner, although they soon found out that it was not blood! Nobody would admit having anything to do with it, so forty pounds of good black cherry jam was lost.

Many years later, after the untimely death of our parents, we found glass jars in the kitchen cupboards containing different jams, our names still pasted on the sides. We sent them to the local hospital. None of us felt like eating any of it with our beloved parents gone. It would have reminded us too much of those wonderful days.

CHAPTER 3

Memories of My Family

At one time, two of my brothers were students at the university in St Petersburg. The elder one, Tonia, was rather shy, very studious, would rarely go out and passed his evenings at home or, occasionally, at the theatre. The younger, Mulia, was lively, extrovert, full of fun and *joie de vivre*. He had tremendous success with women, knew it, liked it and revelled in it.

He was the best dancer in the ballroom, a gifted pianist, a chess and bridge player. He also had an innate talent for engineering. At the age of thirteen, his knowledge of electricity was so well-developed that grandfather Berlin gave him the freedom of his house to install electricity, then something of a rarity. That successfully achieved, Mulia also invented a device which automatically turned out the electric light at a certain time on Friday evenings, and then restored it on Saturday night. This was important, for grandfather was deeply religious, and strictly observed the rules of the Jewish Sabbath, including not switching on electric lights.

My brother asked father to let him have a shed in the factory grounds for his electrical experiments, and many a time he played truant from school. He would go to his shed in the early morning and come back in time for tea. It took weeks for the school to discover that he was not ill at home. My parents were most annoyed when, after many weeks, they found out from the management of the factory, where the staff were his best friends, that he passed all his truant days there.

Mother had a beautiful silver fox stole. One day, she was amazed to discover that the fox had lost its luxurious large tail. Months later, it was discovered under a glass cheese dome in my brother's shed. Mulia's explanation was that you could get the best electricity from this tail. By this time, of course, most of the hair had gone, and the tail presented a sorry semblance of its past luxury.

Students at that time wore uniform, and the richer the student, the more luxurious the uniform. My eldest brother did not believe in flashy attire, but my second brother most certainly did. The numerous buttons of the uniform had to be gold, and the trousers royal blue, but the tunic could be dark navy with a dark lining. My eldest brother's uniform was as discreet as possible. Mulia, however, had his uniform in the brightest blue, lined with white satin, and, when out in the afternoon for a stroll, was dressed to kill. No wonder all the girls on the Nevsky Prospect knew him, and smiled at him, trying to attract his attention. It was sometimes embarrassing to walk with him. My eldest brother despised all this flashiness, but most probably envied him his success.

My sister Raissa was eighteen when the question of marriage came up. She had finished school, and passed all her examinations. The French and German governesses had done their best, and, as neither of them ever learned a word of Russian, which they considered barbaric, we children were forced to speak to them in their native tongues, something which had become quite familiar to us. Now, well 'finished', Raissa was ready to be married.

The marriage-broker came many times with eligible young men. The young men were brought to tea, sometimes from far away. The whole family was present, all later giving their opinion. The young lady was also asked her opinion. Not that this made any difference. The opinions of parents, grandparents, aunts and uncles were the ones that counted. One aunt had a younger brother who was rather shy, but had met my sister several times and found her rather attractive. My uncle came with the marriage proposal and a meeting was arranged. My mother was not happy about this young man. His manners were not good enough; he could not speak French, but women's opinions did not count. My sister had no opinion, but listened to what she was told. The marriage was arranged, the wedding dress ordered, and that was that. Whether rich or poor,

Jewish tradition demanded that parents and family knew best when it came to match-making. My sister's marriage was no exception. There were no exceptions to the rules.

The day of the wedding came, complete with Jewish canopy, the ladies all adorned with jewels and finery. The bride was there, the Rabbis – everybody except the bridegroom. Messengers were sent to his home, telephone calls made, but nothing helped – he had just vanished! Several hours later, towards evening, the bridegroom arrived in a rather crumpled condition, pale and rushed. The workmen who were supposed to have given him a wedding party in the morning, had detained him instead and put impossible conditions to him with regard to their wages and work. It had taken a whole day of negotiations to appease them.

The honeymoon was spent in Venice. Neither the bride nor the groom had had any previous sexual experience. This was quite normal for the bride, but the bridegroom, aged twenty-six, also knew nothing about the facts of life. The inevitable happened. The bride flew out of the room into the corridor in the middle of the night, crying and screaming hysterically that her husband had become raving mad and obviously wanted to kill her, and that someone should get a doctor quickly to take him to an institution. A doctor came. Handicapped as he was with no knowledge of languages other than Italian and a very little English, he took until the morning to explain to both of them what life was, what marriage meant, and so on. Their married life did not start smoothly, and left a bitter feeling ever after.

My parents' marriage had also been arranged. When their fathers had finished with the 'arranging', the two young people met for the first time. The great step came when father was introduced to mother. There entered two young men. My mother and grandmother asked a passing relative if the smart, rather good-looking young man on the right was the bridegroom. 'Oh no. That is his elder brother, married with a son. The other one is the bridegroom.' My father had just recovered from a very serious illness, typhoid fever, which not only left him extremely thin and pale, but also deprived him of most of his hair. Although he was almost nineteen years of age, he only looked fifteen.

Mother and grandmother both fainted and had to be taken to the next room and comforted, and the story had to be hushed up. Ladies of better-class society easily fainted and nobody took any notice of it. Yet there never was a happier marriage than that of my parents. Not for a day were they apart. Fifty years later, they celebrated their golden wedding and went for a second honeymoon to a hotel in Italy. Everybody was under the impression that they were honeymooners and Chaliapin, the great Russian singer, who was staying at the hotel, asked them why they had waited so long to get married!

It was no wonder, then, that young ladies got quite a shock when they were eventually married, for sex was never mentioned in our education, and more often than not, the young men were just as naive. One wonders how large families sprang forth, but of course nature will always find a way. Still, there must have been shocks and surprises, especially on the wedding night. It would be quite correct to say that couples grew to love each other, and even if they hated the sight of their spouse, they just had to grin and bear it.

But in most cases parents chose well, and newlyweds knew at heart that they just had to make the best of it. There were none of the trial 'marriages' of today; such a thing was unheard of. For all that, I believe families were happier then than they are now.

CHAPTER 4

Trouble in the Land

The year was 1905. The Russo-Japanese War had just been lost. The sense of shame was enormous and the country was in a state of unrest. A scapegoat had to be found, and the oldest of them all was inevitably chosen. The pogroms began. In the villages, police would tell the peasants that for two days from Monday they could kill and rob the Jews. For those two days everything was permitted. On Wednesday, at two o'clock, everything had to stop. The inhabitants of whole villages would come to the little towns and hamlets, rob and rape, and for two days slaughter as many people as they could, taking away everything they could carry and burning the rest.

The reasons given for allowing all this were, first, that the Jews had killed Christ, and second, that they had made Russia lose the war, and so had to be punished. The fact that these Jews had neither killed Christ nor lost the war was quite immaterial. On Wednesday at two o'clock the police would restore order and everybody had to go home. The dead were buried, the half-dead killed, and everything was all right again.

Not everybody in Russia, however, believed that it was the Jews who had made Russia lose the war, and young people began to be resentful of many things, apart from the treatment of the Jews, who were of no great interest to anybody.

With the help of wealthier Jews, the great exodus started. Committees and societies were formed, money was sent, help was desperately needed – and help was given. But there were millions of Jews and the need was enormous. Not everybody was rich and not everybody was willing to go. Only a few people reached America, the land of plenty. Some were stuck in England, in Liverpool, not knowing that Liverpool was not in America.

Unrest was rife throughout Russia. Strikes broke out in the

factories, and the director of father's factories was carted out on a wheelbarrow – a sign that, if he ever came back, he would be killed. Father, notwithstanding the advice of those around him, went alone to speak to the strikers, leaving his family crying with worry. Eventually, after explaining many things, and promising others, his was the only factory which started normal work again. We continued our sheltered existence, surrounded by governesses and nannies.

CHAPTER 5

My Brothers and Sisters

The nanny who looked after Raissa and Tera, my two elder sisters, was now very old and retired but still lived in the house, rather like a house guest. She had no responsibilities, but helped sometimes in the kitchen, and the cook accepted it only to give the old lady pleasure. Sometimes her eagerness to help was not too welcome.

Once, the two elder girls were ill with dysentery. The doctor tried everything, including putting them on a strict diet. Nothing helped. They got steadily worse until they were on the danger list. Mother then discovered by sheer chance that Nanny, who came daily to comfort the girls, had been bringing them a large piece of salted herring and a slice of black bread, as they were hungry and miserable. Nanny's visits were forcibly stopped, and the children were soon out of danger.

Tonia, my eldest brother, contracted typhoid fever, and the nurse engaged to look after him contracted the disease herself and had to be sent to hospital. Mother then decided to look after Tonia herself, complete with a special white apron and gloves. It was beautiful summer weather, and we were staying in our villa. One room was converted into a hospital and locked with a key that mother kept in her pocket.

We five children, seven cousins and lots of friends living close to our villa were regularly in and out of the garden for croquet, other games and general entertainment. At tea-time there might be as many as thirty children enjoying a splendid tea of sandwiches, cakes, fruit and sweets.

We felt sorry that poor Tonia was missing all the fun, and found a way of easing his loneliness. His room was on the ground floor with windows overlooking the garden. The door was always locked, but in the summer heat the windows were wide open. What could be easier than placing a bench next to the window and jumping in and out? Buba, our baby brother, had to be helped by two children to come and sit on Tonia's bed. Somebody would keep watch for mother and everybody would jump out quickly if she were heard approaching. Tonia was ill the whole summer, probably because some of the children brought him sweets, but he recovered and no-one was any the worse for these forbidden visits. Had mother known, however, we would have been in terrible trouble.

The adults would play croquet or Kegli, a bowling game, with mother the champion, while in the morning there was swimming in the sea with, of course, separate hours for men and women. In the evening there were always numerous friends, and the table on the veranda would seat more than thirty people, who were there almost every evening. At the weekend several people stayed overnight, and the ballroom on the top floor was arranged as a dormitory where all my brothers' student friends could pass the night.

In the summer, when so many relatives and friends stayed at the villa, my room was invariably given to a relative and I had to stay with Buba and his French nanny. It was not very comfortable, but better than sleeping on a couch in the drawing-room, through which people were constantly passing from the garden. In any case, one hardly minded in those happy days. Little did we know how few of them we had left.

My second sister, Tera, wanted to study in Paris, and as it was quite impossible for a young unmarried lady to do so alone in the town of Toulouse-Lautrec, Zola and the Folies-Bergère, it was necessary for my brother, Tonia, to accompany her. Tera studied French, literature and history, and Tonia, chemistry, for which he was gifted. They both graduated with first-class honours.

Tera was different from all the other children. She was envious and intolerant, and could not forgive me for being many years younger, blonde, and for playing the piano quite well. After my first concert, at the age of twelve, she forbade me to play Beethoven because, she claimed, she alone could and should play it. It needed all mother's tact and understanding to explain to her that now, at the age of twenty-six, and still unmarried, she should leave home, find an occupation, study something. Her dowry would provide sufficient income for her to live on. She declined the proposition. More and more marriage-brokers came to the house, and more and more young men were brought to tea, only to depart disappointed.

Father employed many people in his office. His patience was proverbial, and such was his dedication to teaching them the intricacies of the timber trade that they were all very successful afterwards. Father had one such office boy who was vaguely related to him, but came from a small Jewish settlement. He was shy and rather simple. He would look at Tera in the rare moments when they met as one would look at a queen, or even, perhaps, a goddess. In time, father advised him to leave as he was now mature enough to start a business of his own. He guided him in his first purchases, sometimes losing money on him, but knowing that he would soon be able to stand on his own feet.

When the young man had become successful, he went to live in St Petersburg, where he had a large office and a flat. Tera decided to marry him. My parents were flabbergasted. She told everybody that the marriage would be purely platonic. As proof, she arranged separate bedrooms on either side of the very large flat. It was quite a journey from one bedroom to the other, and became something of a family joke. She would get furious at the tiniest suggestion that all was not quite platonic. When their daughter was born, Tera even tried hard to make people believe that this was some kind of miraculous conception!

My brother Mulia was the most gifted of all the family. Whatever he attempted, be it languages, the piano, chess or bridge, he mastered. Many years later, we sometimes read in the newspapers about his success as a grandmaster in chess, or as the best Australian bridge player. His life was complicated. There was plenty of variety, some happiness and much sorrow.

After 1914, during the First World War, he was sent to London by the government on a special mission to buy important parts for war machinery. He was rather lonely away from his family and friends, especially having left his true love behind. She could not travel with him on a government mission, but promised to follow as soon as possible.

In Archangel, ships were arriving from England with war ammunition and returning empty. With much difficulty and quite a bit of bribery, a few persons, very few, could leave for England. It was arranged for Mulia's young lady to be taken on a certain convoy. She was to go to Archangel and wait, as there was no proper schedule and nobody knew when a ship would arrive. She decided to smarten herself up for her imminent marriage, and ordered a new coat. When news came that she was to be in Archangel on a certain date, the coat was not ready and she decided to postpone her departure until the next ship arrived. The 'next ship' never arrived, and she never reached London.

Mulia waited patiently. He had prepared everything and had even bought a house. Having received news that she had missed the last boat, he was in despair. He started to drink and went out too much with girls.

One evening, he met a very young inexperienced girl. She immediately fell head-over-heels in love with him. He took her home, played the piano to her, charmed her as he well knew how, and, in due course, the inevitable happened.

Notwithstanding his flippancy with women, he had never before found himself in a situation where a virgin, a nice, clean girl, was made pregnant by him. The only right thing was to marry her, which he did. However, he took some time to arrive at this decision, the girl starting her labour pains on the way to the registry office!

Tonia, my first brother, was a straightforward, honest man with no special qualities. He could not play the piano, did not take part in games, was very awkward and even clumsy when dancing, and extremely shy with girls. He was a complete contrast to Mulia. He was quite good-looking, but made nothing of it. He finished school with all the necessary grades and even with a gold medal, but this was nothing unusual for a boy of Jewish origin.

In those towns where Jews had to have a special permit to reside, schools and universities all had a *numerus clausus*, restricting the number of Jews admitted. People with university degrees could live in all the normally prohibited towns, but to get to university was almost impossible. Even people living in such towns in Russia had great difficulty in getting their children into good schools.

The government schools had somewhat rowdy and boisterous children to cope with. The better-class schools, half-private, were all under the supervision of government directors and a very strict *numerus clausus* was applied. With father by then having to place six children, three girls and three boys, into the better schools, it was hard work and very costly.

In the exclusive school where we three girls finished our studies, the arrangement was that each child paid three times the normal school fees which, in a private school, were already several times higher than in a government school. No parents with means would have dreamt of sending their children to a government school. The anti-Semitism was appalling and not only the children, but also the teaching staff, made a point of making the lonely Jewish boy or girl the target of hatred and humiliation.

CHAPTER 6

Lausanne

I left school and music college at a very early age. As the youngest child but one in our family, I had to prove that I was as clever as the others. So, after enormous effort, I finished school at the same time as my brother, who was four years my senior. At fifteen I was too young for university, and so went instead to a finishing school in Lausanne, in Switzerland. By a strange irony, Switzerland was to feature dramatically in my later life.

Here they taught French and English, which I knew, as well as the history of music and art. I passed the examination at the local Conservatoire and was taught by a well-known professor of music. This was much better than being taught by the house teacher, an old maid who played very badly, less well, in fact, than either I or the other girl who passed the examination with me. The two of us went to music lessons accompanied by a governess from the school.

Yet what really preoccupied us was this: how could we buy some chocolate! Strict rules prohibited it; no-one was permitted to buy anything in town. Chocolate was given, just once a day, and then only a very small piece to each girl. In Switzerland, where the chocolate is so good, it really was not enough, especially as all the girls came from wealthy families and were used to a lot. So, while one of us had her lesson, the other would ask to go to the lavatory, but instead would slip out to the shop next to the entrance of the Conservatoire and buy as much chocolate as possible, concealing it in large special pockets under her dress. Then we would reverse the process and so there was plenty to distribute amongst all the other girls.

The school was run by a very orthodox Jewish couple in a very traditional manner. Religious observance was strictly adhered to, and we were totally sheltered from any contact with boys. There was a large boys' boarding school a stone's throw from our school and this mere fact must have caused many a headache to our teachers. Boys for us simply did not exist.

During my stay the unthinkable happened. The headmistress, a married lady, became pregnant. For many months she carefully hid the fact by wearing incredibly concealing clothes and was convinced that no-one knew her secret. She managed this very well. None of the girls noticed anything untoward, except me. I watched fascinated as the dresses grew wider and wider. There came a time when concealment was no longer possible. The headmistress addressed us all during morning assembly. We were always known by number, and not by name. And so it went: 'No 1, have you noticed anything unusual?'

'No, Madame.'

'No 2, have you noticed anything unusual?'

'No, Madame.' And so it went on, until she came to No 37. This was me. I'm afraid I answered her question by saying, 'I certainly have, Madame.' This remark did not go down well, and the headmistress threw me a very black look. She then proceeded to try to explain the situation to the girls. The result of this explanation was a disaster for the school. The girls excitedly wrote home about the great event, and a considerable number of parents arrived at the school in order to remove their daughters. Many of my friends were whisked away in great haste.

In later times this attitude of parents might seem incomprehensible, but in those days the very mention of a pregnancy in an establishment for young ladies was taboo.

I was at the Swiss finishing school for a year, before spending a further year in London, improving my English.

Both my elder brothers had studied at two faculties. Mulia studied both mechanical and chemical engineering. Not wanting to be outdone, I enrolled at the same time at the University of St Petersburg, where I studied law, and at the Conservatoire, where I studied music. At a later date, I studied at the Faculté des Lettres at the Sorbonne in Paris.

CHAPTER 7

Reflections on Russia

August 1914. War was declared, and all the children had to return home – my sister Tera and my brother Tonia from Paris, where they were studying at the University, my youngest brother from Frankfurt in Germany, where he was at school, and I from London. The government provided trains and, after we had closed down the factories and packed all our belongings, including the Venetian furniture and the grand piano, we left Riga for St Petersburg.

On arrival, I went to the University to study law, and the Conservatoire for piano studies. I did not require to pass an examination for University since matriculation was sufficient, but the Conservatoire set a stiff examination, twelve professors examining each entrant. Fortunately, I passed. I studied under the well-known composer, Glazounov, who was the director of the Conservatoire, and got to know Jasha Heifetz, who was a pupil, though already established as a virtuoso. I was taught by his brother and had the same piano teacher as Vladimir Horowitz. Pursuing the study of both law and music at the same time was quite difficult, but one managed somehow.

Life was pleasant in St Petersburg during the war. The Front was far away, nobody knew much about it, and nobody cared. Of course, one could not travel abroad, which was a nuisance, but there were plenty of nice places in Russia itself which nobody had previously bothered to visit. In the summer months, with the children grown up, my parents had usually gone to a spa in France or Germany – Vichy, say, or Baden-Baden, and every winter, as a ritual, to the South of France. Since this was no longer possible, we went to Yalta on the Black Sea, where we took a villa, bringing all the family, servants and governesses, and discovering many beautiful places. The region was normally out-of-bounds to Jews, but in St Petersburg we had all the rights, and used them.

I remember meeting four young ladies with a governess on the promenade at Yalta, all dressed in white with hats to match. Two were rather good-looking, the other two less so. I remarked that one of them had a crooked heel which needed mending. These were the daughters of the Tsar! I never met the Tsar or the Tsarina. They lived very near Yalta, at Sochi, but Sochi was out-of-bounds to any Jew, whether rich or poor.

Sometimes, regiments of soldiers marched past us along the road, singing beautifully, outwardly happy and gay, but often with long sticks instead of rifles, and very poor-quality boots. We were so sorry for these young people who had been torn from their homes, but we were equally sure that they would all come back with medals, and would be only too grateful to have had the opportunity to show their heroism.

The Russo-Japanese War was long forgotten, apart from the memory of the well-known hero who captured ten or twelve soldiers single-handed. The Russians firmly believed that nobody could beat the heroic Russian soldiers. When they were defeated, everybody knew that it was 'all the fault of the Jews'!

So life went on. Charity balls for soldiers, charity theatre performances for soldiers, big dinners and receptions all in evening dress, every lady trying to outshine the other. Business was good. Everything was available, and well paid for. News from the front was reassuring. The Russian hero proved himself to be as good as ever. We had a box at the Opera where the best artists and ballerinas performed, and to attend twice a week was an absolute necessity. We saw Pavlova, Kshessinskaya, Karsavina, Nijinsky, Fokine, and all the well-known dancers and singers.

As time passed, however, although the government had been hiding the true situation from the people, news from the Front leaked through. Despite the censor, it was clear that everything was not going too well. The losses were enormous. Wounded officers were brought to the hospitals in St Petersburg and people would go to the railway stations to meet them. Then things began to happen. The marching and the shooting at crowds, the discontent, the arrests. Everybody was a revolutionary. Everybody knew exactly how to save the Fatherland – what had to be done and what should not be done!

Children from the age of eleven knew the difference between the political parties – knew what the KD, the RD or the RS meant and stood for. Every child had a different idea of how to save Russia, and discussion was heated and intolerant.

While in St Petersburg, we sometimes saw Rasputin, the mad monk, in the street. Whenever we did so, our governess would hustle us away into the carriage. Sometimes, when she had gone into a shop, my friends and I would gaze at this fascinating character, watching him as, usually drunk, he chattered to his friends, and were intrigued by his penetrating eyes, eyes which sparkled with an uncanny spirit and seemed to look right through you. He was very tall, with a long black beard and a thick mass of hair.

Rasputin was known to be a healer, and it was on account of this that he was introduced by a society lady to the palace. The young son of the Tsar had a small cut on his finger, which would not stop bleeding. He suffered from haemophilia. Rasputin approached him and prayed. The boy was cured and from that time the monk visited the palace frequently.

He used to drink, even at the palace, something which caused a great scandal. People then began to accuse the Tsarina of having a love affair with him, or at least that is what we heard. As for the goings-on in his house – these were the talk of Petrograd (as the city was known from 1914 to 1924). Had our governess known what we knew, she would have fainted on the spot!

The scandals continued to grow around Rasputin, and Prince Yusupov, a daring young man married to the niece of the Tsar, decided to get rid of the mad monk. Having invited himself to

Rasputin's house, he waited until the monk was completely drunk. Then he shot him. It was said that, even though wounded, Rasputin still managed to walk to the entrance but fell dead at the gate.

The episode came as a terrible shock to the Tsarina, but the whole family subsequently breathed more freely. Prince Yusupov and his wife were frequent visitors to our grand balls in Paris many years later. However, although Rasputin scandalised all Russia and was the talk of Petrograd, there were many ladies in high society who shed more than a few tears when he was killed.

CHAPTER 8

Scandal in the Family

When my grandfather Hindin died in the Baltic, he left a vast fortune to his children and grandchildren. He also left a large sum of money to charity. This was left to my father for him to divide amongst the Jewish charities. The money was duly distributed.

Some of the forests in the Baltic belonged to my father, and in the midst of one such forest lived my uncle with his family. He was the supervisor of a very large enterprise and the organiser of the felling and transport of the trees. They had a large house, complete with staff, and my aunt, a wonderful lady, rich and beautiful, played an important role in village life.

At that time, a young Russian attorney, his studies in St Petersberg completed, was assigned, much to his dismay, to a post in the village. For some reason, it annoyed him intensely to find a Jewish woman so popular with the local governors and people of influence. He himself had rather grand ideas of running the businesses, and was totally frustrated to find my aunt such a competent person. It was obvious he was an anti-Semite and was not going to take orders from a Jewish woman.

He had hoped to be offered a high position of authority in St Petersburg, and was furious at only getting as far as Toropets. His fury turned to bitterness when he found himself in only a relatively unimportant position. He tried very hard to make trouble between the governors and the local inhabitants, but without success, even being castigated for his rudeness. He was outraged and vowed to take revenge upon my family.

He busied himself studying all the affairs of my father and the role of his brother. He tried his best to find something amiss in the business transactions, but could uncover nothing. This made him even angrier. Then he discovered about the money grandfather had left to charity, and set about making a ridiculous case out of the whole affair. He had found his weapon.

He made a legal case, and brought charges against my father. Everyone was aghast. He said my grandfather had left the money to be distributed to the Russian churches, but that it had instead been given to Jewish charities. The whole thing was, of course, ludicrous. My grandfather was a strictly Orthodox Jew and well known for his charitable activities with Jewish organisations. It was entirely natural for him to leave the money to his own people, and it would have been grossly inconsistent to have left it to the churches – in fact unthinkable.

Nevertheless, the charges were brought and my father was arrested and placed in the local prison. It was a great scandal. My aunt had had several quarrels with the attorney and had often put him in his place. Consumed with guilt, and presumably shame, she committed suicide by drowning herself in the river. The director of father's factory could not get over the scandal and shot himself. My mother gathered the family together and hired a house near to the prison. She approached the prison director and bribed him into allowing father to have a bed and a carpet, and, most important of all, into letting him have kosher food, as father refused to eat the food provided in the prison. She also engaged the best lawyers she could find: Oscar Grusenberg and Goldstein. It was to no avail. The money was taken back from the charities and deposited in a bank in St Petersburg. It probably found its way into the pockets of the attorneys and judges rather than the coffers of the churches – not that the churches had any right to the money in the first place.

Father remained in prison for six months and, with anti-Semitism still rife, this whole episode typified the trumped-up charges which Jews encountered. The troublesome attorney was transferred to St Petersburg for his 'wonderful achievement of depriving the Jewish people of their rightful money'.

We felt desperately sorry for father, because he had always conducted his business with honour and integrity, and was loved by all who worked for him, Jew and Gentile alike. Unfortunately, honour and integrity were not enough. At least we survived the ordeal. Many Jews had their land, businesses and homes confiscated, and hatred continued to be directed against those wealthy people who were left. After the war, the Bolsheviks did everything to purge the land of people who did not hold their beliefs or could not be made to hold them. It was a crime to be rich and a crime to be Jewish, and a crime twice compounded to be both.

Yet, at the time, there were many Jews who happily joined in the 1917 Bolshevik uprising, because they thought their lot might be happier in a system which aimed to rid itself of the rich. This was understandable because the less fortunate Jewish families were very, very poor and had lived in great poverty for as long as they could remember. They had suffered persecution under the Tsars, and thousands had fled long before we did ourselves.

Often one would hear of long, pitiful marches across Russia and through Europe on foot by thousands fleeing from the pogroms. They had nothing except the clothes they wore, and a few simple possessions on wooden handcarts. It never ceases to amaze me that, although they had so little and suffered such great hardship for so many years, they eventually were successful in life, or, if not they themselves, at least their children were. Their stamina and will to survive were miraculous, their determination to raise their children in new lands without losing their identity unbelievable.

CHAPTER 9

Life with the Bolsheviks

I heard Lenin and Trotsky speak many times, although I never met them personally. I remember an aunt once telling me that, during an outing in the carriage, they had passed the Kchessinska Palace, where some unkempt men were hanging perilously out of the balconies, haranguing the passing people, screaming revolutionary nonsense at the top of their voices. Only a few people would stop, and then only for a short while. The weather was not good, and nobody found the speeches very interesting.

The Duma, Parliament, started its sittings. Unrest was general. The war was going very badly. Shortages of food, fuel and other necessities became more acute. A youngish gentleman, slim and elegant, a lawyer and intellectual, tried to save the country by soft words and good manners. This was Kerensky, a very nice man whom I had the pleasure to meet. But the time for gentleness had long gone by – Lenin and Trotsky had taken over! Life became quite unbearable. There were arrests and executions, especially at night; the hunt for the rich 'bourgeois' had begun.

Father was a very rich man, and his turn inevitably had to come. A newspaper appeared with a picture of my father and the following caption beneath:

'This bourgeois who sucks the blood of the workers and soldiers to be brought to justice, alive or dead, for (so much money – an enormous amount).'

The year was 1918. It was obvious we had to leave the country, but how? Our servants were devoted to us and wanted to help, but, again, how? Police came to our apartment day and night to search and arrest. Each time the bell rang, the servants, all six of them, would place themselves in front of the entrance and shout in loud voices that they had thrown out the 'bloody bourgeois' a long time before. They and they alone occupied this place by force of revolutionary decree. All this time, we were living and hiding in the servants' quarters.

There was no money. The banks were all occupied by the new regime. Nobody could withdraw so much as a penny, especially well-known 'bourgeois' like my father. The servants fed us as best they could.

The family in St Petersburg consisted of father, mother, my brother Tonia and me. My sister Raissa, married to a very wealthy man, also in the timber trade, lived in Moscow. At that time she had two children, a son and a daughter. My youngest brother lived with her in Moscow where things were a little quieter and his school was still open. My brother, Mulia, was in London. My sister Tera, married to her 'platonic' husband, lived in a splendid many-roomed apartment in St Petersburg.

CHAPTER 10

Reflections on the Revolution

Father, mother, Tonia and I had to leave St Petersburg at once. The Jewish question was being overlooked for the time being, and many Jews, mostly revolutionary, had settled in the hitherto forbidden provinces, including Moscow and St Petersburg. Several of my father's employees arrived with one purpose only, to help the family escape. Between them they arranged to smuggle father, mother and Tonia in the middle of the night, disguised, to some obscure railway station, and out of the city. It was very risky and dangerous, but there was no other way. They landed safely in Kiev in the Ukraine where, also in the midst of revolution, nobody knew or had heard of my father's family. I was smuggled to Moscow.

Raissa's husband had left a long time ago. He certainly could not stay in Moscow, and through friends, acquaintances and bribes, reached London safely. Now there was Raissa, her two children, the nanny, a Jewish girl, Buba, my brother, and I. It was not possible to stay in Moscow. Our arrest was imminent and inevitable. One of father's employees, a very crippled hunchback, came to our rescue. He arranged with some of his friends for one woman and several children to leave Moscow for somewhere in the country where food was less scarce. How he did it I do not know, but he succeeded, and we all alighted in a remote little Jewish town called Vitebsk, which we had never seen in our lives.

However, there was one big problem. This little town was on the circuit of father's ships, and everywhere large boards announced that this was the shipping company of .... – my father's name in full! To make matter worse, my sister's husband, wanting to help the poor Jewish population, had installed all the waterworks in the town, and his name was a household word. We had come directly into the lion's den! At once, people hid us in the cellars far away from the main street. We were there for quite a while.

Whilst in Moscow I had met a young doctor who had proposed marriage to me, but I had to decline in view of the circumstances of our lives. He was a revolutionary, but in his student days had been arrested several times, and now, in the Revolution, had become a Commissar with a certain amount of power. When we said goodbye to each other he promised that, should I have difficulty in leaving Vitebsk, he would help me. He gave me an address where a message would reach him.

In Vitebsk, lost in the cellar of some suburban 'dacha', I sent a message to him. He arrived the next day, and at once organised the departure of Raissa, the children, the nanny and Buba to the next town, which was Orsha, on the border of Bolshevik Russia. Part of this town was occupied by Germans and Bolsheviks, and the rules were very strict. No-one could go there without a pass. The doctor organised these for Raissa and the children. I was advised to wait as he intended to take me there himself. We stayed a few more days. He still tried to persuade me to stay with him in Russia but, seeing that I was not willing to do so, took me to the train.

For some unknown reason, the trains travelled only at night. There were no day trains. Thus, in the middle of the night, with no luggage, just a tiny little vanity case with a toothbrush and a spare handkerchief, we arrived at Orsha. As the train stopped, the hunchback appeared, apparently from nowhere, snatched my little case from me, and disappeared into the night. There was a great outcry. Four soldiers with rifles arrested me and demanded to know what was in the case, and who was the hunchback?

My explanations were of no avail – it must have been a fortune in diamonds, and the whole affair was pre-arranged! The position of my doctor had now become most dangerous. If he were held to be a party to some bourgeois saving their diamonds from the rightful government of Russia, he would, as a commissar, be shot at once. He could not help me, especially as he did not know whether behind his back I really wanted to save the family jewels. He then and there disappeared from my life. Many years later, after Stalin's death in 1953, I read of the doctors' purge during the dictator's reign, and of the ordeal my doctor had had to endure before he was shot for 'treason'.

Meanwhile, I was taken to the CHEKA, the Russian secret police. We went into a small dilapidated house. In the front room sat a young man with an open shirt showing the whole of his very hairy chest. The room was lit by one candle stuck in a vodka bottle. He took a look at me and said he was going to search me for the documents and diamonds. I was to go into the next room.

This was a bedroom – filthy, with a large unmade bed. There too was a candle in a vodka bottle. I knew very well what the search would mean. We had heard enough about it. It was not only the shame and horror of this search that was well known. We knew they had venereal diseases and that no girl ever survived. If they did not kill her afterwards, she would kill herself. There I stood, awaiting my ordeal.

In the next room an argument started. A shrill voice was heard and a furious young woman stomped into the room, ordered me to undress completely – yes, chemise and everything – and searched me thoroughly, not forgetting my hair, eyes, mouth and so on. Finding nothing, she confiscated my blouse, which must have taken her fancy, told me that in the Revolution no decent girl should wear a blouse of silk, ordered me to dress, made the young man give me a pass, and threw me out. It appeared the woman was the young man's mistress and that the Almighty had sent her to save my life.

There I was, in an unknown town, in the middle of the night and nowhere to go. I stood in the road not knowing what to do, when, suddenly from nowhere, a shadow passed me, stopped and took me by the hand. It was the hunchback, who had followed me from the station, had seen me taken to the CHEKA, told my sister about it, and had come to see if, by some miracle, I would emerge in one piece. He showed me the way to my sister, who sat crying, mourning the loss of her young sister.

Buba, my younger brother, had caught a heavy cold in the train. It had been very cold, and with the presence of the passengers, soldiers and peasants, making the air rather thick, he had several times found it necessary to go to the window for a breath of fresh air. Undernourished as he was, and not very well-covered, the inevitable had happened.

Worse was to follow. When my sister, her two children, Buba and I were together in Orsha, we found a room in a little suburban house with no comfort whatsoever. There was no toilet, and to go to the woods in such bitter weather was no joke. Buba went down with double pneumonia and typhoid fever, a contagious illness. The landlady at once told the authorities (a commissar and a few soldiers) that there was a contagious illness in her house and the people must be thrown out.

A barracks stood on the outskirts of the town, where all the peasants, soldiers and anyone with a contagious illness had to be taken. There were no beds. Each person lay on a filthy mattress which was not changed from one dying person to another. There were no toilets and no running water, just a hut with a candle in a bottle for light.

Raissa said that she was a trained nurse. She had undergone a short course of training, lasting some two weeks. It had been arranged for young society ladies to enable them to comfort the officers when they arrived from the Front. Even the Tsarina had taken the course. Therefore, she would go to this hut to tend our brother. Upon hearing this, the authorities said that she would have to look after all the patients or not be allowed to go there at all. As a result, she did nurse all the patients, certainly saving our brother's life by so doing.

The question of the children became urgent. Bella was now nine, and Lionel about twelve. The town was full of contagious diseases. It was essential to get them out. Raissa said I had to do it. She could not leave Buba and the children could not stay.

At the station, I discovered that the only possible way to leave the town was to be able to prove that one came from a town to which one wished to return. There were refugees from Kiev, Minsk and another town across the border. We came from St Petersburg. I knew nothing about any town beyond Orsha. A commissar provided permits for the stationmaster to issue tickets for trains which left at two o'clock in the morning. It was winter, and, if snow fell heavily, trains often became stuck and unable to run for several days. I asked people for the names of the main streets in Minsk, and decided to be a refugee from Minsk.

I went to the Commissar with a trembling heart. I had to wait quite a while. A young man in a short, black leather coat – the uniform of the revolutionaries – received me. He sat behind a desk and listened to all I had to say. He then issued permits for myself and the children to go to Minsk as refugees.

When the paper was signed and I was ready to take my departure, he rose and said in a quiet voice: 'Now listen carefully, Miss H...... [which was not the name I gave in my request for a permit], I am a Commissar, a revolutionary, and I am doing very well for the time being. It will be all right if the Bolsheviks hold on, which I sincerely hope they will, but should the regime not be able to survive and the old regime comes back into power, tell your father that [he gave his name] helped to save the lives of his daughter together with those of her niece and nephew, and, should I need help, let him not forget it. I was one of your father's employees in his factory at Riga. I was well treated and have never forgotten it.'

We departed for Minsk and arrived safely. From there we joined my parents in Kiev. When I told them of Raissa and Buba, they were stricken with grief. Somehow, they arranged for a soldier to take food and clothing to them. It took some time for Buba to be well enough to travel, but the soldier was a constant help and eventually brought him and his sister to Kiev. Poor Buba was in poor shape. Although seventeen, he looked more like a twelve year-old, a bundle of bones in a thin skin. He could neither sit nor walk. It took a long time for him to recover.

Kiev was most dangerous. There were eleven governments during our time there. They 'governed' the town by looting, killing and burning until they were thrown out by another company of looters, killers and arsonists. They called themselves the Green Army, the Red Army, the Machno Army (the latter after a bandit of that name). Occasionally, the White Army, which was still fighting the Bolsheviks, would temporarily occupy the town. The looting would continue – and Jews were persecuted and killed.

Each 'government' issued passports which every citizen had to acquire on pain of death. These were very expensive. Regular searches were made in entire streets and woe to the person without one. With each change of 'government', we quickly had to find out who had taken over and prepare the necessary passports. There were eleven for each of us buried in a tin box in the garden of the house where we were staying.

This house was a very special one. At one time it had been the best establishment in the town for physiotherapy, mineral baths, mud baths, massage and so on. During the Revolution, and the reign of the 'bandits', one professor and several doctors stayed on – where else could they go? – and used the building as a boarding house.

My parents were helped by their employees and could afford to stay there. Many others hid there too – refugees and even people from Kiev itself who were too well known to be able to stay in their own luxurious houses. There were one hundred people altogether. To give the building the appearance of a hospital, a Red Cross flag was flown from the roof, while it was known as a madhouse, or, at least, a 'psychiatric establishment'.

The doctors taught us how to feign madness. Sometimes it was funny, but, mostly it was distressing. Searches were frequent. Then, everybody had to be in their room, assume the role, sit with a wet towel on their heads, and remember not to answer any questions put to them by the intruders.

CHAPTER 11

The Bolsheviks and the Bourgeois

One afternoon, marines invaded the house. Everybody had to go to the dining-room. All the rooms were searched, some people arrested, and quite a few valuables 'confiscated'. I had influenza, and lay in bed in a small room. Suddenly, the door burst open and a young marine in black leather was demanding to know why I was not downstairs. I said I had influenza and could not get out of bed. He looked me over and announced that he would do the searching himself – 'Where was the key of the room?'

The doctor had the keys. So, the doctor was to come at once and give him the key; he did not want to be disturbed while searching me!

The doctor saved my life. He calmly announced: 'This patient has a very contagious illness. The spots are just starting to come out and it is my duty to tell you, comrade, that whoever touches this patient will most certainly get the illness.' The marine listened and must have been frightened, but, to avoid losing face, he demanded the key, locked me in, and put the key in his pocket, announcing that he would return later. The marines stayed until eleven o'clock that night, searching, looting and arresting, and all this time my parents were fretting – would the marine come back or not? At last they all went, the marine still with the key in his pocket.

We were in Kiev for several months. Life got more and more dangerous. Bandits came and went. The White Army was in and out of the town. The Bolsheviks were in and out of the town. To the Bolsheviks we were bourgeois, and had to be got rid of. To the White Army we were Jews, and had to be got rid of. It was simply impossible to stay in Kiev. But what to do?

With great skill and bribery, father secured a promise of a cattle truck to be attached to a train leaving for Rostov, or even Kharkov, towns which were nearer to the Black Sea. The Black Sea and surrounding towns like Odessa, Novorossiysk, and Sebastopol were under the supervision of the White Army and the British. If we could only reach a port on the Black Sea and approach the British, there might be hope of leaving Russia altogether.

The cattle truck was hired under an assumed name to transport some cattle from Kiev to Kharkov. The problem, however, no small one, was that no Jew ever passed alive between Kiev and Poltava. The bodies of Jews hung on trees all along the route. That was bad enough. But, to add insult to injury, they hung not by the neck but by the genitals.

Father approached an officer in a café we sometimes frequented, and asked him if, in return for payment, he would be willing to take some old people out of Kiev to their relatives in Kharkov. It was a dangerous thing to do. Some time before, the officer had taken an obvious fancy to me, and had invited me to a meal. I could not accept and therefore avoided this café. I was not to know that this was the officer whom my father would approach. At all events, the officer was willing and agreed to provide eight soldiers with rifles to protect us.

The departure was arranged for the following Tuesday at five o'clock in the morning. It was December 1918. The snow was so deep that we could only walk in single file, each one stepping in the footprints of the one before. Arriving at the cattle truck we found, to our amazement, a crowd of about thirty people including the local Rabbi. A rumour had spread that a truck was being hired. The officer and soldiers raised their rifles, ready to shoot. Father stopped them, saying that they all belonged to the family. The officer looked at me, and I inclined my head. Yes, they belonged to us.

One fat couple, the richest of the group, arranged themselves on the wooden planks which had been specially prepared for the 'comfort' of my parents. The officer was about to displace them, but was stopped by father. On the wagon in large chalk letters was written: 'URGENT DELIVERIES TO THE TROOPS'. What troops? Nobody asked!

The most unpleasant aspect of the journey was that the eight soldiers, by arrangement, had received half their money on the previous day and, not by arrangement, had been drinking ever since. Anything could happen! Why should they guard Jews when they could easily kill them all, take their money and continue their drinking? Nobody would ever be found out or punished! Everybody knew it and everybody thought of it. The only person quite sober was the officer. He was rather handsome, very well-dressed and carried a most unusual golden sword encrusted with diamonds and other precious stones. He told me it was the sword of the Tsar. Maybe it was – how could one tell?

The soldiers, ordered by the officer to be quiet, arranged themselves to sleep off their drink, but before they could do so, were all violently ill. In the commotion, the two planks fell down into the vomit and the two fat people emerged in a rather sorry state. No-one said a word, and the journey continued. After some sleep, the soldiers stood guard at every stop.

At one of the stations, a little man in a bowler hat, easily recognisable as a Jew, proved unable to control his natural functions, and jumped out, for just a few seconds, to relieve himself. He was noticed at once. People on the station started to scream that Jews were in the truck. 'Stop it! Get them out!' To our immense relief, the train started to move, one of the soldiers putting out a hand and lifting the little man by the collar back into the truck. The bowler hat was lost. Thereafter, bottles were used, one of the men emptying them at the tiny little opening in the wall of the truck.

The journey took two days and two nights. The officer spoke to me in a serious tone. He showed me a half-litre Vichy water bottle full of diamonds – how many people were robbed and killed for them? – and said that I did not belong to what he called this miserable crowd of Jewish people, that he would give me the life of a princess. He was, besides, quite learned, having finished his studies at Moscow University, spoke perfect French, and belonged to one of the best families. How he became a bandit I never knew!

He told me that he had arranged the whole journey purely because of me, and insisted that I prove my love for him by letting him make love to me here and now. The other people being there did not disturb him. Nobody would notice anything in the middle of the night and he insisted that it should take place now. In his excitement, he stopped whispering, with the result that everybody soon understood the situation.

The Rabbi approached me and said that thirty lives depended on me – that sacrifices had been made in Jewish history on many occasions and that I should think of the people around me, including my own family. I felt lonely and forlorn. What was I to do?

The officer had once been more in life than a bandit. His feelings towards me were perhaps not wholly dishonourable. With this in mind, I begged him not to start our love life in the dirt and vomit of a cattle truck in full view of everybody. Why not wait another day till we arrived in Kharkov? I would leave my family and go with him wherever he wished, and have a clean love-life in pleasant surroundings. My words must have impressed him for he understood, and promised to wait until we arrived in Kharkov.

CHAPTER 12

We Make Our Escape

Kharkov was in the hands of the British. At the station one could directly approach a British officer. I wasted no time in doing so, explained my difficulties, and, without luggage, without even my handbag, which the officer kept for me, was put on a train which was leaving for Rostov immediately. In an instant I had left everything and everybody.

Many years later, I met this British officer in the Majestic Hotel in Harrogate. He had ginger hair and, apart from being much older and heavier, was quite recognisable. We had a very pleasant conversation and I once again thanked him for his prompt action in Kharkov which helped to save my life. My family found me much later through the British Military Intelligence. Now it was easier to get to a port on the Black Sea.

From Rostov we hoped to reach Novorossiysk. This was a very small town full of refugees trying to leave Russia, something which was almost impossible. Sometimes a ship would arrive, but it would depart without anyone being taken. The joint 'government', as we eventually discovered, was headed by one Russian admiral of the White Army and one English captain of the British Armed Forces. They sat on either side of an imposing desk. What they did no-one knew, but everyone knew that the White Army was in the town.

Meanwhile, the journey to Novorossiysk would have to be undertaken by ship, and since nobody knew to whom the ships belonged nor who travelled on them, this was certain to be dangerous. Once again, father was able to engage two soldiers with rifles to see us through the hazards of the voyage. As we were rather suspicious of each other, and as rifles were such an important commodity, the two young soldiers slept on their weapons with me between them. It was not very comfortable for me, but even less so for the soldiers. My father stood beside us each night to safeguard his sleeping daughter.

At last we arrived in Novorossiysk. The whole journey from St Petersburg had taken us a full twelve months. It is probably made now in a couple of hours by air. During this time, my father became very thin, and had lost so much weight that his shirt collar could have gone twice around his neck.

On arrival, however, accommodation was almost impossible to obtain. My parents hired half a room from the local washerwoman, in which there was a small single bed. Disease was rampant, typhoid fever, black fever, cholera, and the dirty linen of almost the entire town came to this hut. To reach the back room my parents had to pass the mountains of filth. That nobody caught anything shows that miracles do happen!

Indeed a first miracle had already happened a while before when we were in Kishinev on our way out of Kiev. There, we had two rooms in a small suburban house. The daughter of the house, a girl aged twelve, had her hair shaved off and looked rather odd. We asked what had happened. She said; 'We had black fever, all of us; my two brothers and one aunt died. I survived but lost all my hair.'

'When was that?' my mother asked.

'Oh, more than two weeks ago; the boys were buried last Friday. That is why the rooms you occupy were empty.' Mother asked very quietly; 'Have you had the house cleaned?'

'Oh yes. We put all our bedding in the sun – the pillows you sleep on, the boys' pillows, were several hours in the sun.' That was their idea of 'cleaning'.

One night I awoke suddenly. A large white louse had bitten my arm. I caught the louse and killed it. Everybody knew that black fever, as the peasants called it, was contracted through white lice. I woke mother and showed her the bite. In the morning, with great difficulty, mother found an army doctor. He looked at the bite and gave his verdict: 'Black fever!'

In a house where three people had died of the disease only a few days ago, the bite of a louse was fatal. 'What will happen now?'

'You have three weeks till the illness develops. There is absolutely nothing I can do. Try to find a place where you can put her in a hospital. Here we have nothing and cannot help you. Goodbye – and, by the way, during the three weeks of incubation the patient is most contagious. '

And here is the miracle! This white louse was not contaminated. How this was so is not for me to understand.

In Novorossiysk, while the Russian admiral was at lunch, we went every day to speak to the English captain. Our knowledge of English helped a great deal. We explained the situation, emphasising that we could not approach the Russian admiral since he would not help a Jewish family to escape from Russia, and would most probably arrest us for a trivial reason, or for no reason at all. We developed a great understanding with the captain. He told us that only on a British ship could he exercise complete authority. At this time, however, what British ships were there passing Novorossiysk? The year was 1919.

Nevertheless, the British captain advised us to be ready at all times of the day or night, should a Dreadnought pass. At last, after several months, a soldier came in the middle of the night to tell my parents that we were to go to the harbour at once. It took some time to gather the family together, as we were not all under one roof. My brother and I, for instance, slept in an office on two desks placed together. It was far from comfortable, but to be indoors was in itself a blessing.

Yet in no time, it seemed, we were on board a British Dreadnought amid cheerful, friendly midshipmen and officers. Their kindness was wonderful. It was like paradise after all we had endured, and I look back on it as probably the happiest period of my life. When the journey was finished, we arrived in Constantinople (later Istanbul). My brother-in-law heard we were there, and came from London to organise everything. We stayed six weeks, trying to get visas for France.

At that time, life in Constantinople was quite uncivilised. Admittedly, the problem of the hundreds and thousands of rabid dogs roaming the streets was just starting to be tackled – a wonderful achievement in the light of such a generally blasé attitude to hygiene. But the rubbish of every kitchen was thrown onto the staircases or into the streets. We always knew what the neighbours were cooking, be it a rabbit, fowl or a goose; feathers, offal – all flew from the windows.

My brother-in-law rented an office in the main road in order to stay in contact with his office in London. By the entrance to the office were two boards covering a small entrance to a tiny space where a moneychanger used to live and work. Why was it boarded up? Oh, nothing. The man died of plague, and, naturally, the police boarded the place up. Was there no disinfectant arrangement in the town? What is disinfectant? And what is it for? That was the answer. In our entire family, only my nephew caught typhoid fever, and he withstood that very well.

The journey from Russia was ended. The nightmare was behind us.

CHAPTER 13

Paris Between the Wars

After our escape from Russia, I began a new life in Paris. We lived in grand style and St Petersburg seemed a million miles away.

Many members of the Tsar's family lived near us, and many of the Russian aristocracy who had managed to escape came to visit us. It was as if we had transported a part of Russia with us. We talked nostalgically of our visits to the Opera, of Pavlova and Nijinsky, and the other well-known artists of the day.

From time to time I would hear from relatives about how things were for Jewish emigrants in the East End of London. Their lot was not a happy one, and every so often I experienced a twinge of conscience about my own luxurious existence. Having timber company offices in London, Paris and Berlin had enabled us to get our money out of Russia. Later the company traded with Russia and had a monopoly on all the softwood imports into England. This supported our lavish lifestyle. Sometimes I gave a charity concert and sent the money raised to England to help my less fortunate brethren, most of whom had been forced out of Russia not because they were rich, but simply because they were Jews.

Meanwhile, we were soon busy sending out invitations to grand balls. All the Russian aristocracy would come, the gentlemen even dancing with young Jewish ladies – something unheard of in St Petersburg. But the lavish life of the Russian exiles could not last for ever. Some panicked, and actually looked for work. None of them had done a day's work in their lives, but they could not live on fresh air. Life in Paris was expensive, even in those days.

So, in the 1920s, young Russian officers became chauffeurs, and since the law was that taxi drivers had to attach a card inside the cab showing their name and address, the most illustrious names were displayed. Indeed, on one occasion I noticed the name of a well-known Prince in the car which I had hired to take me home. When we arrived he said he would not accept a tip from 'a lady'. I had to remind him that he was no longer in Russia!

Many titled Russian ladies tried to become cooks and domestic servants without the slightest idea of what would be expected of them. Sometimes families would hire them for the sake of prestige, but little work was done. A few ended up in hotels. All of them hoped simply for the Bolshevik nightmare to end and to be able to return to their country homes and palaces. That was not to be.

Life in Paris went on, and every year I organised a function with the help of society ladies – in fact three grand balls, for Russian writers, painters and musicians. We hired the best hotels and invited the 'best' people. Several Grand Dukes attended, something which could not have happened in Russia – a Jewish woman inviting a Grand Duke! In Paris they came willingly and graced the occasion with their presence. Even Yusupov, the murderer of Rasputin, was there.

The Tsar's family had arrived in France with a vast array of diamonds and jewellery. They longed for the revolution to be over, and continued to lead lavish lives, being always happy to 'grace' an occasion even when their treasures had begun to dwindle. There were many hosts in France who welcomed them to their soirées and great occasions; their names on an invitation card always sounded grand, even though they hadn't got a penny.

I looked forward to the visit of the Ballets Russes on a tour arranged by Sergei Diaghilev, the famous impresario who was the group's founder. He introduced Russian ballet to the West with a glittering season in Paris. We society ladies had something to talk about, something to do, and much thought was given to what we were going to wear. After all, Anna Pavlova, Fokine, Mathilda Kchessinska and all the famous dancers were coming to Paris.

A theatre, the Châtelet, was hired and work began on a new pine floor. Everyone took a great interest. The well-known painters Alexandre Benois and Leon Bakst were engaged to paint the scenery and backcloth. A special embroidery salon was organised by a friend and this kept us all very busy. Jean Cocteau wrote a beautifully illustrated book heralding the arrival of the ballet.

A new ballet was composed by Cherepnin, to be performed alongside the well-known ballets of Tchaikovsky, Rachmaninov, Ravel and Albeniz. The success of the ballet was overwhelming, and again Jean Cocteau wrote many articles praising its great beauty. The opera was also popular with the bass Chaliapin, then pre-eminent among many famous musical celebrities.

We had endless parties and receptions, and I became very friendly with Mathilda Kchessinska who was later to teach my daughter Irène to dance.

Alexandre Benois and Leon Bakst gave me some beautiful paintings, although these, alas, were stolen some years later by the Nazis. Banquets abounded, and with the social life in Paris at its peak we felt free, young and happy. In winter we would go to St Moritz in Switzerland and enjoy the snow, the sun and the night life. We had experienced so much since leaving St Petersburg, so much danger and insecurity. There in Paris, for us at least, life was good.

CHAPTER 14

London

Quite often in the inter-war years I would visit my sister Raissa in London. She and her husband had a mansion on four floors, with a very large garden, in Arkwright Road, Hampstead. This became a meeting place for well-known Zionists, and somewhere to hold grand balls. It was a splendid house.

Raissa was a great organiser, and it was usual for upwards of two hundred people to attend the fashionable balls. These became the talk of the town, and anybody who was anybody used to come.

During the week, it was a gathering place for Zionists visiting London. I became friendly with Chaim Weizmann, Jabotinsky, Sokolov and many other Jewish personalities.

I was always fascinated by Weizmann's character. He was so vibrant and full of energy. Of course, our conversations tended to centre on Zionism, but from time to time we would drift on to another topic – timber. His father was also a timber merchant and made his living by floating logs along the Vistula and exporting them in Danzig. I recollected how father's trees would sometimes become dislodged, with whole consignments being lost in the Baltic. I remembered once having seen every tree lost in just this way. More often than not, though, Zionism brought our conversations about timber to an abrupt end.

In between times, we nearly always managed a conversation or two about music and literature, and of course, the anti-Semitism we had earlier encountered in St Petersburg. He was most anxious for me to visit Palestine, as it then was. The desert was far removed from my life in Paris, but I promised I would, and, in due course, did.

Weizmann had already made two allies by gaining the support of Balfour and Lloyd George. I well remember the great importance that Weizmann attached to the Arab question; he wanted cooperation and friendship between Jew and Arab. He loved to remind people at these gatherings of the occasion when Balfour had remarked, 'London is the capital of my country,' to which he himself had replied, 'Jerusalem was the capital of our country when London was a marsh.' It was said that from then on Balfour became a firm supporter of the Zionist dream. This story always received loud applause.

I visited my sister's mansion on and off during those years, and I was always carried away with the enthusiasm of the meetings. They were dynamic.

Another frequent guest was Vladimir Jabotinsky. I can only describe him as being full of fire and flame. He was a handsome and determined sort of man, and very friendly with my family, renewing contact with many of them when he visited the Baltic states. I always admired him for his exploits as a lieutenant in the 38th Battalion of the British Army. He was decorated for heading the first company to cross the Jordan. We talked of the pogroms we had gone through in Russia, and about poetry and literature. He was himself a very prolific writer.

The Zionists who came to my sister's house for the meetings were all so dynamic that my life, associated as it was with music and ballet, seemed to pale into insignificance. But for all that, I enjoyed the fiery enthusiasm, and the atmosphere which they created. It was electric.

I passed my final examinations at the London Academy of Music but, alas, it was not possible for me to do what I really wanted – to become a concert pianist. At the age of twelve I had given a concert. This was a success. After the concert, mother had had a serious talk with me and explained to me that it was unthinkable for a daughter in our family to consider a stage career. She would allow me to continue my musical studies, but only on condition that I gave her my word of honour that I would never, ever, go on stage. With sorrow in my heart I gave my word. My teachers were aghast as they had predicted a brilliant future for me. I gave concerts for charity, but never got over my disappointment.

CHAPTER 15

Music, Meetings and Marriage

When, in 1922, I studied at the London Academy of Music and obtained a gold medal, I lived at Raissa's home in Hampstead. At one point, she had to leave London with her son who had developed glandular tuberculosis. The household, her little daughter, the seven servants and the gardeners were left under my supervision. As she was away for eight months, this proved quite an awesome task, but I somehow managed to combine it with my studies.

My brother-in-law, Lipman Schalit, was a gifted and successful businessman, with a well-developed sense of responsibility towards his employees and his business. My father kept up a regular correspondence with him, business letters often being written in verse, in Hebrew, and supported by quotations from the Bible!

With my sister away, the days were hectic. The Zionist gatherings continued, and many a time I would return from the Academy to find groups of men hovering around the rooms talking excitedly, the air heavy with smoke. Sometimes I would quickly slip into the music room to practise, but more often than not I would have to organise vast amounts of refreshments. The maids would scurry from room to room, carrying large silver trays, and the doorbell never stopped ringing. How my sister coped with it all I shall never know.

In fine weather, the men would sometimes walk in the grounds, the servants trailing behind them with endless cups of coffee and tea, not to mention mountains of home-made cakes.

Through it all, I managed to enjoy my musical studies, and my love for composing increased daily. Music has always given me so much pleasure. I cannot, in fact, imagine life without it. The sheer joy of making music 'at home' was, and remains, something which I truly enjoy, and enjoy, moreover, with the whole of myself. It is such a rewarding experience, and I am sure there is a special relationship between people who are musically minded. Perhaps it is the total harmony which appeals. It revitalises the soul.

I had studied the piano in Russia with Felix Blumenfeld (where Vladimir Horowitz was a fellow student). I had private lessons for several years with Wanda Landowska. She was by then a world-famous virtuoso of the harpsichord, in fact the first modern virtuoso of this instrument. She played an important part in the musical life of Paris.

She became a dear friend, and tried to talk me into abandoning the piano in favour of the harpsichord. She insisted that the rather unusual hands that I was blessed with were particularly well-suited to the harpsichord. My hands were extraordinarily supple, so supple in fact that it was believed that I was double-jointed until X-rays showed that I was not. She used to show me how she would put coins between her fingers in order to stretch her hands and increase their span. She did these exercises daily. All of this I did not need.

I had by then already received my gold medal for piano and she offered to train me to virtuoso standard. It was a wonderful offer, but my great love was the piano, not the harpsichord, and Beethoven. One cannot play Beethoven on a harpsichord, and so I did not take up her offer.

After my studies in London, I returned in 1923 to France, and met Senia, my husband-to-be. Certainly I shall never forget his proposal.

We were at the Café de la Paix in Paris. Senia proposed while pouring out a cup of coffee for me. Looking deeply into my eyes he was quite unaware that he was pouring the coffee not in the cup, but onto my knee. The coffee soaked into my new dress. Fortunately the coffee was not very hot, and I was able to control myself until he finished his proposal. I could not bear to inflict him with so much embarrassment. The proposal over, I gently suggested that I had had enough coffee! He was most apologetic, and we often used to laugh about it in the years to come.

Senia and I were married in 1926. The speeches at my wedding were very lengthy. The family was well known in Jewish circles and rabbi after rabbi made speech after speech.

I have a painful memory of sitting on a dark-red brocade armchair and being bitten non-stop by a flea. Much later in the evening, when I took off my wedding dress, I found my tormentor, who by then looked fat and well-nourished.

We all stayed at an hotel in Nice that night, and only left for our honeymoon on the next day. A grave mistake. When we finally got away, a young nephew insisted on joining us for a chat. He was too young to know that wedding nights are generally spent without company, and did not see why he could not use this opportunity to have a chat with his favourite aunt.

He sat down on the bed in our room, and told us all about his school, his lessons, his friends, the sports he liked best. The clock ticked on and on, and Senia my new husband, who was a shy man, did not muster the courage to ask him to leave.

In those days young ladies did not take the initiative, so I too sat patiently and learned a great deal about football and cricket.

Above: Jacob Hindin (grandfather) in Riga.
Left: Siskind Alexander Berlin (grandfather) in Berlin.
Below: Schneur Schneerson (uncle) with Aunt Esther in Hedera.

Above: Raissa and Tera.
Below: Bella (niece) Lionel
(nephew) and Siskind Alexander
Berlin in Riga.

Above: In St Petersburg.
Seated, Zalman and Rebecca
Hindin (parents). Standing, left to
right, Vera, Buba, Lionel and
Raissa.
Below: Sholem Aleichem.

Above Bella.
Above right: Tonia.
Below: Summer villa in the Baltic.

The family all together in St Petersburg.
Above right: Zalman Hindin.
Above: Buba.
Centre: Vera.
Below left: Lipman Shalit and Raissa in their honeymoon period.
Below: Tera with her husband and daughter.

Left: Vera and brother-in-law Lipman walking in the park in London.

Below: The ballroom at Lipman Shalit and Raissa's house in Hampstead, London. Raissa and Vera are on either side of Lipman in the centre of the photo towards the back.

Facing page:
Vera on her
engagement in
London.

Right: Vera in her
'coming out' period in
London.
Below: Zalman and
Rebecca Hindin in Nice.
Below right: Vera in
London.

Above right: Vera and
Irène in Paris.
Above: Senia and Irène
in Nice.
Right: Irène during her
school year in London.

CHAPTER 16

Our Daughter Irène

My husband and I had been married for three years when we decided the time had come to start a family.

My daughter Irène was born in Paris on 20 December 1929. She weighed nine pounds and was a beautiful baby. The birth took under four hours. She immediately began to feed happily, and I had ample milk. In fact, I had so much that it was arranged for some of it to be taken in a bottle to a frail little boy whose mother had none. Everything was perfect and we started thinking of home and the nanny awaiting us.

On the eighteenth day something went wrong. I could not breathe properly and had a fearful pain in my chest. My temperature rose to 104° and my pulse rate to 160. Alarmed at this sudden development, my doctor called in a specialist, who arrived at ten o'clock in the evening. After examining me, he requested a private conversation with my husband. He told him that I had no more than three hours to live. I had puerperal fever, septicaemia and an embolism in the lung. Nothing, absolutely nothing, could be done to save my life. Puerperal fever is now rare in developed countries. There were no antibiotics in those days and the unfortunate women who contracted it and the resultant septicaemia were doomed.

There had been an influenza epidemic in Paris at the time, and the private nurse attending me had caught it. Not wanting to lose her income, she had tried to conceal it and had worked on, surreptitiously blowing her nose in my presence. She had obviously infected me. The specialist felt that I should be told the truth. With so little time left, I may have wished to write my will.

My husband decided not to tell me. He came to my room with an ashen face and paced so incessantly around my bed that my headache increased unbearably. I did not appreciate the fact that I was dying, and thought that I must have caught a cold when they took me in haste to the labour room.

The ordeal began. Camphor, morphia ... camphor, morphia. There were no antibiotics. I lay on a special bed known as a *lit Dupont*, a weird contraption with ropes and pulleys to enable a patient to be slightly raised, if necessary, without actually moving.

They brought in my baby for a last farewell. They held her close to me. I could not hold her in my arms as I could not move. I looked at her. She was beautiful. She needed me. I decided that I must get better as quickly as possible.

In Paris a friend, Dr Emile Coué, was developing the new concept of auto-suggestion. I had attended his lectures and read his books. I believed in his theories and decided that this was the time to put them into practice. I could not speak, but I could think, and so all through the day and night, I mentally repeated to myself Dr Coué's words, 'I am getting better. Every day, in every way, I am getting better and better.'

Eighteen little cushions were tucked around me to prevent the slightest movement. Where the cushions would not fit, pounds of cotton wool were tucked into the spaces. I wore a hospital gown open at the back and still remember the enormous cold and clammy hands of the male nurse on my bare back every time they raised the bed. He was a young man with curly hair, full of life and given to cracking jokes. He considered himself very witty and was popular with the nurses, but I found it hard to appreciate his jokes. The clinic also booked another private nurse for me, telling her in confidence that she could accept the next booking almost immediately as I would not live.

The morphia and camphor injections continued endlessly. I could not breathe properly, but I was at least alive. Slowly I improved. After seventeen weeks I was brought home on a stretcher. I had confounded the specialist's gloomy predictions!

It was wonderful to feel my own sheets in my own bed, the silk coverlet, the lace on my pillowcase. Everything was so lovely, so pleasant, so comfortable, after the heavy, rough sheets in the clinic.

In the drawing-room stood a glass cabinet containing antique china, the collection of which, especially cups and saucers, gave me much pleasure. I told Marie, my maid, to take the most beautiful cup and saucer and to put it on my breakfast tray as a symbolic way of celebrating my survival. Marie had a holy terror of this china, which was very valuable.

The next morning she gingerly took out a priceless *Tasse Napoléon*, and brought it in on the tray, walking as if on eggs. Alas, for there was an obtrusive corner rug. The *Tasse Napoléon*, the tray and poor Marie, in that order, crashed to the floor. The coffee gently soaked into the pale pink carpet.

Marie picked herself up, burst into tears, and announced that after such a disaster she was, of course, giving her notice. Madame would not want her in the house after this. I could not care less. I had just returned from hell, and a piece of china, however valuable, meant nothing to me. I comforted Marie and decided thereafter to have the ordinary breakfast cups on my morning tray.

My lady doctor suggested that a couple of friends visit me to cheer me up and prevent the depression which often follows an illness of this kind. I asked her to drop in that evening at nine o'clock and she did. I was sitting up in bed, dressed in silk and lace. Around my bed, the rows of chairs and armchairs were filled with people drinking and chatting, the air heavy with cigarette and cigar smoke. In the adjoining drawing-room, my brother was listening to a record of ragtime music, and trying to keep up with it on the piano. Normally a good player, his synchronisation was not always accurate and the noise was appalling.

This was the normal pattern of my evening. 'This is madness,' she said. 'I was talking about a couple of people!' How could I explain that I was celebrating my survival!

In Paris, the inter-war years seemed to be spent in the pursuit of pleasure. Everybody felt that life was lovely. Everything was wonderful and people were happy and content. They danced, whatever their ages, took up various sports, simply tried to amuse themselves. The aim was to be happy, to forget and forgive the past, for now the peoples of the world were brothers and sisters, and there were no more enemies. There had been a war, of course, but it had been the only one of its kind, one which could never happen again. It was considered bad manners to talk about such a thing; one must forget, and live, live, live, the misery caused by the Great Depression of 1929 and the early 1930s notwithstanding.

The happiest years were those sufficiently far removed from the first war yet not close to the second. We lived opposite the Bois de Bologne. We had an apartment which was quietly luxurious without being ostentatious – subdued colours, good Persian carpets, English and French antique furniture and a library of rare books. Although certainly not millionaires, we had quite enough to enjoy life's comforts, including a good car. We employed a cook and two maids.

My husband and I had been married for three years before our daughter was born. That time had been used profitably. I studied law and philosophy at the Sorbonne and played the piano at the Conservatoire under the direction of Wanda Landowska. We had an evening of chamber music at our home every Thursday and our friends consisted of writers, painters, musicians – indeed most of the intelligentsia.

A few months after my illness, I revisited the specialist. I could not walk very well and was using two sticks. He did not recognise me. I gave both my name and the name of the private clinic I had attended. He stood up in anger, completely misunderstanding. I was obviously referring to someone I knew, but why come and see him? The poor woman had been dead for some time. It had been a very sad case, in which the woman had died in childbirth. Why did I look so pleased about the matter? Was I a relative?

I took hold of my sticks, stood up and said that I was very sorry to contradict his diagnosis, but was still, as he could see, very much alive, and fully intended to stay so. The specialist stared at me in amazement. He got up, came towards me and kissed me on both cheeks. Never, he said, had there been a case this this. It was just physically impossible for me to be alive!

A few days later, I called in a children's specialist to see that the baby was well. I was waiting in the drawing-room when the maid opened the door, and I heard him asking, not for me, but for my husband. I could not understand why he expected my husband to be home at such a time in the week. When he saw me, however, he lifted his hands in amazement and turned deathly pale. Helping him into an armchair, I asked him if he felt ill. 'Madame,' he said, 'it is you! You must understand me. My friend the specialist told me some time ago of the tragic circumstances of your death. Coming in and seeing you, I naturally had a shock!'

Medical opinion at last seemed to have accepted that I had survived the ordeal.

CHAPTER 17

Growing Up

As time went by, the baby thrived. She was plump and cheerful and soon began to walk. When she was nine months old, I noticed her nanny had a cough. Alarmed, I called in the doctor to attend her in case it was catching, but he only pooh-poohed my fears.

Still, despite his assurances, as the nanny's cough worsened, the baby too began to cough. This was bad enough, but my mother also was just back from hospital after a major operation, and soon her maid, a woman of seventy-odd, and even my mother's little terrier, began to cough. They all coughed terribly, the dog worst of all.

As soon as the doctor heard the coughing, he made an instant diagnosis. 'Whooping cough!' he said. 'Everybody has whooping cough!' He turned to me. 'I can tell you that you too will have it, and after the illness you have had, this can be dangerous.'

'I asked you many times,' I said. 'I asked you every time you came about nanny's cough. How is it you didn't recognise it as whooping cough before?'

'Well, a women of your age very seldom catches it, and a baby of nine months even more seldom.'

I decided to consult another specialist, who agreed with some reluctance, not wishing to dispute another doctor's diagnosis. After seeing the baby, he told me would have to take an X-ray of her lungs because she had a very serious case of whooping cough.

We brought the baby to his consulting room. The light was switched off and the baby was put on the X-ray table. Irène lay on a table and a large board on rails was pushed up to cover her chest.

Instinctively I covered her little face with my hand. The doctor pushed the board up forcibly in the dark and it hit my hand, the sharp edge cutting it deeply. Imagine if my baby's face had received the impact! The doctor was most apologetic, saying he had forgotten how small the baby was, thinking he could push the board higher than it could really go.

One evening I noticed the baby sitting in bed moving her little head in a strange manner, to and fro, to and fro, not even crying, just moving her head.

I telephoned the doctor and he said, 'Get a specialist.' The doctor arrived at ten in the evening and diagnosed the complaint as otitis. The child's ears were punctured until the pus emerged. She cried all night with pain and fright, and it was three months before she was well again. By that time she was a year old and had begun to talk, not very distinctly but in a charming way.

A year went by and Irène not only walked but danced. I now found that she was a *born* dancer. She danced all day and, whenever possible, stood on her toes. Her little white shoes were spoiled by this habit, with black stains in front, but no matter what nanny or I told her, she simply could not refrain from standing on her toes to dance.

She waved her little arms and, although she had never seen a real dance, she instinctively possessed the right movements and the grace of a ballet dancer. Everybody in fact told me to make a dancer of her, giving me addresses of ballet schools, but she was only two years old and I considered her far too young and fragile to begin the hard training of a dancer.

Irène was extremely pretty, but thin, with tiny feet and hands, although tall for her age. With her large green eyes and blue-black hair, all curly and soft, she looked like a real doll. She even behaved like one, with never a cross word to anybody, always willing to do exactly what she was told, never breaking or spoiling her toys, never dirtying her dresses.

She loved dolls, but only baby ones, never a dressed-up girl doll, even when dressed in frills and fineries. With these, we had to take off all their normal clothes and put nappies round them. This alone made her happy. The baby dolls had all her care and all her love, and she could play for hours, alone, in a corner of a room, disturbing no-one.

She liked everybody, and everybody liked her. She was so good-looking, I was proud of her, and her nannies all loved her dearly and were heart-broken when they had to leave her. Every time a nanny left it was a real tragedy for the child, who could not get over the departure for weeks, crying through the nights, becoming thin and pale, not eating or sleeping. A great deal of diplomacy was needed to make her accept a new nanny, but once accepted, her love was whole again, and she was happy and smiling, listening to every word she was told, eager to please everybody, including her dolls.

Irène was two when she began to find it difficult to digest her food, becoming very ill in time. The woman doctor I called came every day, while a specialist attended her twice a week. Still nobody could find anything wrong with her, although she grew thinner and thinner.

During this period she was particularly loving and clinging. Sometimes she would say she would like to cry a little, but I should not be upset as she had just a little tummy-ache. Her pathetic face would fill with tears and I found the way she forced herself to smile particularly heartbreaking.

One afternoon the specialist informed me that I pampered her because she was my only child, but if I did not worry so much the child would feel better. In despair, I telephoned yet another woman doctor, a friend of mine. She came at about six in the evening, examined the child thoroughly, listened to my story, and after a while confessed she did not know what was actually wrong.

Because of this she could not help me, although she felt the child was dangerously ill and would not survive the medical treatment she was now receiving. She suggested that I should consult a professor in Switzerland, her teacher at the university where she had studied. He might help me, and the sooner the better.

I wasted no time, and next morning I was on the train for Switzerland with my child and nanny. We arrived in Zürich and telephoned the professor. We learned that he was on holiday at his villa, which was two hours away by train, and that he would not be receiving patients for a month. I told them I had come from Paris especially to consult him, with a very sick child who might not survive a month. After I had told him my story over the telephone he agreed, as an exceptional favour, to see me at his villa – two hours by train plus one hour by bus.

I was received at the villa by a rather old and powerfully built man with a crew-cut, wearing heavy hobnail boots – the Professor. He was very abrupt and cross in his manner, looking more like a farmer than a doctor.

After examining Irène, he pronounced that he did not know what the doctors in my country had done to her, but she was certainly being starved to death, her digestive tract being so wilted that she could hardly swallow anything. I said that in Paris she had been treated for a liver complaint because her breath had smelt of acetone. The Professor immediately lost his temper and shouted that anyone who was as starved as this child had been would smell of acetone, a symptom of hunger, not of liver trouble.

He admitted that he did not know what to do with the girl except forget about her, for she was not likely to live. As I was young, I should have another child and start it off in the right way. Then there would be no reason why the new one should not be healthy.

He must have noticed the expression of utter misery and grief on my face, for he went on; 'I am going to give the child a TB test. Should it be positive, I shall ask you to take her home, because I will be unable to be of any help to her. Should it prove negative, however, we might think of something and try it out. '

I asked him how I was to know what was positive or negative. He replied that the incision he would make would show positive if it became red, negative if it stayed white. He then made the incision and I took my little daughter back to our hotel. I sat beside her bed all night, watching the colour of the incision. But it was white, and it remained white. I telephoned the Professor and gave him the good news. 'Come and see me with the child,' he said, 'and we will discuss what to do next.' The journey was wearisome, but I was eager for advice.

I reached the villa only to be advised to go home and give Irène two soupspoons of milk. When I told him that Irène could never stand milk, which upset her stomach badly, he demanded to know who was the doctor and who the patient. He would tell me what to do and I should please obey him. This I agreed to do.

At the hotel I reluctantly gave Irène two soupspoons of milk. Before long she began to scream with pain in her stomach. Everybody, including the staff, demanded to know what was happening, wondering why I was punishing her so severely.

In desperation, I telephoned the Professor, asking him to listen to the cries of my child. After he had listened in astonishment, and perhaps with some pity, he told me to come and see him the next day.

From then on, the Professor and I really started our work on the child. I bought a letter scale and a set of doll's kitchenware, saucepans, frying pans, etc, and every morning consulted the Professor about the menu for the day, which was never the same two days running. I acquired a notebook in which I noted each day's diet, and the results it gave. I also had to send a daily specimen to be analysed at a laboratory. The baby, he would state, could have half an ounce of this and one ounce of that, and such items I measured on the letter scale to the precise amount.

We tried everything possible and impossible. Irène, who had been so strong and healthy that she had started walking at the age of nine months, now, at the age of two, could not manage to do even this. She was too weak to stand and had to lie in bed from sheer exhaustion. Her hair and teeth stopped growing. The Professor and I worked hard for nine months, but only in the tenth month did Irène start to gain weight.

When this continued on a regular basis, the Professor shook my hand in delight and told me that we had won the battle. He could state with certainty that there could never have been anything wrong with Irène – just the misfortune of having had doctors who did not understand her case, an intolerance of milk and certain foods.

'Without your help and loving care,' the Professor said, 'we would never have achieved what we have now done. Go to the mountains, stay in a nice place, for you do not need me any more. You know exactly what to do and how to do it. I shall come to visit you, but only in the capacity of a friend, not as a doctor, and not for money.'

We stayed in the mountains for about three months and Irène grew happy and healthy. She could walk and she could eat almost normally. At last we could go home!

Now we began a normal life again in Paris. My baby was out with her governess in the Bois de Boulogne every day, she ate and slept well, and was altogether a happy, healthy and beautiful child. Every summer I took her to the mountains for a holiday and, on our way, we would visit the Professor, who looked like an angry farmer but who had a heart of gold. He loved Irène and asked her to call him grandpa, which she did with delight.

At the age of five, during a holiday in Nice in the mid-1930s when we were visiting my parents, Irène suddenly contracted appendicitis and the resulting illness set her health back again. The doctor who attended and operated on her advised me to send her to a Swiss boarding school for a year in the mountains when she was a little older.

The Professor was of the same opinion. She was too fragile, he said, because she was pampered by her mother and nannies. 'Send her to a school in the mountains to learn to ski and skate and swim,' he said, 'to forget for a while that she is an only daughter and always alone. The company of healthy children will do her good. Sacrifice your own feelings for the good of the child!'

He gave us the address of a school in German Switzerland, high up in the mountains. I agreed to this and found the school was nice, the director and his wife being quite young and efficient, though perhaps a little too efficient for my liking. In 1937 Irène spent a year at this boarding school. I suffered terribly when leaving Irène but knew it had to be done for her good.

The child did profit by her stay and became rosy, plump and sunburnt. She could skate and ski wonderfully. As for learning, she acquired perfect knowledge of the local dialect, which was completely useless to her. She had a great facility for languages. Brought up in Paris by German and English nannies and governesses, she spoke, read and wrote three languages perfectly by the age of six.

Naturally, in this little village in the mountains where no-one in the school could speak English, let alone French, she became the general interpreter at the early age of six. But her moral sufferings were severe for she believed that everybody was good and wanted to be nice to her, just as she herself wanted to be nice to every else. But when the boys took away her dolls, her own beloved babies, and trod on them and broke their faces and laughed at her tears, her heart almost broke.

She later told me that she had wanted to kill herself. She decided that the best way of doing this was to stop breathing. And so every evening she would hold her breath, on one occasion for so long that she very nearly fainted. Her stay in the school was an ordeal and she never forgot it. I went to see her many times, but always regretted doing so, our partings being so unhappy.

Irène went next to a school in London for one year. She became a proper little English schoolgirl, with school uniform and all, eventually resuming her attendance at her school in Paris. Despite all the setbacks, Irène, my sensitive and gifted daughter, was growing up.

CHAPTER 18

Bürgenstock

I saw the world in the 1930s and travelled extensively, to Austria, Egypt, Italy, Palestine, Greece and many other places. Every summer I would spend some weeks in Bürgenstock in Switzerland together with Irène and her nanny. Situated above Lake Lucerne and reached by funicular, this idyllic place had a style of its own and had always been one of the pinnacles of the Swiss hotel industry. It was a quiet place, consisting of just three very grand hotels. There were no shops apart from a newsagent's kiosk and a couple of boutiques. Cars were not allowed.

Bürgenstock was a privately owned estate, and the three hotels were under the same management. It boasted a famous collection of Old Masters, which hung in the public rooms. The latter were furnished with the most exquisite antique furniture. In the Thirties, when I was a regular visitor, this quiet place was a retreat for many of the great musicians of the day. I remember one wonderful summer when my fellow guests at the hotel included Vladimir Horowitz, the pianist, Nathan Milstein, the violinist, and Igor Piatigorsky, the cellist. All three were of Russian origin, and we became very friendly.

I will never forget the Kreutzer Sonata played for me by Nathan Milstein and Vladimir Horowitz, who told me with a smile that this was a unique occasion. It certainly was. Soloists of this calibre do not often perform together.

Irène was a quiet and well-behaved child except when she had to have an enema, when she would scream most dreadfully. The doctor had ordered these to be given regularly and nanny wondered what could be done to avoid the tears and the trauma. I had an idea. I told Irène that nanny was going to give me one too, and that if she listened carefully she would see that I did not scream at all.

Nanny and I went into my room. When we came out, I found my child on the balcony waving her little arms about excitedly and having a conversation with an elderly professor who had befriended her. The Professor was seated on his balcony across the courtyard. Irène was shouting, as the Professor was rather deaf. 'Herr Professor! Herr Professor! It is really wonderful. Nanny is just giving Mummy an enema and she is not screaming at all!' This bit of news was much enjoyed by all the hotel guests, who were sitting downstairs on the terrace having tea.

On another occasion, I came down for dinner and was greeted by one of the guests, who, grinning mischievously, said, 'Aha, here comes the treble tummy.' Most of the other guests were grinning too. In a flash I remembered. That morning Irène had come into my bathroom and had seen me in the bath. This was the first time Irène had seen anyone without clothes on. 'What is it?' she wanted to know, pointing at my bosom. In those days it was believed that little children should not be informed too early about the facts of life. So I told Irène that it was two little extra tummies, and that when she grew up, she too would have them. Irène had shared this interesting news with everybody!

CHAPTER 19

Palestine and Egypt

In the 1930s, I was asked by the Jewish societies ORT, OZE and WIZO to attempt to persuade the Egyptian authorities into accepting an invitation to one of the very large annual exhibitions held in Palestine. These were becoming increasingly popular. In 1929, no fewer than 121 foreign firms had participated, and in 1932 foreign governments were officially represented for the first time, including those of Great Britain, Switzerland, Rumania, Turkey, the USSR, Latvia, Bulgaria, Poland and Egypt.

It was my first trip to the Middle East; I was keeping my promise to Chaim Weizmann to visit Palestine. The Egyptian Consulate was most emphatic that I would not need a visa.

Packing the right clothes was a complicated business. Certainly my Parisian style of dress would not have been suitable for a family visit to my Aunt Esther and Uncle Schneur Schneerson. They were deeply pious, and my uncle was the son of the Lubavicher Rebbe, a famous Orthodox religious leader. I thus had to select clothes that would be regarded as 'modest'. This meant long sleeves, and a long dress to conceal, rather than reveal, my figure. My neck and shoulders should also be covered. In short, I would have to look rather like a peasant – complete with headscarf.

I set aside a small case for this special family visit, and packed a variety of clothes for the grander occasions, not forgetting that in Egypt, a Muslim country, one still had to exercise moderation.

When I arrived in Palestine, I went straight to my uncle and aunt's house. Aunt Esther was my father's sister. My paternal grandfather had given the whole colony of Hedera to his sister and her family. Most importantly, this enabled my uncle Schneer Schneerson to continue his beloved and devout studies of the Torah and the Talmud.

I found my uncle quite well advanced in years, with a long beard, very dignified and full of good humour. He was surrounded by his sons and daughters and a veritable stream of grandchildren. I had to behave with strict decorum; there were so many rules and regulations to be observed at every minute of the day. It was as if I had been transported into another world. All the children appeared delightfully happy, the little boys busy with their studies – their *payot* (sidelocks) dangling down their cheeks. There was a feeling of holiness in their home and all about them.

My aunt seemed content, and very happy to see me. Their way of life was so different from my own and, indeed, from our earlier life in St Petersburg, but then they had chosen a way of life which demanded constant devotion to God.

I looked at the smaller children playing in the hot dusty sand, and thought how different it was from Irène's childhood in Paris, with her nannies, ballet and bows. They lived in two different worlds, and in a way I envied such a simple and good existence with its almost total freedom from material things. The memory of this visit still lingers.

I went on to the King David Hotel in Jerusalem, which was luxurious even then. The only thing which confused me was a special button on the bath, which had to be pressed continually in order to make the water run. I rang to complain.

The maid was quick to explain that water was scarce in Palestine, and the button had been installed to discourage waste. She continued with a detailed explanation of the bath water going through special pipes, connected to tubes, and eventually finding its way into the garden, where it watered the strawberries and vegetables. I understood – and ate no salads or strawberries in Palestine!

I found Jerusalem utterly fascinating. With such a diversity of people and faiths, it was like being at the centre of the world. Everybody was so busy. I had seen nothing like it.

I then sought to make my way to Cairo, to open negotiations

about the forthcoming exhibition. Contradicting earlier assurances, however, the Egyptian police said that I would need a visa. I was politely told to reurn to Paris to obtain one. This was, of course, impossible. I made a fuss and was eventually taken on a special police boat to Cairo, something which proved quite frightening, although the scenery was beautiful.

I got down to work in Cairo. In the event, I was successful, and on my return the newspapers announced that the delegation from Cairo included a Mr and Mrs Zadek Bey and a Mrs Vera Chesno of France. The exhibition was held in Tel Aviv, and a banquet was organised to meet the Egyptian delegation. I felt quite proud of myself, because negotiations had not been easy.

At the banquet, I was beside the Mayor, Meir Dizengoff, who struggled in his attempt to converse with me in French. To his astonishment and relief I whispered to him that I would be delighted if he spoke Russian!

We became great friends. He visited us in Paris and went also to my sister's house in London. Palestine was then very poor, with sand everywhere, and water was at a premium. Life was very tough. When I visited Israel in more recent years, I could hardly believe the transformation that had been wrought. The deserts bloomed with trees and groves. Whole towns had sprung up, universities thrived, and some of the best hospitals in the world had been built.

It had been but a dream during those meetings in London, when Chaim Weizmann and Jabotinsky had worked so hard to fire enthusiasm into the Jews. What I saw in later years was far from a dream, but a reality. Through their hard work, those early pioneers laid the foundations of what is now Israel, with all its greenery and modern technology. All I yearn for is peace in that area, so that both Jews and Arabs may share its prosperity.

CHAPTER 20

The Bereavement

When father and mother went to live in Nice, in the South of France, after their escape from Russia, the first thing that father looked for was a synagogue. The local French rabbi was a very young man, and this was his first post. He still had a lot to learn and my father who, although a businessman, had had a full rabbinical training, did not like the young rabbi's lack of experience. And so the local rabbi would call upon my father every day at eleven o'clock in the morning for a lesson in rabbinical matters. This went on for some time and father was still not satisfied with the style of the young rabbi's religious service.

Father finally decided to set up his own synagogue. He bought a small house, furnished it with chairs and carpets and set aside a separate area for the ladies, as is traditional in an orthodox synagogue. Each of us contributed a carpet, some furniture and some prayer books. The Sefer Torah (Scroll of the Law) belonged to the family. It had been written in our house in St Petersburg and was immensely precious to us. This Sefer Torah was the only thing that my eldest brother brought with him when he was smuggled out of Russia.

It was the first Yom Kippur (Day of Atonement) in father's new synagogue. It was absolutely crowded. All those people who wanted to worship in the traditional way had come and the synagogue was completely full. Father gave a long and learned address in Hebrew. When he finished, it occurred to him that probably ninety per cent of the congregation would not have understood a word of it, so he quickly translated the whole address into French and said it again.

It was hot and stuffy in the smallish room. With so many people present there was not much air. Father was very tired. He sat down, had a stroke and died, there and then, in his new synagogue. There were seven doctors in the congregation. None of them could do anything. An ambulance was called, he was taken home and laid on a bed, still in his white Yom Kippur robes.

I was staying at my sister's house in London, where I was studying music at the Academy. Mother phoned us from Nice. To telephone on the Day of Atonement is unthinkable for any Orthodox Jew. When we heard mother's voice on the telephone, we knew something terrible must have happened. She asked us to come to Nice at once because, as she put it, 'Father is not well.'

We did not understand this at all. Mother had always been the one who was not well. She suffered from a heart condition and was frequently seriously ill, getting better again by sheer willpower. We left for Nice at once and told mother that we would be there at three o'clock in the afternoon. Using transport, any form of transport, on Yom Kippur is once again quite unthinkable for any Orthodox Jew. In those days the planes were not very reliable, and, unfortunately, our plane was grounded in Marseilles. After a long wait, we had to take the train and arrived at eight o'clock in the evening.

Earlier, at three o'clock, mother asked her Catholic maid to leave the room and request her Jewish doctor to come in. She told him that she was now going to her beloved husband and that she could not wait any longer. The doctor frantically tried to explain to her that her daughters were coming and that she must wait for them. 'I waited till three o'clock,' she said, 'I cannot wait any longer.' She said the last prayer in a loud voice, closed her eyes with her hands, and died. When we arrived, we found both parents dead.

My sister, prostrate with grief, could do absolutely nothing. Everything fell on me. I had three brothers. One was in Australia, one was studying in Germany, and the eldest was on holiday in the mountains in Czechoslovakia. I spent all night trying to contact them by telephone and finally, towards the morning, was able to speak to the eldest one in Czechoslovakia.

I knew that father had always wanted to be buried in the old cemetery located above the town. He had tried very hard to buy a plot there, but was told that this was an ancient cemetery, that there was only one plot left, and that this would have to be allocated to some long-established Nice residents. When the authorities heard about the circumstances of my parents' death and all the charitable work they had done over the years, the Municipality of Nice presented us with the plot.

People of all religions followed the funeral cortège. There were Catholics and Protestants and Jews. Among them walked an extraordinary assortment of beggars. It was as if all the beggars and down-and-outs in the town were following the hearse. It was only when we went through father's effects that we discovered the reason for this. In a locked cabinet we found a collection of ledgers, and in those ledgers, in his own spidery handwriting, there was a detailed and meticulous account of monthly allowances to a vast number of beggars. This had gone on for years, but no-one knew anything about it. He had kept this to himself.

The burial presented yet another set of difficulties. An orthodox Jew has to be buried in a certain way. I remembered that my father had to be buried wearing his woollen *tallit* (prayer shawl) and not his silk one, but I was not absolutely sure. I put this question to the young rabbi, along with many other questions, but he could not help. When faced with such questions he had always turned to my father. I had to telephone Rabbi Abramski in London, and found out that, indeed, a woollen *tallit* was necessary.

Upon my return from the funeral I was so desperately unhappy that I felt I could not go on living. I was in charge of my sister's sleeping pills. These had been prescribed for her and I kept them to avoid the possibility of her taking too many by mistake. I put sixty tablets in a glass of water. Just as I was about to drink it the doorbell rang. It was a telegram. My daughter, now aged four, was on holiday in the mountains, in Switzerland. Her governess was telling me in the telegram that the hotel was closing and where did I want her to go with the child? Suddenly I remembered that I had a daughter. So great was my grief that I had completely forgotten about her.

I took the glass to the lavatory and poured the contents away. And how my daughter needed me during all of her life!

CHAPTER 21

Our Little Ballerina

In 1938, enthusiasm over the Munich agreement between England's Prime Minister Neville Chamberlain and Germany's leader, Adolf Hitler, began to wane and people started talking about war. I went to Switzerland to fetch Irène, now aged nine, and found the boarding-school half-empty, most of the children gone, the windows darkened, blue lights and blackouts in force, and a general atmosphere of fear.

With my husband having business to attend to in both Paris and London, I accompanied Irène to London to give her a taste of life at an English school.

On returning to Paris, Irène began her ballet training. I enrolled her at Mme Kchessinska's ballet school. She was in her element. It was as though she had come home, to a place where she belonged. Her ballet class became her life.

I took her to an old friend of mine, a famous ballet critic, for his opinion of her progress and ability. Irène changed into her tutu and began to dance. He watched her carefully, then took me to one side.

'Yes,' he said, 'the child has talent, great talent.' But there was something wrong with her. She was strangely inhibited. Had I not noticed that she danced in one tiny circle, keeping her limbs so close to her body? There was no exuberance, no life, she was not 'giving'. There was something wrong psychologically, and the sooner I took Irène to a child psychologist, the better.

I could not understand. The usual Irène would leap around like a whirligig, a mass of arms and legs. Dancing was as natural to her as breathing, and such things as stage-fright did not exist. I went over to Irène, who was sitting quietly and rather sadly in a corner. I questioned her gently. Two large, tear-filled eyes looked up at me. 'But mummy,' she said, 'what else could I do? No knickers.' In a flash, I understood it all.

In the rush to be on time, I had forgotten to pack the satin panties. These were a very important part of the costume. This first tutu had not been made by a theatrical costumier, but by my own dressmaker, and neither she nor I had realised that unless a tutu is cut in a certain manner, it will ride upwards, as it were, instead of downwards, and, rather like an inverted lampshade, show much more underwear that it should.

It was a very cold winter's day, and nanny, a great believer in 'sensible' underwear, had dressed Irène in her warmest clothes. These included a pair of knickers which she had knitted herself. They were made of very thick, ribbed brown wool. Irène, realising that the combination of tutu and brown knickers was not quite the costume for a ballerina, decided that she had better wear nothing underneath, dealing with the decency problem by keeping her limbs close to her body. The critic roared with laughter when he found out.

In one of the last happy moments we spent before the war, a film producer saw Irène and liked her so much that he asked for my permission to allow her a role in his film, to be produced in Paris, tempting me with a promise that he would give me a copy of the film. As Irène had only recently returned from school in London and had not yet started school in Paris, I agreed.

Irène was delighted. To her it was all good fun. She had no idea of earning money for doing something so pleasant.

At one point, Irène was reluctant to play a scene which required her to grieve over the absence of her mother, whom she loved dearly. We had to explain that she was pretending to be somebody else, a 'pretend girl' who had been left alone because her mother would never come to see her. As soon as she understood, she started to cry bitterly in sympathy for the unhappy girl, and the camera hurriedly filmed her childish sorrow. It was so genuine that it even touched the heart of the producer – a hard-boiled man with many unhappy childhood memories of his own.

On another occasion, a scene required all the children to perform gymnastics in a gymnasium. I left Irène busily doing gymnastics and went to do an urgent errand in town. Upon my return, I found that the scene had changed to one where there were only grown-ups. I looked for Irène, and found her at the back of the gymnasium set, hot, bothered, perspiring and exhausted, still doing gymnastics. Nobody had told her that the scene was over and so dutifully she had continued.

This episode remained in our memories throughout our lives. Each time Irène attempted to force herself to do more than was required of her, I used to say, 'Gymnastics again?'

I was present when the rushes were shown to the American film producers, buyers and talent scouts. Again and again I heard them say, 'Who is that child? Who is that child?' On learning that I was the child's mother, they immediately approached me and several people offered me long-term contracts for her. They insisted that she must go to America where, they felt, she would become what they referred to as 'a brunette Shirley Temple'.

They told me that it was extremely unusual to find a child whose acting was natural. This, they said, was a great contrast to the usual parrot-like performance of a child actor. Irène, they said, seemed to live her lines, not just say them. Upon learning that Irène was a pupil of Madame Kchessinska and had a training in ballet and, in addition, could speak three languages completely accent-free, their enthusiasm knew no bounds. Since I would be needed to look after her, they offered me a contract too.

I thought about it for some time, weighing up the advantages of her having a very interesting life against the disadvantages of her no longer being able to enjoy a normal childhood.

Senia was very much against the idea and practically accused me of selling our daughter. The decision was taken out of my hands. The contract was to be signed on the 1 September 1939, and on that very day war broke out when Germany invaded Poland. I have often bitterly reproached myself for not having taken this opportunity. Irène would thereby have been spared the horror of the war and its aftermath of illness and poverty.

CHAPTER 22

In Tune with Nature

Irène was an unusual child. She had a strange affinity with nature. It was as if she could commune with nature in a mysterious way, and I would often find her quietly and lovingly chatting to a plant or flower. She also had a great love of trees, and would stand with her arms around one, whispering endearing words. Years later, in the course of our psychic studies and development, we discovered that this love of trees is shared by many healers.

We also read of the experiments of a Canadian doctor who claimed to have discovered that trees emit a form of radiation, beneficial to human beings. He used instruments to measure this radiation and wrote a learned paper which he read at a medical congress.

Healers, of course, have always felt this radiation instinctively. Many healers gather strength from trees and recharge their own energies by placing their hands on the trunk of a tree. The famous healer Harry Edwards, for instance, would meditate under a tree before his healing sessions.

Irène also had an extraordinary affinity with animals. This was at times quite uncanny; it was as it she could communicate with them in some strange, non-verbal sense.

One day, she informed her governess that as she was sitting quietly in her nursery, a little old lady had tripped through the room and vanished through a wall. She described the old lady, her face, her hair and her clothes, the latter grey in colour and worn in old-fashioned style. She was a friendly lady, Irène gravely informed the governess. But why did she not use the door to leave the room?

Irène was severely reprimanded for this and made to stand in a corner in disgrace. Little girls were not to tell silly tales like that. My child was psychic, but in those days, neither I nor anyone else who came into contact with her knew or understood this. Years later, as she developed her gift of healing, this sympathy with plants and animals became even greater.

CHAPTER 23

Rumblings of War

While Irène lived in her own little world, tuned in to nature, protected and loved, I was not to know that our lives were to be altered almost out of recognition.

Maybe I should have had more sense, for had not my own life been torn apart when the Bolsheviks came to power? Yet, one never knows in this life what is just around the corner. Irène was happy and content, and though the auguries were not good, I was not going to allow them to spoil it for her. Maybe I just hoped it would all blow over.

By the mid-Thirties, Hitler's threat was looming over every Jewish head, yet many still tried to ignore it, hoping that what he and his Nazi followers were saying were just words. When these words turned into violent action people began to fear for their lives – sometimes too late. In Germany, things got steadily worse while even in England Mosley and his Blackshirts were ranting against the Jews in the streets of London.

There was a widespread upsurge of Fascism, and people began to fear a war; you could even smell something in the wind. The men kept it from us as much as possible, but, of course, we read the papers. Already in Germany they were rounding up Jews, and smashing and looting their shops.

My thoughts went back to Russia and I thought, 'My God, not again. '

During the months before the outbreak of war, my husband Senia was conspicuously quiet. He seemed totally absorbed, looked worried, and said little. He often went out to see somebody, yet would never say where he was going. A strange silence seemed to surround him. I had never known him so quiet before. It was as if he knew of some impending disaster.

Little did I know that he was thinking and planning it all to perfection. He had not just sat back as some did. He too could smell the wind of war and, far worse, he knew that Jews had no chance in France, Germany or anywhere else where the Germans might gain a foothold. As it turned out, he was right.

CHAPTER 24

Yellow Stars in Paris

A German soldier offered Irène a slice of pineapple speared on the
tip of his dagger. The gesture was symbolic. Such kindness was
short-lived. Soon there would be only daggers for the people of
France.

****

We went to the Spanish Consulate to try to obtain a visa. Thousands
of people were besieging the Consulate. We stood for many days,
but there was no possibility at all of getting one. We had to leave.

Then darkness came upon us with the defeat of France in the
summer of 1940 and the Occupation. We had vacated our Paris
apartment in the first wild panic, but decided now to return. The
Occupation army had begun to take over empty apartments and we
had to fight with the authorities to get ours back.

In August 1939, we had been on holiday in Le Touquet, and in
September war had broken out. I telephoned my family in London
and asked for advice. 'Stay in France,' they said; London would be
bombed. Go to Vichy. It would be safe there. Unfortunately, we
took their advice.

The air-raid sirens began to wail day and night. Every time this
happened, a dear old lady who lived in the adjoining villa in Le
Touquet came out and, adjusting her hearing-aid, told us in dramatic
tones that this indicated gas, that we were all doomed, that our last
moments had come!

It was the *drôle de guerre* – the phoney war. Nothing happened
and life appeared more or less normal. My husband and I returned
with Irène to Paris. We all knew the Maginot Line was impregnable.
There was no danger to Paris.

When the Germans reached the Maginot Line and it fell at once, people began to panic. With the enemy getting nearer, most Parisians were leaving – by car, lorry, bicycle, anything on wheels.

The chaos on the trains was indescribable. No-one was able to pass through the carriage doors, which were chock-a-block with standing passengers and luggage. People had to climb in through the windows. At least there were many willing helpers, especially if the passengers were women. We went to Hossegor, a place near Biarritz.

Three days later, the first motorised German troops arrived. They were the advance units of the army. There was no fighting as everything had already been conquered. They were perfectly groomed, and at this stage were under orders to be polite and friendly. This was shortly to change. There were no more pineapple slices. We returned to Paris.

We sent Irène to school and for a time life seemed to settle down and become almost normal. But for us this could not last. We were Jews. Special rules came out. No Jewish person was allowed a radio, or a telephone, or a car, or a bicycle. No Jewish person was to leave home after eight in the evening. All Jews had to queue at the police station and write down their names, addresses and occupations.

From the age of six, Jews had to wear a yellow star sewn on their clothes, and to get these they were obliged to queue again, and pay coupons – textile coupons, which were themselves almost unobtainable and had to be bought or bartered for. We ourselves received three stars each, and as soon as Irène started to wear one, she was automatically expelled from school. No Jew was allowed to buy food, except for one hour in the afternoon, and as the shops in Paris were all closed during this period, life became very difficult. With food scarce in any case, queues formed all over the town.

Then came more regulations. No Jews could enter a theatre or cinema or be in a café. No Jew could sit on any bench in a park or square. A Jew could ride only in the last carriage of the underground train. If found in any other carriage, the penalty was instant deportation.

For the sake of our safety, Senia had gone into hiding. I suffered restless nights wondering if he would be safe. Anyone could give him away – or give us away for that matter.

My mind wandered to the Friday nights at my parents' home when we gathered around the table for the Jewish Sabbath and my mother would say the blessing: 'Blessed art thou, O Lord our God, King of the universe who has sanctified us by thy commandments to kindle the Sabbath lights.' The beautiful glow of the candles was far removed from the Nazi terror that haunted us now. It seemed we were to be hunted down like dogs, but, even then, we still knew little enough of the full horror to come.

On the night of 16 July, at eleven o'clock, Olga, a Gentile friend, sent word that Jews were to be arrested that same night. She advised me to leave my apartment immediately and to hide in some place of safety. As it was already well past the curfew, there was no possibility of our going anywhere, let alone to a 'safe' place. We had no choice, so I packed a small suitcase with a few things for my daughter and myself, and waited all night for the Gestapo.

Five times they came to our block, and each time a family was taken away and seals put on their apartment doors. Irène sat shivering with fright in the corner of the room. The thudding of heavy boots shook the building, and the slamming of doors jarred every nerve.

The screams pierced our ears as families were dragged along the corridors and down the stairs. The Nazis were shouting, 'Come on, you dirty Jews. Schnell! Schnell!' My imagination ran riot as I heard anguished pleas for mercy. I heard baggage being thrown and old men praying. Then small children crying, 'Mama! Papa!' – and several dull thuds, followed by silence. Was this to be our fate?

Irène clutched hold of me and began to scream, 'Mama, mama, have we Jews done something bad?' I pushed my hand over her mouth. One sound and we could have been discovered. I held her close, and could find no answer to her question.

Outside, soldiers were struggling with families as they were herded on to lorries. In those moments, I could find no words to explain pogroms, persecutions, anti-Semitism. With jackboots on the rampage, fuelled by Hitler's madness, my mind went blank with fear. Together, we whispered the age-old Jewish prayer: 'Hear O Israel, The Lord our God, The Lord is One. '

After what seemed an eternity, the screaming died down as the lorries drove off with their pitiful cargo. Sleep did not come any the more easily. As Irène turned restlessly, I thought of my husband. I prayed God he was safe.

In the morning, an Italian friend of Irène from what now seemed far-off ballet school days, came to see if we had been arrested. Finding us sitting with a small suitcase, she asked why we had not taken refuge in the home of a Christian friend. I explained that all our Christian friends were afraid to hide us, that we had nowhere to go. She told us that she would run home and consult her mother. An hour later, she was back to say that they were already stretched to capacity sheltering some twenty of her friends, but would try to make arrangements with another 'safe' family.

Towards evening the little angel came back with an address. I thanked her warmly. Little did I know that this was the last time we would see her. With the Italians still at war, the Germans were keeping to their agreement with Mussolini not to deport or kill Italian Jews. Thus, the members of this little girl's family, including her brothers and sisters, had all received special passports stamped with the word 'Aryan'. Later, however, after Italy's surrender, Italian Jews lost their protection and were deported and murdered, including this splendid family and the little girl who had done so much for us.

The address she had given us was near the Place Victor Hugo. As it was now seven o'clock in the evening, we had to hurry to beat the curfew. After a breakdown on the Métro, we finally alighted at the Place Victor Hugo just a few minutes before eight o'clock. The Gestapo had already begun their rounds to pick up Jews, easily recognisable by their yellow stars. I looked frantically for the house we were seeking – number thirty.

There was no such number. The last number in the road was twenty-eight, and there it stopped. I looked around me. It was past eight o'clock. I had nowhere to go and could not possibly return home. I stood helplessly, holding Irène's hand. What could I do to save us? I could ask for directions, but what if I picked the wrong person – a German in mufti or a Gestapo man? On the other hand, if I stayed like this I would be arrested anyway.

In despair, I decided I had to take the risk. A man passed. There seemed something friendly about him. It was now or never. 'Where is number thirty?'

'Oh,' he said, 'don't you know that this road has been given another name? Number thirty would be number two in the new road.'

I thanked him and started to walk quickly towards the house, the number of which I could now see. As I was entering the courtyard, and turning my back to the street, I spotted a Gestapo man on a motor-bike. He was looking at me suspiciously. Another minute, and I would have been arrested.

The door of the apartment was opened and there stood a woman who was obviously blind. I asked for her name. When she told me I fell into her arms, half-faint with relief. She said in a soft and refined voice, 'This is certainly Madame C, the lady who has come to see me. I can feel by the beat of your heart that you are the lady I am expecting.'

She invited us into the house. She was the widow of a barrister who had died some years before, leaving her with very limited means. Totally blind, she had learned the art of giving ladies a special slimming treatment, consisting of paraffin baths administered in a type of wicker chair containing bags of paraffin. The ladies passed a few hours in these chairs each day. At night, Irène and I slept in them. We had to avoid the customers for fear of being denounced, hiding in the lavatory or, when it was in use, in the kitchen.

In this way we passed four days, being fed by the old lady. When I offered to pay, she would say simply, but indignantly, 'I don't earn money from persecuted people. '

During our stay, we contacted a man who was earning a good living smuggling Jews out of Paris into so-called 'Free France'. France, at the time, was divided into two halves – Occupied France, where the Germans were in uniform, and behaving quite openly as conquerors, and 'Free' France which, as we soon discovered, was free in name only.

The people there looked dejected, and those who were not shuffling along in despair scurried with eyes down for fear of being stopped by the police. Everywhere there was an overwhelming feeling of bewilderment and confusion. We found later that the Germans were there too, but in mufti, and that they behaved exactly like their own counterparts in Occupied France, only more subtly, arresting people but making no boast about it in posters and newspapers. Later, when Italy was out of the war, the whole of France and Italy were occupied by uniformed Germans unashamedly intent on showing their true colours.

Now, though, we contacted our man, who promised to take us over to Dax, the frontier of Free France, and from there to Pau, where, we thought, life really was free. He gave us false papers. They were so badly made that it was risky to use them. Some months previously, when my husband had been with us, the same man had brought us identical papers. My husband had taken them from me, torn them up and thrown them down the lavatory. This time, there was no husband with me. He was hiding in the centre of Paris at a small boarding-house, where the proprietor, at a price, was sheltering him.

Senia and I would meet in the street, our yellow stars on our chests. We spoke only of Irène, there was no other interest in our lives. Our meetings were brief. Sometimes, he would pull us gently into a doorway, and the three of us would huddle together. Irène would cry when her father had to leave. The fear and unreality of it all were beginning to take their toll.

Both Senia and I were so weary and unhappy that we really did not care what happened to us, but the child was so young,and had to be saved, had to be given an opportunity to live. We discussed the possibilities of escaping from Paris and decided that it was I who would have to take her over the frontier. I would have to go alone with her because a family would be so much more conspicuous than just a woman with a child, and, having blue eyes and a very fair skin, I could pass as non-Jewish. It was dangerous enough for a woman, but almost impossible for a man.

CHAPTER 25

Once Again We Make Our Escape

Utter despair and loneliness gripped me when I said goodbye to my husband. I wondered if I would ever see him again, and began to panic. There was no freedom for the people who had to wear the yellow star. Would there ever be freedom again? Yet something deep inside told me that nothing could crush this ancient symbol of ours – the Star of David. Our people had survived many persecutions down the years. I prayed that it would be so again.

Now, I would have to make my own decisions about the false papers, and the train journey to the Free Zone frontier. I decided that the smuggler should take Irène and me to Dax. This would be very dangerous, but at least he was used to these journeys, and he was making a good profit. We agreed that my husband would pay him 6,000 francs on his return. To prove that I really had arrived in the Free Zone, we also agreed that I would send a letter to my husband.

At last, Irène and I left our gentle guardian, the blind widow, and at nine o'clock in the evening set out with just our false papers and one small holdall. We tore off our yellow stars and destroyed them, and went to the home of the smuggler, en route to the Gare de Lyon. Looking at him, however, it occurred to me that the Gestapo must have noticed his frequent appearances at the station. That could prove disastrous. I asked if his daughter, aged fifteen, could accompany us instead. She was acquainted with all the arrangements. He was only too pleased. This would allow him to take on a new case. After all, fortunes were to be made with people like us on the run!

At the station, we immediately noticed two rows of Gestapo. They were obviously waiting for any Jews trying to leave Paris. My heart was in my mouth. Some were dressed in black leather coats, and others in uniform, but all looked very sinister as they stood eyeing each person. I instinctively knew that if we were to get past them in spite of our fear, we would have to act.

Taking the two girls by the hands, I told them such a funny story that they both doubled up with laughter. I forced myself to laugh loudly too. The Gestapo, seeing such apparently happy people, a mother and two daughters, could not possibly imagine that we were Jewish, and let us through without questioning.

Once in the train, however, I realised that the Gestapo would be at every station to question us. I decided to feign to lose my voice. It was a necessary deceit. Both girls believed me and were upset at this sudden loss of speech. That, of course, made it more effective. Now I need say nothing that might give us away. They would thank me later.

All the people in our compartment commiserated with me too. The Gestapo came several times to question me, and it was left to Irène to answer them. Our lives depended on her. She did not let us down.

In the morning, we arrived at Dax, the frontier between Occupied France and 'Free France'. We found it full of uniformed German soldiers, everybody looking at everybody else with suspicion. We hid in the back room of a café for about eight hours.

Later that evening, a peasant came to take Irène and me to a farm. There, we sat until one in the morning. The young girl had already left to return to Paris. I felt some relief at having come this far, but we were fugitives and could only pray that nobody would give us away. We were, after all, not the only ones fighting for survival.

I thought of my husband and whether or not he was still free. I knew it would not be easy for him, and yet I was constantly aware that his thoughts were with us, that he would be wondering the same things as myself. In our position, that was the only comfort any of us could draw. We were not alone in this nightmare – there were thousands of us. I had never thought that blonde hair could have been such a blessing, but a blessing it was. Sometimes I felt guilty about it, but in the end I consoled myself with the thought that this was simply how the Creator had made me.

I wondered what had happened to those poor families who had been dragged from their apartments. I also wondered how all this would affect Irène. In short, I could not stop thinking about this terrible war. My mind went back to the pogroms in Russia; it certainly was not easy being a Jew. I tried to comfort myself with thought of the good times in between, but they seemed so far away.

Not at any time did I blame God, as some did in their anguish. I just blamed the inhumanity of man, which had reached an all-time peak with Hitler's rise to power. His hatred of Jews was completely beyond my comprehension, but anti-Semitism has long been, and remains, something which rears its despicable head when fanatics get into power.

The frontier consisted of a main road between two fields. There were two ways of crossing it, the peasant told us: either you crawled on your stomach till you reached the road and then made a dash for it, or else you crawled through a disused pipe which passed under the road. The danger above-ground was that the Germans hid in the long grass in the field and shot at any point where they saw grass moving. The danger below ground was that the Germans had discovered the existence of the pipe and would let the traveller inch his way almost to the end of it and then aim a machine gun into it and let go. We chose to go above ground. The possibility of being shot at in the open seemed less terrifying than being shot at in a pipe.

At two o'clock in the morning we began the perilous journey, crawling on our stomachs over fields and under hedges. The ground was full of thistles and Irène, who wore ankle socks and a short skirt, tore her skin as we crawled towards the frontier.

Suddenly the peasant motioned us into a ravine, urging us to lie quite still. To my horror I heard the barking of a dog. It was well known in France that that on the frontiers the Gestapo had fierce Alsatian police dogs who searched for refugees and tore them to pieces. There I was, holding the hand of my child, alone in a field except for the guide, near an Alsatian who would certainly maul us to death. I could not even pray, reproaching myself for bringing Irène here, for not finding a better way to save her young life. My mind a whirl, what did I not think of in these terrible few minutes as I listened to the barking of the dog, waiting for what I believed to be the end . . . .

The peasant told us in a whisper to crawl quickly over the road. We did so, and saw what had caused the commotion. There was a herd of cattle with a dog – a good old-fashioned farm-dog, not an Alsatian at all. He was running round the cattle. How I loved that dog! In the middle of the herd of cows was a small vehicle containing two German soldiers, rifles in the air, cursing and shouting, unable to advance or reverse.

Had they looked back instead of sideways, we could not have saved ourselves. 'Run, run for your lives,' whispered the peasant, 'but do so bent double.' We obeyed as best we could, and reached the other side, to what we believed was our refuge.

We sat in the peasant's farm all night, downing glass after glass of green water. The ordeal had left me parched and I was too exhausted to worry about the colour of the water. Later, we discovered that the farm's drinking water came from a small muddy pond shared by ducks, cows and numerous frogs. Never mind, we were alive. We just had to survive.

The smuggler from Paris arrived on the following morning. With him was a Jewish lady. He brought a small piece of paper on which were written endearing words from my husband. Had Irène not been with me, I would have made my way back to Paris just to be with him – whatever our fate might have been. I wept as I read the note, but we had agreed that the first priority was to save our child. That was a plan we could not change.

My husband had already gone through a great deal of danger to get us this far. There could be no turning back now. I read his note over and over again, and felt desolate. Yet I knew that, however great our danger, his was greater.

I regained my composure, and awaited instructions. We were to go to the main road. A taxi had been arranged. This would take us to Pau in the Pyrenees. The Jewish lady would go with us. He himself was going back to Paris. We stood in the road and waited.

CHAPTER 26

Hunted Like Dogs

'Your papers?' A French policeman suddenly approached us. I felt sick inside. He stared hard at me. It was difficult not to show fear, but one had become accustomed to putting on an act, even though one's very nerves trembled. He snatched the papers from me as if I were a criminal. I wondered if the false documents would really bear close examination. They contained a false name and address. A simple telephone call would reveal everything.

The lady with us was of Polish origin. She had lived in Paris for over thirty years but had never bothered to learn to speak correct French. Her French passport was genuine, but her name was absolutely unpronouncable: Schmazkerton-Shazkelowitz. The policeman certainly could not pronounce it and, furthermore, could understand not a word of what she was saying. Then it dawned. 'But you are Jews. Come with me, we go to the Germans – they will sort you out.' That would mean certain death. Once in the hands of the Germans, we could not hope to escape.

At first, I felt like appealing to him, but quickly changed my mind. I just had to keep up the pretence that we were not Jews. How, I did not know. My heart pounded against my chest, but I couldn't show how I really felt. I dared not. My mind was in a whirl, and his words, 'The Germans will sort you out', kept ringing through my head. I was half-inclined to make a dash for it, but realised that would have been stupid.

Later on, I was told that the first three hundred metres of Free France was supposed to be still in the hands of the Germans. As we walked, I had only a few moments to think. Trying to make my voice very quiet so as not to show my terrible fear, I said, 'I notice that you are wearing the Croix de Lorraine.' This was a special cross worn by the people of Lorraine. Alsace and Lorraine were now provinces of France, but at one time had belonged to Germany. Consequently, the inhabitants very often spoke fluent German, but very poor French. 'I am Lorrain and I am proud of it – but I hate Jews!' he replied.

'Oh,' I said. 'You are Lorrain and you did not realise that this poor woman is not Jewish at all but Alsatian, which is why she has an unpronounceable name and very bad French. You, a Lorrain, take an Alsatian woman to the Germans! You know very well what the Germans do to the Alsatians who run away from them – they kill them on the spot!'

The policeman thought for a little, and then said, 'You are right, run for your life!'

We ran!

We arrived in Pau and checked into a small hotel. We were, of course, relieved in one sense, but ... soon it would all be starting again.

There seemed no let-up. It was terrible being a fugitive. One experienced the sheer hell of feeling totally abandoned.

There were a number of people staying at the hotel, and it was apparent that some of them were on the run, although, like us, they had learned the art of composure under stress. Yet a sense of unease still hung in the air. There was an elderly couple in the corner, and I noticed that the man was swaying vaguely to and fro. His lips were moving slightly. I was sure he was a Jew and was praying as inconspicuously as he could. Only a fellow-Jew would have noticed.

By the fireplace, a family glanced nervously towards the front door every time it was opened. The children were subdued and looked extremely tired. They were certainly not on holiday. I was sure a number of these guests had false papers. There were one or two couples playing cards, but this did nothing to make for a carefree atmosphere. Not that one was to be expected but, generally, people tried to stay cheerful. For Jews, it was harder than most. The proprietor told us that the French police and the Gestapo arrived at seven o'clock each morning to check the papers of new arrivals. Anyone arousing suspicion would, of course, be arrested.

The Polish lady certainly could not stay, and my own papers could hardly be guaranteed to pass muster. I would have to leave early the next morning. But where would I go? I had never been to this part of France before, and knew no-one.

Before we left Paris, the smuggler had told us that his brother-in-law lived not far from Pau. He had given us his address in case of emergency. I had seen a car in the drive of the hotel, and, in despair, asked the proprietor if he would be willing, for money, to take my daughter and me to this village. The distance would be some fifty kilometres. He agreed, though only for a sizeable fee. I had no choice but to pay it.

We left at five in the morning. I held my breath all the way to the village. Would we be stopped on the road? I told Irène to say nothing, but to try and look cheerful and happy, however little she may have felt like it. She wondered what it was all about. How could one explain? We saw a few people on bicycles, and although they looked quite harmless, I felt very much on edge, and did not enjoy the run at all.

In due course we reached the village, and found the place, a small wooden house, more like a hut than a house, and were greeted by the brother-in-law, a workman employed at a small local factory. He told us that he had lost his wife, and was left with three children. The youngest had been adopted by a wealthy family in Marseilles, while the second was staying with an aunt. Only the eldest, a boy aged thirteen, remained, and he ran the house while his father was at work.

There was no lavatory. A small hut at the bottom of the garden contained a makeshift seat fixed to the wall, but waste had accumulated to within inches of the sitter. The stench on this hot summer's day, with the flies buzzing around, was indescribable.

The workman very kindly gave us his bedroom and shared his son's room during our stay. In the former, the mantelpiece served as a kind of shrine to his departed wife. There were several photographs, each one covered in about an inch of dust, a very dirty handkerchief, last used by his wife, and a comb full of her hair.

There were so many flies in the room that Irène decided to escape them by hiding in the bed and pulling the blankets over her head. Unfortunately, there were so many fleas in the bed itself that Irène's entire body was covered with bites, and she had a rash which looked like scarlet fever.

CHAPTER 27

The Letter

We stayed there for six weeks, desperately waiting for news from my husband, who was to have taken the next train and met us in Pau. I had left my address with the hotel proprietor.

At last, a letter arrived. It was addressed to the workman and was from the smuggler in Paris. When the workman came to my room, he simply stood there, ashen-faced, twiddling the letter in his hands. Finally, he blurted out the news. My husband, it said, had met with a fatal accident on the train to Dax. My heart stood still. This had been our code. 'Accident' stood for arrest. 'Fatal accident' stood for deportation. My beloved husband had been arrested on the train, and deported to Germany. We were alone.

Many years later, Irène told me how she had gone out by herself into the garden that day, prayed and vowed to try to grow up quickly, work hard, look after me and replace her father to the best of her ability. She was twelve years old.

A few days later, the workman knocked at my door. Again he looked uneasy. I asked him why. The question was this, he said: would I marry him? He realised that it was a little soon to put such a question, but there had been gossip in the village. People said that Irène and I did not look like working folk, and they did not believe him when he assured them that we were relatives from Paris. If I married him the gossip would stop, and everything would be all right. If I did not, it would be dangerous for us to continue staying there.

The authorities, he went on, paid a large reward to any villager who informed on a Jew or a possible member of the Resistance. Sooner or later one of the villagers would be tempted to denounce us, even inventing a story if necessary. Since I was now alone, and he was a widower, the ideal solution, in his opinion, was for us to get married.

The time had clearly come to move on. But where to? It was my husband who had constructed the itinerary. The workman gave us a letter of introduction to his son's foster-parents in Marseilles. Perhaps they could help me. I decided to risk travelling by train once again. We said our farewells.

After a gruelling journey in a filthy train, we arrived in Marseilles at six o'clock in the morning, tired, hungry and trembling with fright and exhaustion. The family, though charming in manner, were horrified when they heard the purpose of our visit. They explained that we had landed in hell itself. We could not stay even a single day, and should return to the station immediately. Marseilles was full of Gestapo agents and arrests were taking place day and night. They themselves were leaving in a couple of days to hide in a village. Life in Marseilles had become impossible.

They gave us coffee (a rarity), with milk (a still greater rarity), and let us have a good wash and a rest, but that was all they could do for us. I considered trying to board a foreign ship, but the port was in the hands of the Germans and nobody could leave without passing a security check by the Gestapo. Realising the danger, I had to say goodbye to these kind people. When I went to fetch Irène, she was de-fleaing herself in the bathroom, surrounded by tooth-mugs filled with water, busily drowning fleas.

What should we do next? To stay a night in Marseilles would be sheer suicide. The Gestapo were everywhere and there was absolutely nowhere to hide. We had to leave as soon as possible, and not later than that evening! Yet where were we to go? I remembered my husband having spoken in Paris of some business friends in Lyons. I decided to seek their help.

CHAPTER 28

We Move on in Terror

Reaching Lyons proved a gruelling affair. A journey normally taking four hours by train and about half an hour by aeroplane, took us two days and nights. As usual, the compartments were filled to capacity. As usual, the windows were the sole means of ingress. As usual, they were very high. As usual, benevolent passengers helped us through. At one point, Irène's face turned pale and she gave a little gasp. I anxiously inquired whether she was all right. 'Of course I'm all right,' she said. 'But I forgot to empty one of the glasses in that bathroom, and it's there with a flea in it!'

In the train at night, Irène, very tired, would sleep on me. She had rather long legs and would push them into other people's faces. A young man next to me, thus inconvenienced, had a gentle way of removing them from his face. It seemed to say a lot. I decided to ask him where a mother and child could go for a 'holiday'.

He told me of a little place, one hundred kilometres from Lyons by the River Loire, where a stationmaster and his wife might be willing to take a guest or two for the summer. The prices were reasonable, and the food, if not luxurious, was at least wholesome. There was, of course, no real comfort – not even a lavatory in the house, no running water, and so on. In the circumstances, though, considering the general shortage of food, it was a nice place for a short stay. I memorised the address.

We arrived in Lyons at about eleven o'clock at night. At the station, I telephoned the people I had come to see. My heart sank like a stone when a servant told me that they were away on holiday and were not expected back for a couple of weeks. He could not give me their address as letters were not being forwarded.

There I was, in a strange town, at eleven o'clock at night, all alone with Irène, with nowhere to go. It was impossible to stay the night at the station. Not only would police and Gestapo be searching it every hour or so, but we had been told on the train that it was infested with bugs and that various diseases were consequently being picked up. I asked a porter if there was any possibility of finding a room. 'Oh no,' he replied; it was absolutely full up everywhere. By now, Irène was so exhausted, she could hardly stand.

Opposite the station was one of the best hotels in Lyons. If a room was to be found, it would be there. The hall of the hotel was very large, and one had to pass down the length of it to reach the receptionist's desk. When I finally reached the desk, I saw a prominent notice: 'Jews are prohibited from coming to this hotel'.

As I read it, I saw the receptionist watching me with small inquisitive eyes. Taking my courage in both hands, I asked whether they had a room to let. He scrutinised my face, looked at my fair hair, fair complexion and blue eyes, and told me that I was very lucky and that they had a room for one night. I forced myself to ask how much it would cost. It was sixty francs, which was a lot of money, but I did not argue.

The room was clean, and had hot and cold running water, a luxury we had not enjoyed since leaving Paris, and were not to enjoy again for some time to come. There were clean beds, and clean sheets. Irène's excitement was absolutely overwhelming. She immediately started to wash with the hot water. 'Look, mummy, clean towels, two clean towels!' There was, as usual, no soap. Instead, we had to manage with our own rations – some kind of pumice stone, which tore off the skin and left red marks over us. But that did not matter. Hot water, clean towels! What more could one want!

A telephone call came through from the receptionist. He had forgotten to ask for my papers. 'The police', meaning, of course, the Gestapo, would be calling at seven o'clock in the morning. He had to have the papers by then. It was now midnight. I decided we could not risk giving in our false papers. This meant we had only a few hours before us. I told Irène to go to bed at once and sleep. I then went over to the station and found out that a train would be leaving for the little place near Lyons at five o'clock in the morning. This suited us well.

Back at the hotel, I paid my bill, and told the receptionist that we would be leaving early in the morning. If he was suspicious, he said nothing. At four o'clock, I roused Irène. It was agony for me to do so, and even worse agony for her to have to leave the so-rare warmth and comfort of a clean bed. It had to be done.

The journey took several hours, and we arrived at the village in the late morning. There we found the stationmaster and his wife were eager to put us up. Their small, wooden house was right by the station, and the trains caused so much vibration that it was as though they were passing through the building itself.

We had, of course, been warned not to expect comfort. Those warnings were justified. There was no running water, and no proper lavatory. What we did have, however, was a cosy little room with quite a comfortable bed.

On going down to the dining-room for lunch, we were surprised by the strange combinations of people we saw there – a lady and a policeman sitting together at a small table, a couple and a policeman at another table, a gentleman with a policeman. Every table had a policeman with whoever else was sitting at it.

This confused us. We asked our landlady to explain. 'Oh, these are all Jews.' There was a camp by the main road, a barracks, where Jews who had been arrested were assembled prior to being deported to concentration camps.

'But why the policeman?' I asked.

'Well,' she replied, 'if a Jewish person wants to have a proper lunch, he has to invite a policeman so as to be able to leave the camp.'

'A Jewish camp? But I thought this was Free France?'

'Oh, the Germans do not wear uniforms here, but that is the only difference.' Whatever they wore, the full impact of their vile deeds gripped me with terror.

Coming back from lunch, I passed the station just as a train approached. It did not stop. From it came terrible screams, shouts and cries. 'What is that?' I asked, aghast.

'Oh, nothing,' came the reply, 'only Jews being deported to Germany.'

I began to feel that I could not have chosen a worse place. It was full of police and Gestapo; it was a small village; everybody knew everybody else; I was a stranger and staying near such a camp. Then, on the day after my arrival, a gendarme stopped me in the street, asked to see my papers and wanted to know from where I had come and what I was doing.

We returned to the guest house and there the landlady saved me. She was a relative of the gendarme, and told him to leave me alone and 'not to interfere with my guests!' But the incident terrified me. Clearly, I could not stay.

After much thought, I recalled a friend in Paris having told me of a Polish lady friend she knew in Grenoble. The lady would sometimes send her provisions, even an occasional chicken, and did not charge exorbitant prices. The address was still clear in my mind. I decided to write and ask if she could help us. I hardly expected a reply, but, to my amazement, received one in under a week.

The Polish lady herself had left for America three months before, but her mother wrote to say that there was a vacant room in the house where she herself was staying, and that it could be let to us. We left for Grenoble at once.

War-weary, tired of being on the run, having no answer to Irène's questions, having terrible dreams almost every night of the Gestapo bursting in on us – life was one long nightmare. I made up my mind that we would pretend to be going for a holiday in Grenoble. We had grown accustomed to such 'games'. I even found myself believing in them. What else could we do?

CHAPTER 29

The Gestapo in Grenoble

Grenoble was a picturesque town, surrounded by mountains. It had a university and a number of schools and colleges. For the moment, the war seemed far away. Such thoughts were short-lived.

We were well received. The Polish mother, elderly and white-haired, was a widow, having previously been married to a doctor. She had left her native land before the German occupation, but was only recently established in France. She lived there alone, although the landlady, who resided on her farm outside Grenoble, would use one of the three rooms when she was in town. Our room contained only one bed, though it was otherwise comfortable.

The Polish mother promised to show us where we could buy food – what little of it there was. She asked me why we had come to Grenoble. I told her that I wanted my daughter to go to school here. At this stage, I did not dare to talk more intimately. We left it at that, and settled down to our first night in Grenoble.

Suddenly, we were awoken by a ring at the door, a strong, persistent ring. It was four o'clock in the morning. The mother answered it, and came face-to-face with a group of people. It sounded as if there were about five or six of them. The Gestapo had come to arrest her. We heard her cry out, then make a request to go to the lavatory.

'Leave the door open,' came the reply. 'We know you dirty Jews – throwing yourselves out of the window and depriving us of a Jew! We must round up seven hundred Jews tonight, and you're one of them!' The poor woman sobbed loudly as she dressed, I heard one of the men ask who was in the next room. My heart missed a beat. 'Oh, some people here for a child to go to a local school. '

'Jews?'

'No. '

Before they left, one of the men knocked on my door. As I was speechless with fright, I made a sign to Irène to answer it. 'What is it?' she asked.

'Oh, excuse us,' he said, 'we are arresting a dirty Jewish woman and she tells us you have no key to the front door. Here is her key.'

We did not sleep for the rest of the night. We did not know what to do, where to go, how to live in this unfamiliar town where we knew nobody. In the morning I had to go out for some bread and apples. The day dragged through to evening. We were lonely – lonely and forlorn, and went to bed very early.

At five o'clock the following morning, we were aroused by loud knocks and a furious ringing of the bell. Now it must be us they wanted. Had they come to arrest us? I could hardly speak. I knew that the Gestapo never broke down the doors of Gentiles, but if the concierge had a key they would not need to. If the concierge had no key, they would wait until the morning and then return with a locksmith. I decided not to answer, to let them ring as long as they wanted to, and, after they had left, to leave the apartment altogether.

Then, I heard a familiar voice. 'Let me in. It's me. Please let me in.' It was not the Gestapo at all. I jumped out of bed and opened the door at once. There stood the Polish mother, her clothes torn, her face dirty, her hair dishevelled. She told us that she was taken to a square, a sort of park, where lorries were waiting for the seven hundred Jews to be arrested that night. She was the first. When the soldiers threw her into the lorry, she had a heart attack and very nearly died. Seeing her condition, one of the Gestapo men had kicked her out of the lorry and left her to die, or so he thought.

When she came round, she crawled into a bush and hid until all the lorries had gone. The next night she crawled out of the bushes and came home.

We decided to leave, and the sooner the better. But now came the eternal question: where to go? How could we know that we would not be betrayed wherever we went? How could we know who lived next to us and what their connections were with the Gestapo? Any person who denounced a member of the Resistance or a Jew could be certain of receiving a very handsome sum of money as a reward, and as money was scarce and life difficult, there were always people who chose this way of making a living.

In a forlorn side street, very provincial-looking but peaceful, we noticed a small house surrounded by an ill-kept garden. It was really more of a cottage, rambling and tumbledown, consisting of two floors. A notice outside said: 'Pension'. The ground floor was almost entirely occupied by a rather large dining-room and a small kitchen. The first floor was the 'Pension' – the boarding-house where a few people lived in small dingy bedrooms. We moved into this place.

The furniture in our room consisted of two beds, a broken wardrobe, a rickety table, and a broken chair. The beds were none too clean, the sheets and blankets torn and stained. We also had an armchair, though in name only, for it was so unstable that it was not safe to sit on. Every time we attempted to sit on it, a cloud of dust rose.

We tried beating the dust out, but one cannot beat out the accumulated dust of several generations, so after a concentrated effort, during which we were nearly choked, we gave up. Still, there was food in the house, and being on full board meant having lunch every day, which was the main meal. The proprietress had connections with some farmers and at the beginning of our stay gave us comparatively good food – even an egg sometimes, and a glass of pale blue milk for Irène.

CHAPTER 30

Madame Arlette and the Menagerie

Madame Arlette herself was a vast woman, with a pleasant face and white hair. The boarders were a very mixed lot. As we soon discovered, some were spies for the Gestapo, others were members of the Resistance, some were Jews, and some were non-French Alsatians. At that time, the latter were in great danger, for every Alsatian not wanting to live under the German heel was considered by the occupying forces to be a traitor to his country, and was to be exterminated.

I told Madame Arlette that I had come here because I had quarrelled with my husband and run away from home. What else could I say? My poor husband would certainly have forgiven me for this lie, for we both decided long ago to do everything to try and save Irène, even to sacrificing ourselves for her.

Besides the boarders, the cottage was occupied by the young son of the landlady, a boy of considerable good looks who, being over forty years younger than his mother, was hopelessly spoiled. Nothing was good enough for him, and the words he used in speaking, shouting, demanding and quarrelling with his mother were quite appalling.

We also learned to live with the dog and a Persian cat, so overfed that Madame Arlette, who loved it dearly, never let it out of the house for fear it would vanish into a neighbour's cooking pot. Many dogs and cats were stolen for food at that time.

In the garden lived a goose, the terror of all the residents, and especially of my little daughter. When Irène went out through the garden, there being no other entrance or exit, the goose would wait for her and attack her bare legs. It really was an ordeal to pass through the garden, and even adults had to fight the goose every time they came in for lunch. All the boarders, especially the people who came for lunch, complained to the landlady, but there was no response, and as the meals were comparatively cheap and not too bad, people still kept coming, goose or no goose.

In the garden were several chickens. It was a lovely sight to see the proud hens walking with their own brood of chicks, and, often, another's. Madame Arlette used to take the newly-hatched chicks into the kitchen and put them into a lukewarm oven to help them grow more quickly. Bringing them out of the oven, invigorated and happy, she would put them next to the chicken she though most deserving of the privilege.

All the time we lived there we had neither chicken nor goose for meals, and I suppose that all those lovely fowls were sold on the black market to more privileged people, or even, perhaps, to the occupying forces, which would explain why we were generally left alone, with only an occasional search and arrest.

The animal population inside the house, apart from the dog and cat, proved to be less pleasant. We had mice, fleas and bugs a-plenty. The bugs were, of course, the most bothersome, and a young girl who lived next to us was so pestered by them – having a wooden bed it was impossible to get rid of them even temporarily – that she decided to sleep in the corridor, next to our door, thus forcing us to disturb her every time we went to the lavatory. Still, this arrangement was more pleasant for her as there were fewer bugs in the corridor than in the bed. But she acquired a boyfriend and sleeping in the corridor à deux gave rise to some scandal. The girl had to leave. The vacant room was promptly occupied by people who heroically put up with the bugs and did not even complain about them.

The mice were another story. I have been frightened of mice all my life, having once had one on my face on a camping expedition, and I have never been able to purge this childish fear. We had mice galore in our room, romping all over the place, and they especially liked to live in the cupboard.

We certainly had no food in the room, for we had none to spare, whatever we had being eaten immediately, but the mice fed on our underclothing, of which we also had little enough. Once or twice we tried to lure the cat to our room, and once I actually managed to put her into the cupboard where all the mice were romping, but she disdainfully scorned them and went to sleep on our bed instead, shedding all her fleas around her. This cat was so adored by our landlady that she never went hungry, and mice were of no interest to her.

There was one maid for the whole house. She had to clean the rooms, help the cook, serve lunch, wash up and look after the goose, among other duties. How she did it, nobody knew, especially as she was young and very interested in the opposite sex. Of course, she never cleaned our room, but this we did not expect, since she had little time. In any case, we preferred to do our room ourselves.

The floor was not touched all the time we were there. What could we have used to clean it? There was no soap; the so-called soap we received every three months on our rations was, as mentioned before, no better than a pumice stone.

We lived in this house for several months, as the food situation gradually deteriorated. Sometimes, for two days and nights, a terrible smell would permeate the house. At these times, animal entrails were being cooked. Hungry as we were, we could not force ourself to eat things which needed forty-eight hours of cooking to make them tender enough for human consumption.

Life went on. I suffered from insomnia, no doubt caused by anxiety, and during the long still hours of the night my mind would wander back longingly to my early years in Russia, my life in Paris, my daughter's childhood.

CHAPTER 31

Our Life in Grenoble

By now, in 1944, the so-called 'Free Zone' of France had been abolished and German uniforms were to be seen everywhere. For a short time, the town of Grenoble had been occupied by the Italian army, and life was reasonably tolerable. The soldiers and officers were happy people, and reminded me of the chorus of an opera. They wore felt hats with a long feather sticking out, which made Irène laugh.

Soon, many inhabitants wore a feather just for fun. Some went a bit too far, and put feathers in slightly delicate places, but it offered some light relief after what we had been through. A couple of offenders were arrested, so this bit of feathered fun came to an abrupt end.

Still, the Italians were really nice and did not bother anybody. They had a romantic disposition; they liked good-looking girls and offered them flowers and gifts. We found this break very welcome, and it was, after all, a little bit like the 'pretend' holiday that I had told Irène we were going to have in Grenoble. She began to smile a little, and was not quite so nervous.

Certainly these soldiers were very different from the Germans we had encountered. But, alas, all this was to change dramatically the day the Italians were out of the war. Scores of them were arrested, and many were deported and killed. Once the Italian occupation ended, the German terror began all over again. I felt I could not take much more of it. Even the sight of them was making me a nervous wreck, and, once again, the dreaded Gestapo were back. Their atrocities were vile. They had no mercy, no compassion. They were just filled with hate.

The shootings were terrible, and the noise went right through us. We shivered and shook and huddled together as people were dragged through the streets in front of us. There were bodies and blood everywhere. The Gestapo were not human, they revelled in their atrocities. The Resistance would kill a German soldier, and immediately the Germans would take twenty young people, Jews and non-Jews alike, as hostages, and shoot them in the market-place in front of their mothers and fathers, who were forced to witness the massacre.

In the town itself there was something called a *rafle*, a round-up or raid. A few German soldiers would walk around, casually window-shopping, when a red flare would suddenly go off and the street would be surrounded by soldiers. Every passer-by was searched and anyone looking like a Jew or a member of the Resistance would be arrested or shot. I myself was on several occasions caught in such a *rafle*, and only by making my face expressionless and showing no fear could I avoid being arrested.

We lived in Grenoble for many months. Before long, real food was completely unobtainable. Our rations were meagre and the little we had was 'synthetic' – bread made of grass, coffee of nutshells. People who had farms or relatives owning farms were in a privileged position; we, unfortunately, had no such relatives.

The only other way of securing food was by barter. The farmers were not interested in money, for it could not buy anything, but if one had something to exchange, then they would sometimes be prepared to make a deal. Such deals were quite amazing – grand pianos were exchanged for eggs, precious china for potatoes. We ourselves had very little to exchange, except my mink coat which had somehow been smuggled to me from Paris through a relative. This I exchanged for butter, which, although made only of some kind of candle-grease, was at least fat, and helped to keep us alive.

Our strangest form of barter, however, was one which consisted of 'music for sausages'. I exchanged giving piano lessons to the local butcher's daughter for sausages provided by her father. The arrangement was for a section of sausage per lesson, so that it took quite a few lessons to make up one sausage. The butcher guaranteed that the sausage, although containing *des substances variées*, a variety of things, was not made from cat or rat meat. So that was something!

I wonder what Brahms would have thought of his waltz being exchanged for a sausage! For it was his waltz that I tried to teach Lucette, the butcher's daughter. She was nine years of age, and the waltz was to be performed at the second wedding of her aunt. Even today, I only have to hear the first notes of that waltz for the ghastly memories of the war to come back to me.

On the day before the performance, I told Lucette that if she forgot a few notes, she should just carry on as if nothing had happened; nobody, I was sure, would notice that anything was amiss. Should she forget everything, she was to repeat the beginning, thus giving herself time to remember the rest.

The great day came and went. The following day, Papa Butcher brought Lucette to her lesson in person. Taking a long, thin and rather wet sausage, a whole sausage, out of his pocket, he presented this to me and said, 'Formidable! Absolument formidable! Magnificent! Not one of my relatives can understand how a child as young as Lucette could play so long a piece. Formidable! You are a wonderful teacher, so wonderful that I would like you to give me singing lessons, so that I too can perform. There is another wedding in the family in three weeks' time. Teach me to sing and I'll double the sausage.' Being basically honest, I started to tell him that I was a pianist, not a singer, but the thought of the sausage was too much for me, and I agreed to give him singing lessons.

Papa went home jubilant, and Lucette then proceeded to give her version of the event. She had forgotten the whole piece, and could remember only the first four bars. So she repeated these. She repeated them nineteen times, receiving thunderous applause!

And so the Bel Canto lessons started. I asked Papa what type of voice he had. Papa was offended. 'Type of voice?' he said. 'Type of voice? A voice!' The voice proved to be a mediocre and extremely shaky baritone.

We started work on it. What would the song be? Papa had made up his mind already. As it was a wedding it must be something cheerful. He fished out of his pocket a small sheet of music, on the cover of which was a picture of a fat lady with scarlet lips and a large bosom. The title, as he happily informed me, was 'La Tristesse de Chopin'. I was somewhat surprised. 'I thought you wanted something cheerful,' I said.

'But,' Papa said, 'it *is* cheerful.' He sang it then and there. Cheerful it certainly was: the editors of this ten-centime edition had jazzed the thing up.

Papa's performance at the wedding was a triumph. They clapped and cheered, he gleefully informed me, brandishing a huge sausage in payment. And then they had roared for more. Alas, there was no encore, since Papa knew only one song!

That was one cheerful interlude, but in Grenoble we also passed through many gruelling experiences. The Czech soldiers, who had been forcibly incorporated into the German army, revolted, and one night I sat up in my bed counting the shots I could hear ... 365, 366, 367 ... I knew that every shot meant a lost life. But who was being shot, and how many? Irène suddenly woke up, and seeing me sitting up in bed in the middle of the night, hearing me counting in a loud voice, thought I had gone insane, and started to cry.

In the morning, we learned that there had been fighting between the Germans and Czechs and that many hundreds of soldiers had been shot. One could see that the streets had been freshly washed, with traces of blood only in the gutters.

On another occasion, a young man of the Resistance, a hero, stole a German uniform, went into the German barracks, locked himself in the arsenal and put a match to the explosives. The ammunition was destroyed, but so also was a large part of the town. As the explosions began, the French police toured the town in cars with loudspeakers, urging people to leave their houses and to save themselves if possible – indeed to leave altogether, for the entire town was expected to blow up. Those who had cars, lorries or bicycles fled, but what could we do?

We went out into the street. There was a small shop around the corner owned by a large, very fat lady, who sometimes sold a little cheese and butter on the black market. She saw us, called us in and threw a chunk of cheese at us. It was a huge piece, something we had not seen for years. Her teeth were chattering, her ample bosom heaved like a mountain so that she could hardly utter a word. We were all going to die, she wept, we *were* dying, so what did profit matter? 'Take as much cheese as you can while you are still alive,' she urged.

We went back home and sat in the hall beside a main wall which we hoped would stand the explosion, and looked at the cheese, which was so beautiful, cheese worth a fortune, and not paid for. We decided to wait until the end was very close before biting into it, and then to depart in style. As it happened, we later returned the cheese to its owner. Although half the town was destroyed, the destruction came to an end two streets before our own.

On another night, there were more explosions near our house, and I remember pulling Irène away from the window where she was looking at the explosions. She said afterwards that I tore at her by the hair. This was quite possible, since the danger was so great that I may have panicked a little.

CHAPTER 32

Bombs and Ballet

Some days, bombs fell from the sky – English and American bombs. This did not happen often, but caused many casualties whenever it did. After each of these raids, posters went up to tell the population that the Free French from London and America were killing French people. Such bombs were called 'Churchill Plums' by the Germans.

One hot summer's day, at about noon, a raid began as we were preparing lunch. We had no shelters and were now so accustomed to the bombing that we did not go down to the cellar, where the people of our house usually assembled. These cellars were far from adequate, and after a few houses were bombed and the inhabitants buried alive in them, most people would not use the cellar as a shelter.

We ourselves took our coats and our passports with us and waited for the raid to finish. That day, a bomb fell nearby and the windows of our house were shattered, the whole building trembling with the impact. The normally quiet and self-possessed Irène panicked. She tore off her dress, a kind of button-through cotton overall, grabbed me by the hand and ran down three flights of stairs stark naked. I ran alongside her, shouting and screaming, but it was not until we reached the cellar that she noticed that she was naked, and let me put a coat over her.

For a little while Irène went to a very strict Catholic school, but soon she had to give this up as she did not know the prayers and could not risk being found out. Any sign that she was Jewish would have spelt our end.

As Irène had had several years of ballet training in Paris, I was pleased to discover an old lady, over seventy years of age, who had been a well-known ballet dancer at the Imperial Theatre in St Petersburg many years before. Some of the townspeople arranged for her to give ballet lessons in a wooden shack normally used as a meeting-place for old soldiers of the 1914-18 war. There was an old upright piano there, and the floor, although not very even, was quite large and made a fair classroom for ballet dancing. There was no pianist, and, before I met the old lady, they had only one record to play, against which all the movements were taught.

When I visited the shack for the first time, I was amazed by the dust and dirt everywhere, by the old, lonely-looking ex-soldiers and officers sitting around watching the antics of the old lady with delight. Her movements were still full of grace and her face must have been angelic in her youth, although it was now old, tired, hungry-looking, and so wrinkled that her beauty was almost gone.

The evening was wintry when I came with Irène, and the class was in full swing. Three girls and two boys were jumping, running and trying to do ballet points. The lessons were cheap, cheaper still if I would oblige by playing the piano so that the children could have the necessary music for their exercises. The lessons were given twice a week in the late afternoon, and I agreed to play the piano.

Soon many more soldiers began to come during the lessons and it was really a great pleasure for them to watch the young girls in their short dresses romping gracefully around the room.

Sometimes, when a higher grade ex-officer came, the old lady herself would dance a waltz by Chopin, or a mazurka. She would fly about the dusty room, arms outstretched, feet as light as a young girl's, her pathetic face wrinkled and tired, with her ancient clothing flying about her. I would play waltzes and mazurkas at her request and, watching her, I really wanted to cry, so pathetic was her appearance. Having finished the dance, she would take a considerable time to regain her breath before slowly moving forward to resume her lessons.

The time came when all the inhabitants of the town had to go to the police to be issued with new identity papers. I was afraid to show my current ones as they were so obviously false. The Germans were becoming even tougher, the *rafles* (raids) and arrests more frequent. We felt we could not stay any longer in Grenoble, and as there was nowhere else to go but the mountains, we left one wintry day by coach to go into the Vercors, a mountainous region above Grenoble and the most dangerous, the most feared, and the most heroic Resistance centre in the whole of France.

We took a room with a peasant woman. The woods were full of young people, the village was full of the young and not-so-young, and a few Jewish people. All the new arrivals were scrutinised to ascertain whether or not they were German or French spies, since such people occasionally infiltrated the area.

Near us, in a small wooden house, lived a family consisting of father and mother, two daughters (one of Irène's age) and grandparents. They were intellectuals, and spoke with a slight Belgian accent. Irène became friendly with the little girl and we tried to plan something for them to study together. There was no school, of course, but among the people of the Resistance there were many students and teachers and we found someone to give lessons to the two little girls. He used to come from the forest, where members of the Resistance lived in caves, shacks and huts.

CHAPTER 33

'We Are the Wehrmacht – Have No Fear'

The Germans made routine checks of the mountains in low-flying planes. When they spotted movements in the woods, they sent out detachments of soldiers on motor-bikes. These would execute anyone they found in the woods, and usually most of the inhabitants of any neighbouring village. The villagers would hide in the woods when an approach by the Germans was signalled from below. These signals were ingenious and no German ever detected them.

One day we received the signal. Most people left for the shelters in the forest. The Belgian father of the two girls left with the others. It was raining heavily and he had to shelter under a tree all night, thus becoming very wet. At about noon the next day, he decided to come out of hiding, thinking that the Germans would have left. On his way he met two German soldiers in a little car.

They stopped him and asked why he was hiding. He said that he had gone out for a walk. They felt his clothing and found it was wet through, although the rain which fell all night had stopped several hours before. They asked why his clothes were so wet. 'You are probably one of the leaders of the Resistance!' they accused him. The poor man decided he had better tell them he was Jewish, and in fear of the Gestapo. 'We are Wehrmacht,' they said, 'come with us and have no fear.' They took him away and for a long time nobody knew what had happened to him.

When the war ended, his wife spent a fortune trying to trace him, advertising in all the local papers. After quite a while, she received a letter from the priest of the village next to the one where he had lived. He had read her advertisement, and could she tell him if the first name of her husband had the initial 'P'?

'Yes,' she replied. Peter had been her husband's name. She went to see the priest, who told her that a couple of years before, a small

German car had stopped at the entrance to the village, and a civilian was taken out, put up against a tree and shot dead. The priest then told her in more detail what had happened. (One of the villagers, hidden behind a clump of trees, had witnessed the scene and told the priest.)

The Germans warned the villagers not to touch the body and to let it rot, as befitted a dirty Jew. Whoever attempted to bury him would be executed on the spot. The priest had waited a few days, then, at night, with a few villagers, had buried the body, which by then was partly decomposed. He had taken a handkerchief with the initial 'P' from the body, as well as a piece of clothing to help identify the corpse, and they indeed proved to have belonged to the missing husband.

In this Vercors village, an episode occurred which had my life hanging by a thread. One day I was told that two men from Paris had stayed in our village before us. They used to go to the woods and take beer to the young members of the Resistance. These men were middle-aged and had foreign accents, and the young people began to think that they were spies, German spies. They killed them both.

Their names were mentioned and I realized that they were people I had known very well in Paris. They were Russian Jews who, like us, must have been hiding in the village. They were nice, honest people and did not understand that, with their strong foreign accents and middle-aged appearance, they should not have attempted to befriend the youngsters in the Resistance.

One morning, two men and a woman came to our room. They said that someone in the village had told them that I could play bridge and that they had come to play with me. It was an unusual request so early in the morning and rather frightening.

I had no cards, of course, but yes, they had cards and we should start playing at once. We 'started', but not one of them had the faintest notion of how to play bridge. We pretended to play cards for a while and stopped. One of the men and the woman were young, the other man was older. He told me that he was the cook in a local boarding school for boys. I told him that he should come back next day to learn bridge with me, as I had nothing much to do and would gladly give him lessons.

He came and immediately started to put questions to me. Why had I come to the mountains? Why had I brought this child who obviously was not my child – Irène had black hair and I was blonde and we were so totally different? The questions went on and on. I talked to him, trying to make him believe that not all French people wanted to stay in the vicinity of the German occupation. I told him that I was a widow (which I was at that time) and that Irène was the image of her father, etc, etc. He stayed a long time.

The next afternoon the three people, the two men and the woman, came to our room again and ordered me to go with them. Leave the child behind, they said. I explained that I never left Irène alone. Never mind what you always do. Leave her behind.

We went into the woods. We walked for a long time. At last we came to a small wooden house in the middle of the woods. This was where the woman was living.

They sat me on a chair, and went to another part of the house, closing the door behind them. They started to talk, and deliberate and argue, but I could not hear what they said, just the sounds of an ever-escalating argument that went on for a long half-hour. They came out, red-faced and furious. 'We are going home,' they said. And we went.

Very much later, when the war was over, the cook told me that he was not a cook at all, but the chief of the Vercors Resistance and that he had saved my life on that fateful day in the woods. The other two people were determined to kill me there and then, as a spy. They had seen me on the road, the same road that the Germans had taken when they came to raid the neighbouring village. How did I know that the Germans would be coming?

He had told them that after the long conversation he had had with me, really an inquisition, he had a feeling that I was not a spy and that it had taken him half an hour of yelling and violent arguments to persuade the two others to let me go.

'But, tell me,' he asked, 'why did you come to the Resistance?'

'Did you not understand that I am Jewish?' I replied.

'I never thought of that,' he said. 'You don't look Jewish. Why did you not tell us?'

'You should know,' I said, 'that a hefty financial reward was paid to anyone denouncing a Jew. It was a lot of money and quite a few "good" Frenchmen were known to get rich quickly by that method.'

'Yes,' he said, 'that is true. Now I am all the more glad that I saved your life.'

CHAPTER 34

Gestapo Raids

As the war turned more and more against Germany, so life in the mountains became increasingly unbearable. When we heard that the Germans were coming up to the mountains, we hurried down to Grenoble by another route, and as it was impossible to stay there, we would rush back up again. The Germans came more and more frequently. The atrocities worsened. Whole villages were destroyed, burnt, and the people killed.

On one occasion, we went down in an odd type of coach which was supposed to link the mountain with the town. This service was most erratic and, as it was stopped many times by Gestapo *rafles*, people used it only occasionally. Now, however, we were in town again, and wanted to go up the next day, staying in Grenoble one night. The coach was to leave from a certain place at four in the afternoon. I was ready and urged Irène to hurry with her coat. Suddenly she had violent stomach cramps. This was understandable with the food we had at that time. How we survived the starvation diet still puzzles me.

Irène went to the lavatory and could not come out for quite a while. I knew that this was our last opportunity to return to our mountain hiding-place, for the driver told me that the bus service was being discontinued and the coaches taken over by the Resistance.

Irène came out from the toilet, pale and weak, and said in a small, apologetic voice, that this time her cramps were more terrible than ever. I was in despair. I offered to carry her to the coach, but that would provoke too much curiosity and the German sentries would certainly want to know what had happened, where our papers were and who we were.

By this time the coach had gone, and I was furious with the poor child. I was furious with myself too, for I did not know what to do or where to go! We were now in Hell's kitchen and I thought our end was near. With her usual quiet courage, Irène said, 'Don't be so distressed. We can't help it. Perhaps the Almighty wanted us to stay here. We must believe in Him.'

As it happened, on that very same day, the Germans went to our village on a special mission 'to clean up the place'. They stayed several days, killing most of the villagers, including the woman in whose house we were living and her only son. They certainly would have killed us if we had been there. They lined up all the men of the village in the main square and shot them. They crucified a small girl on the church door, and played football with the new-born son of one of the villagers. The mother was made to watch until the infant died in agony.

CHAPTER 35

Liberation

In Grenoble, the Germans put into effect a plan which they took care to publicise widely. All the underground pipes carrying electric cables, water and sewage were mined, and the mines would be set off if ever the Germans evacuated the town.

Everybody knew that although our town would be sacrificed, this would indicate that our allies were gaining ground. We felt both proud and frightened at the thought. Some families had relatives or friends in the surrounding farms and left the town altogether. Others hid in the mountains, but the headquarters of the Resistance was there and life was not easy faced with the Germans' mopping-up operations.

Most of the people stayed on, prepared for the worst, trying to live an ordinary life. What else could they do? The town was well guarded by the occupying forces and, as the end of their stay drew near, they became increasingly savage. Executions, tortures, arrests and hostage-taking were everyday occurrences.

One morning at about seven o'clock, Irène woke me and told me excitedly that something strange was happening in the town. I was well aware of this. Throughout the night the Germans had been leaving, snatching whatever they found useful – lorries, cars, horses, even bicycles. The members of the Resistance were also busy putting sugar in the carburettors of vehicles to make them useless.

Opposite the window of our room was the local branch of the Bank of France, and all through the night the German soldiers had been bringing out from the cellars wooden crates full of currency and whatever gold they could find. There was a rumour that the director of the bank had found a way of hiding the bulk of the gold coins, but enormous sums of currency still remained to be taken. We could not watch them for long, as they fired several shots at our window and others into the house.

These were clear signs that liberation was at hand. In the morning Irène's excited voice told me that everybody was in the street. Strange little cars of a make unknown to us and full of shouting people were coming our way. More Germans, I thought – who else could they be? Reluctantly, I got out of bed and went to the window.

I saw strange open cars with a few uniformed soldiers whilst many civilians with children and babes-in-arms crowded the street. There were shouts, cheers, bottles flying in the air, babies carried by uniformed men.

'Mummy, could it be the Liberation?' Irène cried. 'And what is happening about the mined sewers?' I retorted. Suddenly the men in the cars shouted loud greetings to us. We shouted back, almost falling out of the window in our excitement. Greetings and laughter increased in fervour. 'Vive la France,' called the soldiers, 'that's the spirit!'

Then Irène looked at me and saw that my nightdress had almost fallen off my body, exposing me down to the waist to everybody. No wonder the passing soldiers and civilians had been so pleased with me! Flushed and ashamed, I covered myself, but I had to go on watching. Yes, I realised these were jeeps, a type of vehicle we had never seen before, and in them were American soldiers, debonaire, human, pleasant American soldiers who had come from the south to liberate us!

The most wonderful moment came when the fire brigade put their own lives at risk in order to defuse the mines and save the town.

This was really the end of the war, at least in that part of France. The town went mad with joy. Irène immediately fell in love with the whole army collectively. We went out into the road and started to help whoever we could, translating, explaining, guiding those who needed our English. This service was in great demand as the inhabitants of this provincial French town had very little knowledge of English and the American soldiers did not speak French. We were hard at work all day and part of the night. But the army was not staying in town; it was only passing through on the way to Lyons and Paris, which were still occupied by the Germans.

After two days of rejoicing, with people dancing in the streets and enjoying American cigarettes and chewing gum, the Army left us. Then we had the biggest fright of our lives, for the Germans returned to find the town bedecked with French and American flags, with paper streamers and anti-German slogans! A few minutes before their return, the police toured the town with loudspeakers urging the population to remove the flags and stay indoors, announcing that the Germans, hiding in great numbers around the town, would massacre us all.

I was out when I met one of these police cars. The roads to the house where I lived were already barred, but I had to get through the barricades for Irène was all alone in our room. I was shot at several times, but I took no notice, diving and lying flat, before running on again.

This new horror continued for two days. By then the Resistance had come down from the mountains and was trying to take the town. Numerous people were killed, there were fights in the street, both sides suffered enormous casualties and the dead were lying about with no-one to bury them. This hell ended with the arrival of new contingents of American soldiers. The enemy was cleared out, the corpses buried and a small contingent of the liberating army remained.

Here, at last, was the real Liberation. Again we were able to offer our services as translators. Irène would have done anything to help. She watched the crowds, and when a soldier tried to explain himself or asked a question, she did her best to be of use.

Once she simply forced me to invite home a couple of very young soldiers, who were sitting on the kerb eating an apple and looking rather forlorn. But what could I give themto eat? I decided to invite them for a beer in the café round the corner. They declined, but asked to be permitted to come to our house because, as they explained, they had not seen a home and a mother for many, many months.

I thought I was old enough to be their mother and, with Irène's eyes imploring me, I asked them to come to our room at seven o'clock that evening. We had a small bedroom and a kitchen and we decided it would be more becoming to receive them in the kitchen. I had some dried beans and, with some vegetables added, concocted quite a good broth. This was absolutely all I could treat them to, all I had.

At half-past six the very same evening, seven – yes, seven – soldiers trudged up the three floors of our house and entered the kitchen. They explained that they were all very young, very lonely, and would love to sit in a kitchen, look at the saucepans and stove, and think of their mothers and home!

I had to add a good deal of water to my broth to make it stretch to seven. They loved it and adored every minute of their visit. They told me about their homes, their brothers and sisters and of their aims in life. Irène was absolutely delighted. I was happy, but rather tired. They sat on the floor, on the kitchen sink, on the stove, all over the place, for there were only two chairs.

They left at eleven o'clock and all of them wrote to us, thanking us for the lovely evening. One or two even continued the correspondence long after they had left France. After they had gone we found, hidden under the chairs, the sink and the stove, food rations – absolute luxuries to us – tinned meat, biscuits, tinned milk, even soap!

On another occasion we found out that we could buy a sack of fifty pounds of potatoes if we could find a way of bringing it home from the market. We borrowed a handcart and went to the market which was at the other end of the town. To our delight we succeeded in buying a sack, although the potatoes were a little frozen and some were rotten, but quite a few were good. Potatoes were a luxury we had not enjoyed for years.

Some of the market people kindly loaded the sack on to our handcart, and then Irène and I began the long journey back, dragging the handcart behind us, the snow melting on the ground and making the road slushy and difficult to traverse. When we reached the door of our house we were stuck. How could we carry a sack of potatoes up three floors?

We looked around for help. In the vicinity there were only three American officers in beautiful pale-beige uniforms, probably going to some reception. Before I could stop her, Irène was already explaining our predicament to them in excitable but perfect English. Almost at once, the three were hauling the dirty sack up the three floors to our rooms, trying not to soil their uniforms.

They were high-ranking officers and I was rather ashamed to give them such work, but they were really very kind and after moving the potatoes to our kitchen, accepted the offer of a drink from the only bottle of ordinary red wine we possessed. They settled down to a most interesting talk and stayed for several hours.

There was a music shop in Grenoble, and during the Occupation I had grown friendly with the woman who kept it, sometimes helping her to arrange the little music she still possessed. She had a back room which contained a piano and here I played on occasions.

Once I had been playing the 'Pathétique' when Irène burst into the room, pale and frightened, to tell me to stop playing; two German officers were in the shop and wanted to know who was playing their Beethoven so well. I left at once through the back door and did not dare to return for a long time.

After the Liberation, Irène often passed her days in the shop helping the woman, who could not speak a word of English, with the American soldiers and officers who came to buy sheet music for their military band or their banjos, flutes or harmonicas.

One day, a young soldier tried to explain to the proprietress that he wanted the score of Debussy's 'Pelléas et Mélisande'. This was such an unusual request that I became interested and started to talk to him. He appeared to be a highly educated young man with a professional knowledge of classical music, and I invited him to our kitchen for a simple meal. We were delighted to have met him, and we corresponded for years. We even met him again years later when he was on a visit to Europe.

Some days later, a soldier walked into the music shop and asked if we could find him a music teacher for three weeks. He was stationed here for that period and he wanted to make the most of it by having piano lessons. A teacher could easily be found, but not an English-speaking one, and I undertook the task of giving him lessons for three weeks, refusing any payment. I told him that the Americans were our liberators and if it had not been for them, my daughter and I would not have been alive now.

He proved to have a gift for composition, and many of his songs, jazz and blues, were really exceptionally good. He explained that he could not read a note and had never, as yet, touched the piano. As all his tunes came from his head, most of them were lost, for they were never written down except when the conductor of the military band had time to do this for him. He made immense progress during our three weeks together, but the time came for the lessons to stop. Before his departure, in lieu of the money I had refused, he left at the shop a tin of corned beef weighing at least ten pounds. I often wonder what became of him, whether he is alive and still composes. Perhaps he is now a well-known song writer – he certainly had the makings of one.

With the war over, I wondered what we were going to find back in Paris. What news would be awaiting me about my husband Senia? Everywhere people were searching, wondering, hoping for news of lost relatives. Those of us who had survived considered ourselves fortunate, but we were so very tired in mind, body and spirit.

Our nerves were shattered and we jumped at the slightest noise. Sometimes I wondered if we would ever get over our ordeal. The whole of Europe was in turmoil and the frightening cost in terms of human life and destruction was now emerging. Of course, we were overjoyed that it had finished, but the horrible reckoning was yet to come. Whole cities and entire families had been blown into oblivion, and the full horror of what had happened in the concentration camps was yet to be revealed.

No one could ever have believed such a thing had happened. We asked ourselves how it could have happened. So many innocent lives gone for ever. Millions slaughtered systematically, ruthlessly, simply because they were Jews. How they must have suffered. Could anyone have ever imagined that the final toll would be six million Jews and six million non-Jews?

As news began to filter through the network, those of us who had managed to dodge the Germans, no matter how dreadful our ordeal had been, began to realise how lucky we were to be alive.

A strong instinct to survive had kept me going. Now that it was over, I wondered how we had done it. I thanked God that He had spared Irène and myself.

CHAPTER 36

The Performance

Before leaving Grenoble and returning to Paris, Irène was invited to perform a ballet number at the local Municipal Theatre. It was to be at a gala performance in honour of the Liberation, with Fernandel, the great French comedian, as the star. Irène was approached via her ballet teacher, who in turn had been approached by one of the retired officers at the officers' club where she used to give her lessons.

Irène was absolutely delighted. Then the problems began. How to find a suitable costume? The war had just ended, and not a scrap of material could be bought anywhere. There was no money to buy it anyway. I concocted an extraordinary costume embellished by pieces of ribbon which I had at home, and we borrowed an interesting 'Biedermeier' type of straw hat from a Russian friend of the teacher.

Olga, the friend, was 'artistic' and her flat was a complete shambles. After a long search the hat was finally fished out from under the bed, complete with one protesting cat and three kittens. Olga proceeded to explain to the cat, in voluble Russian, that it was necessary to borrow her abode for art's sake and that it would be returned in due course. Irène appeared at the Municipal Theatre of Grenoble reeking of cats.

There was a further problem. During rehearsals Irène's legs developed a frightening weakness. The teacher explained to me that this was nothing serious, only hunger, but unless I found a piece of meat to give her before the performance, there would be no performance.

I dashed off to Monsieur Léon, the local butcher, telling my tale of woe. Fortunately for me, he liked ballet, and let me have a little piece of meat, which I duly fed to Irène before the evening performance. We felt a great feeling of gratitude to Monsieur Léon, who enabled my daughter to make her début in what I believed would be a brilliant career.

The great moment came. I had asked for the piano to be left off-stage as I wanted Irène to have the stage to herself. The lights went on. The orchestra gave her cue. And suddenly I realized that no-one had thought of providing a lamp for the piano. The piano was standing in complete darkness. I somehow sat down, and thanked the Almighty that I had got used to playing in the dark during the blackouts.

It was a great success, and the applause was deafening. The ballet teacher shook my hand and said that her only criticism was that I had played the second movement a shade too fast. I showed her the black hole where the piano stood. She threw up her hands in horror.

The posters about the performance had been plastered all over town, and among the supporting acts one could read 'Little Irène of the Paris Opera'. I had vainly tried to explain to the management that Irène had never been near the Opera, let alone a part of it. This, they assured me, did not matter in the least. It sounded good, and who was to know!

With this performance, our time in Grenoble came to an end. How we had survived the vile brutality of the Germans, the hunger, the ever-present danger, I do not know. But survive we did, though memories of this fateful period never left us, nor unfortunately did the consequences for our health, especially that of Irène. Little did we know then that we had another battle ahead, a battle that took as long as the war itself to overcome, until Irène's health could be restored.

But, for the moment, we put the horror we had lived through behind us as we looked forward to the future.

CHAPTER 37

The Aftermath of War

The year was 1945. It was summertime. The war was over and we could go back to Paris. It seemed as if life was going to be wonderful after all the dark years we had spent.

We had been issued with free tickets to go back to Paris, which we seemed to have left so long ago. The tickets were for ourselves and our luggage, but we needed none for the luggage, as we had so little.

The train was packed; every seat, every standing place, the corridors, the passages between coaches, everywhere was crowded with people and their dogs, prams and suitcases. The noise was tremendous. People even travelled on the buffers and on the roof, resulting in many an accident when the trains passed under low bridges.

Twelve of us occupied a compartment meant for six. We shared seats, sat on the floor or stood. With nowhere to put one's legs, let alone stretch them, we did as best we could. Although the journey lasted twenty-four hours, nobody was cross or unhappy. Everybody smiled, for the war was over, and we were going home.

Several accidents almost marred the journey, though. There were still selfish people about. A large stout man sat himself on the seat of the lavatory nearby, travelling in great luxury and comfort, with a seat all to himself! He refused to budge no matter who had struggled past the people in the corridors to use the lavatory. He insisted that this was his seat, and he was going to keep it until we reached Paris.

The plight of those who needed to use the lavatory became so desperate that finally they urged three soldiers in uniform, travelling on the buffers, to come to their rescue and induce the man to let them use the lavatory, the only one available in the crowded carriage.

Very reluctantly, the man got up, but he insisted on standing beside it, no matter who used it, man, woman or child. In this way, he could keep an eye on the seat, and claim it after its proper use. No arguments could touch him. There he stood, and there he remained. A pregnant young woman burst into tears, unwilling to undress in his presence, yet all he would condescend to do was to turn his head a little, still grasping the seat, hardly giving her time to adjust her clothes. In our compartment, one man lost his grip in trying to reach his vacuum flask, which he had put on the luggage rack, causing the flask to fall. It opened and coffee – a rarity in those days – spilled all over my beige coat, the only coat I possessed. But he hardly noticed this, only bemoaning his lost coffee, a fact he referred to constantly during the whole of our twenty-four hour journey.

In the corner sat a young woman with an almost new-born baby on her lap which, at regular intervals, she would breast-feed. At similar intervals her husband, sitting on a buffer, would send a sandwich to his hungry wife, begging the crowd in the corridors to 'pass it along'. Notwithstanding the numerous hands the sandwich had to pass through, and the hungry people who handled it, each sandwich reached her safely, so that she was well fed during the whole journey.

As we neared Paris, the woman was changing the baby's nappies. I complimented her on the child's excellent behaviour, for he had not cried once during the long journey. At that very moment he had an urge to pass water and covered me from head to foot! What with the coffee, and now this, the state of my coat was dreadful!

At last we reached Paris. We had only one suitcase between us, and although it was not very heavy, it was far too heavy for us to carry. There were no taxis, so the only possibility of getting our luggage home was to hire a man – known as a 'human taxi' – who would carry it to the Métro station, and from there to our home. There were no lifts and the stairs were usually steep and numerous. Such men handled suitcases roughly, so that they usually arrived minus their handles.

However, there was nothing else for it, and after a while we got a man who, for quite a substantial sum, carried our things to the apartment where we had previously arranged for a small room to be let to us. The landlady lived on the proceeds of renting rooms in her apartment, and was keen to find wealthy people able to afford the high prices she demanded for her front rooms. Irène and I had a very small back room, which carried with it no right to use the toilet paper, which was reserved only for the rich people in the front rooms.

The day after our arrival, we went to the Ministère des Prisonniers et Déportés in Avenue Foch, anxious to learn details of the deportation of my poor husband. The Germans had kept files of all their prisoners of war, together with the people they had deported and killed.

My husband, we learned, had been arrested on the very same train Irène and I had taken in 1942 when we had left Paris on our perilous journey to so-called 'Free France'. He had been trying to join us and had been accompanied by the same man who had smuggled us over.

He had been deported to Auschwitz and gassed. There it was, coldly stated in the document. My heart felt as heavy as lead. Throughout the war we had always hoped, but this was the terrible truth in writing: my husband Senia, his three brothers, their wives and all the children. As soon as I read the word 'gassed', I could hardly pull myself together. My mind was in a whirl, and my imagination ran riot. I prayed to God he had not suffered much, yet I knew that was impossible – all those poor, dear souls gassed together, how could they not have suffered?

People were scrambling around, trying to find details of their loved ones, and in between the scramble, piercing screams could be heard, and some fainted. Others just went quietly away in total disbelief. I sat down on a wooden bench for a moment – I could not really take it in. I began to see Senia in my mind, quiet, gentle, with no malice in his heart. I thought of his brothers, their wives and all the children. It was a nightmare.

I looked up, and saw others just wandering around looking quite blank, shaking their heads in total despair. I realised that had it not been for Senia, neither Irène nor I would even be alive, for he had planned everything for our escape, without any thought for his own life. To think that he had been arrested on the same train as us, and we did not know. It took me time to take in all the details, for they were too horrific to contemplate.

There were more details about him from some people who had seen him at Auschwitz and who had miraculously survived and returned to Paris. My husband, we learned, had spoken only of Irène and me, and his last thoughts had been of us. God rest his soul!

Now we were completely alone, Irène had only me to look after her, to bring her up and educate her.

Much later we learned that at least forty members of our family had perished in the concentration camps.

We discovered too that all our worldly possessions were gone, our apartment confiscated, my safe with all my jewellery looted, my husband's business and everything with it gone. I had a moment of panic. How could we live? I had always been very comfortably off, and Irène had been brought up in luxury before the war. How were we going to live now? We could not survive without work.

I decided to apply to the American Army which, at that time, was engaging civilians for jobs in their Paris Headquarters. My knowledge of languages and my university training proved to be of use and they took me on as a technical translator.

Irène was with me when I applied for the job. When I was accepted she looked at the American officer pleadingly. 'Please,' she said, 'could I, too, work for you?' He smiled.

'As what, my child?' he said. 'You are far too young.' Irène pleaded that, in spite of her age, she was qualified, for she spoke, read and wrote English, French and German, and her handwriting was good. There were many things that she could do in the office. She could translate and interpret. She could distribute the mail around the house and run errands. She told him how she had lost her father in the war, and mummy and she desperately needed the money the extra work would bring.

She pleaded so much that the American's heart was touched. He turned to me and told me that he had four daughters at home, one of them the same age as Irène. 'I'll take her on for a week's trial and see how it works out,' he said. 'Don't worry about her. She'll be well looked after, and no harm will come to her.' Irène resisted a childish impulse to throw her arms around his neck in joy and gratitude. She knew that, as an employee of the United States Army, she had to observe some decorum.

CHAPTER 38

We Begin Work

We started work happily. Irène had her own desk with a large card and her name printed on it. Everybody in the office, in fact, had their name printed on similar cards, but Irène found a source of endless delight in seeing her name on her own card. She was very happy in her new position and put her heart and soul into her work.

She was so keen, so eager, so enthusiastic about even the smallest and dullest of chores, that in the end she was kept on as a sort of mascot. The staff were very good to her. Her pale little face and emaciated body must have stirred many an American's heart, for the quantities of chocolate bars, sweets, soap and toothpaste which they deposited on her desk were quite amazing. These things were all luxuries which for most people were quite unobtainable at the time.

The two jobs solved our financial crisis, and Irène now visited the ballet teacher she had had before the war. The teacher was delighted to know we had survived the horrors of the war and allowed her to join the ballet class again, free of charge. So, in the evenings, Irène would go to her ballet class, a fact which worried me, as I knew she was really far too weak and undernourished to take on this extra physical strain. Yet what could I do? Ballet was Irène's life, it was everything to her, and I did not have the heart to take this pleasure away. And so, reluctantly, I let her go.

Each morning we would go to work, and on two evenings a week Irène would go to the ballet class. But then she began to experience some difficulty. Over the last few years she had started to suffer from a strange weakness of the limbs, with pains in all her joints – the effects of malnutrition. Nothing could be done about it during the war, when neither doctors nor medicines were available; besides, what she needed most of all was food. The limb most affected was her left leg, the pain being most prevalent in her left knee.

The inevitable happened. Ballet did not improve her. The left knee gave way and she severely sprained it. With sorrow in her heart, Irène gave up her ballet classes. She told me she felt too tired in the evening to go on with ballet, but said nothing about the knee, not wishing to give up her job. So we continued to go to work together every morning.

On me, too, years of starvation, of cold, of hunger, of persecution, had left their mark. After a few weeks of work, I broke down and became seriously ill. It was a strange illness. It began one evening while I was in the bathroom. I suddenly lost consciousness and fell to the floor, where I remained in a kind of coma until the morning. Recovering slightly, somehow, I dragged myself to my bed, only to lose consciousness again.

The landlady found me and called a doctor. My illness was due, he said, to a combination of severe anaemia, malnutrition and complete and absolute exhaustion. There was nothing he could do. Perhaps I would get better. Perhaps I would not. He could not be more precise in his verdict.

It was evident that both Irène and I were suffering from the terrible experiences of the war. For three months I was unconscious for the greater part of every day, and during all this time Irène continued to work, leaving in the morning and returning in the evening to look after me. I did not know it at the time, but each day on leaving she would strap her leg up with a piece of rag – bandages being unobtainable – and then take the rag off before coming in at night so that I would not notice anything wrong with her during my few moments of consciousness.

She suffered agony as she walked on her painful knee. At work she hid her pain, carrying on as if nothing had happened. She knew she was the only bread-winner and was determined not to give up. Someone at the office arranged for her to go to the Army Dispensary for an elastic bandage to replace the rag she was using. The doctor examined the knee, but Irène lied and said that it did not hurt or bother her much. The doctor told her to return when the bandage began to wear out so that he could give her another one.

In due course Irène did go back, but the doctor was no longer there, and on this occasion there was a long queue of soldiers waiting their turn to be seen by the new doctor. They looked sad and worried, rare in Americans, who were usually such cheerful people. Irène awaited her turn, occupying herself in studying some colourful posters which decorated the walls.

When her turn came to enter the surgery, the doctor asked her to sit down. 'My poor child,' he said sympathetically, 'tell me the whole story. Do not be shy. I must know how it happened and who was responsible.' The doctor looked at her with infinite gentleness and kindness. 'Now,' he said, 'tell me about yourself. '

Irène told him about her knee, and the ballet class, and how the bandage had helped a lot. Suddenly the doctor smiled. He had misunderstood the situation. He gave Irène two bandages and told her not to come back to this dispensary as it was now being used in a different capacity. It was, he said, no longer the Casualty Department, and was now a place not becoming for little girls. Irène wondered why, but he did not explain. Many years later she realised that the initials 'VD', which had embellished all the brightly coloured posters, had not stood for 'Veterans Defence' as she, in her innocence, had thought!

Time went by. I got better. The periods of unconsciousness became less frequent. Although I was weak, I remained conscious, which was an improvement. I ventured out of bed.

I still knew nothing about Irène's knee, the condition of which had by then deteriorated considerably. She had developed water on the knee and was suffering agony. Yet she still told me nothing and arranged matters so that I never saw her naked and never noticed the swollen knee. Every morning she went off to work, smiling cheerfully as she kissed me goodbye, the journey to the office taking her an hour by bus and Métro.

Early one afternoon, I saw the Colonel's car outside the house after Irène had gone to work. It transpired that she had fainted in the office and her boss had himself brought her home. I looked at the knee. It was immensely swollen, hot and inflamed. My poor Irène. What pain and suffering she had gone through those last three months!

It was just at this time that we had a visit from the son of an old friend of the family, a French paratrooper on leave in Paris for a few days. He immediately took Irène to see a doctor, who decided that it was necessary to make an incision in the knee and remove the water.

This decision, as we later realised, was an absurd one, for it was the cause of the trouble which needed attention, rather than the water itself. Still, that was the decision and at the time we thought it was correct. The young man took Irène to a hospital where the operating theatre was in a frightful condition. There was no glass in the windows, the panes having been shattered by bombing, and there was no glass with which to replace them. The room itself was filthy, and the medical instruments were just as bad.

An incision was made in Irène's knee and the water was squeezed out by hand. A piece of wood, an ordinary piece of rough and very dirty timber, was placed behind the knee to keep it still, held in place by a bandage. Then Irène was sent home. She suffered violent pain in the knee and the journey home – one and a half hours by bus and overcrowded Métro, since there were no taxis available in Paris at the time – must have been a dreadful ordeal for her. After that, she stayed at home, resting on a couch, getting thinner and thinner, paler and paler, as the weeks went by.

CHAPTER 39

The Mountain Village

In desperation at her suffering, I took her to see another doctor. He did not like the condition of the knee at all. It was getting worse, and he recommended a mountain resort in France, where he was sure a doctor whom he knew could help. We could stay at a small hotel, and the change of climate itself would help, he said, to cure the knee.

Fortunately, at this moment, we were able to contact a former business friend of Senia, who told us that before leaving Paris Senia had left seven valuable Oriental carpets and a few pieces of jewellery with him for safe-keeping. The proceeds of their sale would pay for Irène's treatment.

So we went to this place, and stayed there for three months. The treatment proved disastrous. The new doctor believed in the healing virtues of the sun, which previously had never been good for Irène. Yet she was obliged to put her bad knee in the sunshine for two hours every morning, and it grew worse and began to hurt more and more.

Then he decided the knee would have to be put in plaster. When he put the plaster on, he made no provision for the fact that her knee was inclined to swell. This it did, and as there was nowhere for the swelling to go, the plaster pressed hard on it, so that Irène passed a night of absolute hell.

In the morning the doctor removed the plaster, and in so doing cut Irène's leg in many places, so that when at last the knee emerged it looked like a chunk of meat, the pressure of the plaster having interfered with the leg's circulation – making it dark blue and tumescent.

At this point, I refused to let Irène stay any longer and insisted she come home. She could no longer walk, so she was put on a stretcher, the leg cradled into the bottom half of the plaster which had been removed and served as a support to keep the leg still. We then returned to Paris, a journey of thirty hours.

The Paris doctor who had recommended the treatment was aghast when he saw Irène's knee. The condition was now very serious indeed and he thought that TB might have set in. At least, if it had not done so yet, there was a great risk that it might. An X-ray revealed no sign of TB in the bones, but as TB can penetrate into the soft parts of the knee, the risk was great. He advised me to take Irène to a clinic abroad which specialised in the treatment of TB cases of all types.

CHAPTER 40

We Discover Healing

It was at the French mountain village that we first came into contact with healing. It happened in a rather amusing way. The hotel chambermaid had asked us whether we would like the Smuggler or the Healer to call. She explained that the Smuggler was a young man from the village who earned his living by smuggling cigarettes and items of food such as tins of sardines over the Spanish frontier, which was not far away. He would call at the hotel during the week and take orders.

The Healer would call by appointment, to see anyone who required his services. He was, she explained, a very good and very experienced healer and dealt with everyone's aches and pains in the village. And so we ordered a couple of tins of sardines – a rarity in France just after the war – from the Smuggler, and made an appointment to see the Healer.

We knew absolutely nothing about healing except the fact that in Russia Rasputin had been known as a healer. We rather expected to see someone in long flowing robes, with a beard, quoting the scriptures. In due course there was a knock on the door, and there entered a very small, elderly man with a cheerful smile. There were no robes, no beard, no scriptures. He chatted about the weather, and then took a long look at Irène's knee and proceeded to lay his hands on it. As he did so, Irène sank into a deep sleep which continued after the healer had finished his treatment.

The healer turned to me and said, 'I have something to tell you – your child is a healer herself, and a strong one. What you see as sleep a really a form of trance. She is so sensitive that she reacts to the healing frequencies in this way. '

He explained to me that the pain and suffering she had been subjected to in life were all part of her apprenticeship as a healer. A healer, he explained, had to suffer himself before he could use his gifts.

When Irène finally awoke, he showed her some of the various passes and techniques he used. He also told us that whilst he could ease her discomfort, he would be unable to cure this knee. It was, he said, part of her apprenticeship.

We were very taken aback by all this and did not know what to think. I was also, I must admit, rather sceptical. The whole thing seemed so far-fetched.

A few days later, Irène's doctor called to see her. He looked awful, and said that he was suffering from an absolutely dreadful headache. Before I could stop her, Irène said, 'Let me try something,' and laid her hands on his head. I felt more than a little embarrassed and did not quite know what to say. It was the doctor who spoke first. After a couple of minutes he looked at Irène with astonishment and declared that the headache had gone. And it had.

Irène used her gift on a number of occasions, easing people's aches and pains, but did nothing serious with it until years later. She was just fifteen years old and the time had not yet come. Her apprenticeship was not yet completed.

A NEW JOURNEY

SWITZERLAND 1946-1954

The Fight for Health

I had travelled many roads, long roads. My life's journey had taken me from Riga to St Petersburg, thence through the length of Russia to the Black Sea, on to Turkey and finally Paris. London I had known between the wars, as well as Palestine, Egypt and other parts. From 1939 to 1945 Irène and I had travelled through France from city to city, village to village, to save ourselves from a form of organised brutality the world had rarely seen before. Now a new road took us to the mountains of Switzerland.

I had experienced wars, revolutions, the height of luxury, the depth of poverty. I had known joy and fear. I had witnessed bravery and selfishness and kindness. Through it all I had survived. Irène had survived, but at what cost to our health, especially that of my dear daughter.

I had been blessed from early years with good health and a peaceful, happy upbringing, indeed a childhood and adolescence of luxury. That pre-1914 world was more simple, slower in pace, than later years.

There was, at least for me, a sense of wide family unity and support that gave me great security, however harsh life may have been elsewhere. It was those early years that gave me strength to face later disasters and crises, the escape from the Bolsheviks, the constant fear of the Germans, when death walked with us daily.

Irène did not have these advantages. She was only ten when

world war erupted for a second time and the vicious pursuit of Jews became a Nazi mania. She had suffered illness as a baby and as a child, but her years of early adolescence, growing into womanhood, were darkened by our fight simply to stay alive. And what a fight it was! Scraps of food here, a drop of milk there, occasionally a piece of meat, unclean water, filthy rooms, insects galore, medical help rare, whilst for years until the Liberation we lived a life of isolation, of pretence, and of fear.

As an adult, determined to save my daughter, I had felt a sense of mission. As for Irène, although perceptive for her years, open in nature, eager always to please, the full force of our experiences reacted severely on her, especially on her health. She grew up without the foods her body needed, sometimes with the foods her body could have done without, and inevitably her immune defences were affected and weakened.

This led to four years in bed in a clinic and a slow process of recovery thereafter. Irène was also a survivor of a kind, a determined survivor, but the effect of the war never left her.

What I have related so far tells the story of part of my long road. A new pathway lay ahead, different in character. No Bolsheviks, no Nazis, no flight from city to city, but a shared journey that also, in a strange way, had the character of a war, a battle, a resistance movement.

It was the long road to health in the clear air of the Swiss clinics, a battle to overcome adversity of a different kind, yet a journey that required of Irène and myself the same kind of patience and resource, courage and optimism, that had characterised our wartime years.

Inevitably this new road took a different direction. The signposts were marked hope and resistance. The ultimate destinations were designated health and peace. How we travelled that road I relate in the next part of my story, a story that changes in detail, and very much in mood, but a story no less important than the road already travelled.

CHAPTER 41

Journey into Pain and Patience

The train was leaving in an hour. It was a long way to the station, almost an hour's journey. We had our tickets and sleeping-car reservations. Reservations were difficult to get. For two weeks I begged, bribed, demanded, cried, to get these two berths. Now when everything was ready, there was no ambulance to take us to the station. Our frantic telephone calls did not help. The only ambulance, which we had ordered well in advance, was taking an expectant mother to hospital. It could not come.

Having lost hope of being able to catch the train, suddenly, delightedly, we heard the sound of a horn. It was the ambulance. It had come.

The station was crowded, the train about to leave. Seeing us – the stretcher, ambulance attendants, the luggage – and taking all this in at a glance, the stationmaster, red in the face, shouted orders to his assistants, to us, to the engine driver, to everybody, frantically, loud and cross, and yet how gentle he was when helping to push the stretcher through the window of the sleeping-car. It was the only way to get in, the doors and corridors of the coach being too narrow.

And thus started the long, long journey, another journey, the bitter fight for Irène's life and health. I tried to make her as comfortable as possible. The night wore on, without sleep. Irène suffered. I worried.

At three o'clock in the morning, we arrived at the Swiss frontier. Two customs officers came to our compartment. They looked suspiciously at Irène's plastered leg and frowned. What was under the plaster? They were not satisfied with our reply that it was a damaged knee. That very day they had arrested a man smuggling gold and currency concealed in a plaster which encased a perfectly healthy leg. How could they know if this was a genuine case? The plaster, they said, would have to come off. Irène looked pleadingly at the customs officers, the expression on her pale face full of pain and terror. They understood. No more talk of removing the plaster. The two men left our compartment on the tips of their toes.

In the morning we reached the station where we had to change trains. Again the stretcher had to be lifted through the window. Off went the porters with the stretcher down endless stairs, across the street to a hotel where I had booked a room for two hours, the time we had to wait for our next train. The hotel was crowded and we were given a room downstairs in which a couch had been made up.

It was here that we had our first normal breakfast since the war, with real milk, real coffee, white bread, butter, jam – things we had not seen for years. The pleasure of my child was wonderful to see. She ate and drank and spoke all at the same time. A group of American tourists, about thirty of them, spotted her through the french windows which led out into the garden. They came to keep her company, and gave her chocolate, books and magazines, and solemnly promised her that she would soon be well again.

Irène was again borne to the train, the usual procession of porters and on-lookers all discussing merrily, heartlessly, the remote possibility of the child recovering.

There were no sleepers on the train, nowhere to place the stretcher. Irène was put on the floor of the luggage van which was full of trunks, boxes and bicycles. The latter hung on a railing dangling over Irène's head. The journey took two hours, then another change of trains, this time a small climbing train, narrow and shaky.

It had to be the luggage van again! A great deal of luggage was placed in such a way that the sliding doors of the van could not be closed, and the danger of falling out – patient, mother and all – was real and alarming. To Irène's right was a cage with live rabbits, to her left a less pleasant box containing fish. The fish must have come a long way – the smell was appalling.

Finally we arrived. A car was waiting for us. The clinic had not sent an ambulance, but an ordinary taxi, not a good omen. There was no room for the stretcher. Irène had to be lifted off it and put into the car – such a painful process. The chauffeur and his lively young assistant were helpful, matter-of-fact and quick. The young man was almost too bright, certainly too talkative. He looked at Irène and said, 'What is it? A lung or a bone? Aha, a knee. Bad things, knees. I have a cousin here in a clinic, been there over eight years. He's far from cured. He also has a knee. Tricky business, knees.'

Eight years! We were aghast. Surely, we said, this was an exception. 'Oh no,' the young man assured us, 'no exception for this place. Mind you, this is nothing – there are people in clinics fifteen, twenty, twenty-five years and not yet cured. Knees are a nuisance, they do not respond to treatment. It's better to have a lung. None of this business of waiting years for something to cure – if it ever cures.'

My little daughter's face went white with fright. Eight, ten, fifteen, twenty-five years! God Almighty! This was impossible! She was just fifteen. How old would she be if she too had to stay here all those years? Had we not already suffered enough?

The car climbed up the winding mountain road. The clinic was a wooden chalet by the side of the road. It looked neat and clean. An efficient-looking, fat woman in a starched white apron answered the door. She was the owner, also the matron. It was a clinic for younger children, but, on the second floor, were two rooms kept for girls of Irène's age.

The owner/matron explained the strict rules for the patient and her mother. Doctor's visits were twice a week. Visitors were admitted from three to five in the afternoon. I was asked to leave. This was not the visiting hour. I would have to go. Poor Irène.

CHAPTER 42

The Cobbler

I went to look for a room for myself. It was August, the holiday season, when relatives and friends came to visit patients. There were no rooms to be had. Finally, I was advised to try the local cobbler who, it was believed, had a room to let. He lived at the other end of the village and it was dark by the time I got there. I saw a small wooden house, more like a shed than a chalet, with rickety stairs outside leading to the upper floor. There seemed to be no door downstairs. I climbed the stairs with difficulty. They were narrow and there was no railing.

I was admitted by a haggard-looking woman, the cobbler's wife. The room was available, she said. Her husband was out, drinking again, but that did not matter as letting the room had always been her responsibility. The room was reached along a small and shaky balcony. I dared not touch the banister lest the whole thing disintegrate. In the corner of the room was a mattress on legs – the bed! I washed, undressed quickly and went to bed.

I had to think, to review the last months. We had been through a horrifying war, we had been chased, hounded, through Vichy France. At times our very existence hung by a thread. We had starved, suffered, my husband was no more. Why could we not have some respite, some peace? A new and different battle faced me, the fight for my daughter's health. I lay and thought about Irène's illness, the sudden unexpected illness of my beautiful child, an accomplished, gifted, lovely girl with long graceful limbs, so gay, so courageous, so good. I thought about previous journeys to clinics in France, the unsuccessful efforts of doctors, the failure of their methods, the decision eventually to come to this clinic and the difficulty of finding the means.

The first night here, sleepless, alone, somehow passed. Early next

Vera and Irène in Paris.

Right: Senia and Irène in Nice.

Left: Irène during her childhood illness in Paris.

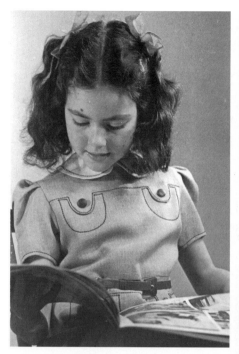

Above: Irène in Paris during her school years.
Right: Irène dressed for ballet training in Paris.
Below: Vladimir Horowitz and Nathan Milstein (right) in Bürgenstock.

Left: Irène in the film that was shot in Paris and which might have led to an acting career..

Below: Irène, in later years, during her singing career in London.

Above: Senia Chesno, Vera's husband who was deported to Auschwitz.
Right: 'Do let me live, I beseech you' - a painting by Arnold Daghani to commemorate victims of all Nazi persecution. The late Arnold Daghani was one of the most famous concentration camp artists and diarists of the Second World War.
Below: Another painting by Arnold Daghani. Fifty of his works are at Yad Vashem in Jerusalem.
(*Both paintings reproduced courtesy of the Daghani Trust*)

Facing page: 'The Rabbi' by
Arnold Daghani.
(Reproduced courtesy of the Daghani Trust)

Right: The original yellow star of
David worn by Vera in Paris and
reproduced here in its actual
size.
Below: The aftermath of war.
Irène during her four years spent
in bed at the clinic in
Switzerland.

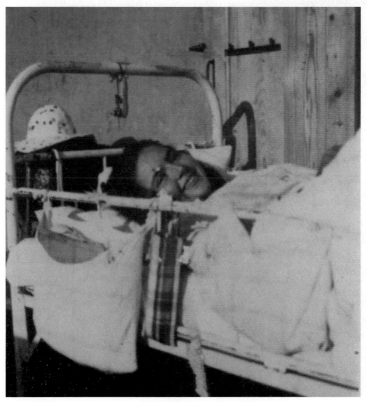

Right: Irène in her consulting room..
Below: Irène's radionic laboratory.
Below right: Fabergé, the dachshund, receiving healing from Vera and Irène.
Bottom:: Vera, aged ninety-four, at her piano.

morning I was at the clinic to see the doctors and hear their verdict. Irène looked pale and exhausted. She was lonely without me and, notwithstanding her courageous smile, I could see she was sad and downhearted.

The doctors entered, one a specialist, the other a woman doctor – followed by the matron and a nurse.

The treatment was severe. Bed, no movement of the knee, nor of the body: no movement at all, in fact. Some months of this to begin with, then one would see. I mentioned that Irène was undernourished as a result of the starvation diet during the war, and inquired whether some vitamins might be good for her. The doctors did not agree. Air and sun were sufficient, also prayers night and morning, which helped a great deal to take away unnecessary thoughts. The doctors' visit was over. I was asked to leave. This was not the visiting hour. An uncompromising and worrying verdict.

I returned to the cobbler's for lunch. He and his wife spoke a local dialect between themselves, of which I understood only a word here and there, but the little I did understand was enough to tell me that they were having a good time at my expense. They would stare at me for some time in silence, then look at each other, make some comment, and roar with laughter.

Downstairs lived a workman who would get violently drunk every night and shout and curse till morning, threatening to rape the foreign lady upstairs and then burn down the house. What had I come to?

Shortly after my arrival the cobbler's wife decided to increase her income by taking in children of unmarried mothers. At one time there were six of these children, some living in one room with the proprietors and some in a small room next to mine. The children were charming, especially one nine-month-old girl, plump and curly, but they were soon going all over the house, often into my room, although forbidden to do so by the landlady. But how can you forbid a child of nine months?

The babies were crawling in as soon as my door was left open for a second. In fact, they watched the door the whole day, and crept in happily as soon as an opportunity arose. There was not much quiet and little privacy. Although I am fond of small children, my nerves were tense, I needed quiet and peace. The cobbler's wife was highly-strung. Quarrels with her husband were frequent and noisy. The atmosphere of the place was unwholesome, but there was no other accommodation at the price I could afford. Anyway, tired, unhappy, miserable, what did it matter where I lived, how I was treated? I had come to try to cure my only child. I had nothing absolutely nothing left but this child.

I loved her and had to cure her. I had to see that she would not become a cripple, like children I had seen in a clinic in France, with deformed legs, deformed hips, short, hideous hunchbacks, all cripples. I had one aim – to save my child from deformity, from being a cripple for life. Nothing else mattered.

CHAPTER 43

The TB Resort

Before fate brought me to this village I did not know, I did not imagine it possible, that so many TB cases existed or that so many could be gathered in one place. TB cases of all ages, all classes of society, all nationalities, religions and colour. Starting with children a few months old up to ripe old age, people on crutches, on sticks, in bed – a whole population – everyone, children, adults, old men and women, all TB sufferers.

There were no healthy people around apart from a few peasants and shopkeepers. Everyone else, doctors, nurses, all were TB or ex-TB cases. House after house, villa after villa, clinic after clinic, hospital after hospital, everything was for TB. There was a Grand Hotel and a Palace Hotel, villas with names of flowers, birds and animals. One or two small boarding houses proudly exhibited notices 'For Healthy People Only, NO Patients Admitted', but still people on sticks came out of these houses. Everywhere there were patients, everywhere there was TB. Talk was about TB, the cure, the sun, the air, the snow – it was all TB.

Coming into the clinics I was struck by the beds, specially hard, narrow beds, fitted with wheels so that they could be rolled onto the terraces where they stayed all day long, and, in summer, all night as well. People were put to bed, often attached to their beds with weights and weird appliances, and stayed there for months, for years, without being able to get out of their beds even for a few minutes.

Twice a year the patient was taken to a hospital to be X-rayed. This was a great event for which one prepared months in advance. The patient was put on a stretcher, the stretcher was put on the bed and the patient was moved onto it with great care and taken by car to the hospital. Every six months their progress or regression was seen on the X-rays. The illness showed clearly on the pictures.

There would be a little improvement or else there would be some more destruction of the bone, more holes and uneven surfaces, more misery and pain – pain, unbearable pain, pain by day and night, worse than toothache, worse than childbirth, persistent, nagging, unbearable pain. Nothing could relieve it, nothing at all – patience and endurance, endurance and patience, for days, weeks, months and years were needed.

And yet, unbelievably, these bed-ridden unhappy people were envied, yes envied, by young, dashing men and women with beautiful complexions, beautiful hair and straight healthy limbs – the lung cases. Bones take a long, a very long, time to heal, sometimes as much as ten years, and invariably leave marks, provoking stiffness, or a shortening of arm or leg, a curvature of the spine – making it impossible to bend down to lace up one's shoes or stretch up and comb one's hair. But, bones get better. With lungs, if they do, there is always the danger of a relapse, of TB coming back, developing after a slight cold, a little 'flu or too much sunshine.

I learned that there were two main kinds of TB – of the lungs and of the bones. The first is infectious, though not always so. The second is not, and once the defective part of the bone is taken away, the cause of the sickness is removed also. Nature does the rest, and within the limits of perhaps a certain loss of mobility, a new and healthy limb is recreated.

An establishment where TB of the bones was treated was known as a clinic. TB of the lungs was treated in a sanatorium. Lung cases and bone cases were always strictly segregated, even to the extent of there being two adjoining TB resorts, one for lung cases, the other for bone cases, a small train linking the two.

CHAPTER 44

'The Bluebells'

Irène's treatment began. In the morning, air and sun-bathing on the balcony – five minutes to start with, gradually increasing to an hour or so. Nothing else. Days went by. Loneliness preyed on mind and body. No sudden improvement. Here things improved in months, not in weeks, let alone days. What was required was patience and hope. Weeks went by. Still no improvement. By now we knew it was futile to hope for quick results. It had to be long, and long it would be.

During the sixth week of Irène's stay at this clinic, the matron's husband, who was also the chef and did all the cooking, had a recurrence of his illness and became dangerously ill. He had to go to bed again for several months, if not longer. As there was no south-facing room available for him in the house, the three girls upstairs were asked to leave at once and find another clinic. Among these girls was Irène. She had been in the clinic six weeks and was just beginning to get used to the staff and the routine. Again, an upheaval, again on the move.

A new clinic had to be found, not so easy as there were not many children's clinics. The woman doctor advised me to take Irène to 'The Bluebells'.

This was a much larger children's clinic, a two-storey building of blue stone housing children aged from a few months to fourteen or fifteen. The boys were in a large ward on the first floor, the girls in three smaller wards on the second. One of the latter was for babies up to the age of two. The second ward was for girls aged two to nine, and the third for girls aged from nine to fifteen.

The babies' ward was the saddest of all, eight little children, all tied to their beds by special appliances so that they could not move. The question of the body's natural functions was a permanent problem: children had to lead the lives of untrained tiny tots as they could not be moved at all. Everything happened in nappies, which were not changed at night.

They were such sad little creatures, mostly good-looking with beautiful curly hair, but with thin, matchstick-like arms and legs. When I visited them – and I would do so almost every day – I would give them sweets, and speak to them, and comfort them. Those who could already talk would call me 'Mother', and tried to kiss and hug me and express their need for love and the embrace of comforting arms.

I would leave broken-hearted, every time. Their real mothers seldom came to see them – their husbands, their other children, their homes, kept them away from these unfortunate children for months, sometimes years. No wonder they could not recognize their real mothers and, feeling that I was good to them, they called me, a stranger, 'Mother'. I had witnessed enough suffering, enough loneliness, caused by human beings to other human beings, but here were innocent children, attacked by no human hand, only by disease and illness.

Irène was put in the ward for the older girls. The matron promised there would be no more than eight girls in the ward, but in time she forgot about this. Beds were added and new cases admitted, and most of the time my daughter spent in this ward there were at least fifteen patients. There was room for eight girls, perhaps nine, but certainly not fifteen. The beds were so close together that they looked like one more floor.

The entrance door to the wards, which was always open, had a special permanent adornment, a small boy of about six who rode on top of it, to and fro the whole day, and, if the nurse did not see him, part of the night too. This was Pete, the curse and amusement of the ward.

He was a bone case, a very serious one, thin, pale, anaemic. The more ill he became, the more his mischief grew, and, being absolutely unable to cope with him in the boys' ward, they had sent him up to the older girls' ward, hoping that there he would be less boisterous and easier to manage. This proved to be a mistake.

Why should he behave in the girls' ward? If anything, he became more impossible. Nights were his most enjoyable time. He played practical jokes on all the girls, loved to pull their hair and their sick limbs. He was a curse! Every new arrival was sure to have him as a neighbour for several nights. His chief relaxation was riding on that door, high up, near the ceiling. He enjoyed himself splendidly. He was very happy with the girls, who indeed were sorry for him, and rarely complained to the nurse. He stayed in the ward for several months until his parents, exasperated with the treatment he was getting, took him home, where he soon died of generalised TB.

The ward nurse was an old woman, at least seventy, with a constantly dripping nose. She was too old, too tired, to attend to all the young patients. She did as little as possible, was often cross and demanding. She had a way of explaining to girls of fifteen that life was short and that everybody must die, so one had to prepare for death and one should think more of the inevitable death than of present brief earthly events. Encouraging, especially when I was doing all I could to keep up Irène's morale. We had not survived the Nazis to be beaten by TB.

The second nurse who attended to the babies, occasionally helping the old nurse, was a girl of about twenty-one with an artificial foot. The first night, at about ten o'clock, when the lights had been out for some time, my daughter had an urgent need for the bed-pan. She asked her neighbour how she could ring for the nurse. The neighbour's answer was simple and curt. There was no possibility of ringing as there was no bell and, anyhow, wanting the bed-pan at night was prohibited. Irène needed it badly and asked her neighbour what she must do. The neighbour said there was nothing to do but wait for morning. This was impossible for poor Irène, so she started to call the nurse by name. She knew that the second nurse slept in a room on her floor.

After a while a furious nurse in a floral dressing-gown came in shouting that one had to train one's functions, that there was no night nurse in the clinic, that she also had to sleep sometime, that wanting to go at night was absolutely prohibited. Finally she gave Irène the bed-pan, urging her to finish quickly as she would not wait more than a minute. She began to pull it away when Irène was only halfway through.

What was there to do? Irène started to entertain her with politics, music, films. She spoke to her about jazz, cooking, the theatre. Nothing interested the nurse and she was getting ready to go. Then Irène had an inspiration.

'Have you seen the new fashions the Parisian couturiers have created this autumn?' she asked. Interest showed in the face of the nurse. 'Which new fashions?' she wanted to know. 'Don't you know?' Irène went on urgently, 'that skirts are half an inch shorter, and sleeves are all three-quarter length?' 'Oh yes? How interesting! What else is there new in the collections?' Irène sighed with relief. The battle was won. She was saved. The nurse would wait until she had finished telling her all the news about the Paris fashions. Irène's quick and inventive mind helped her on this and many future occasions.

Early in the morning Irène was awakened by the clatter of bed-pans and a loud command from the nurse 'to finish everything quickly'. Bed-pans were handed out. For a new girl used to gentle handling by a loving mother, this mass-distribution came as a shock.

After the bed-pans came the thermometers. They were kept in a large jar filled with dirty-looking disinfectant. Actually, the brown water in that jar had once been white. It was changed every spring, and that was part of the spring-cleaning. Penny, a new girl, noticed that the girls kept the thermometers under their blankets. She asked the nurse why they did not put them in their mouths.

'In their what?'

'In the mouth, where else can I put it?'

'Don't be silly,' retorted the nurse crossly, 'put it where everyone else puts it.' She really had quite enough to do without being bothered by someone asking unnecessary questions. So Penny asked her neighbour where one had to put it. The neighbour said that there was naturally another place to put it. Penny did not know and by now was flushed and confused. The neighbour indicated her behind with a finger.

'Push it in,' she said. With astonishment, fright and pain, Penny proceed to push in the whole thermometer. At last, with pain and embarrassment, the wretched thing was well on the way to the inside. There was nothing left of it when the nurse came to collect it. Red and flushed, Penny could not get the thermometer out. The nurse glanced at Penny's flushed face and said that she most probably had fever. The thermometer was finally retrieved.

Each girl was given a small basin of water in which to wash whatever part of herself she chose to keep clean. The nurse insisted that washing be done under the blankets in order to keep some decency in the ward.

Then came breakfast. Now the day really started. The beds, which were fitted with wheels, were pushed out onto the balcony, a large terrace shared by the three wards. There the patients lay, having their sunbath, some only on the tips of their feet, others on their legs, others on the whole body, depending on how ill they were and how much sun they could stand.

There they passed their morning, there they had their lessons, if any. Some of the foreign girls were learning the language spoken in that part of Switzerland. After lunch everybody had to sleep for an hour. At three o'clock tea was brought in, consisting of a cup of rather tepid milk. Thus the hours came and went, day after day.

The afternoon was spent on the balcony or, if the weather was bad, in the ward. Some of the smaller children were convalescent and could get up. They would come to the older girls' ward and play blind man's buff or similar games under the beds. The other girls resented the noise and the bumps under their beds, but nothing could be done about it. The little ones had to have some amusement, and there was nothing else to do.

If there were several convalescents, an outing was arranged, and the boys with their nurse, and the girls with theirs, would go out for a walk. These outings were a sad sight as none of the children could walk normally. Each had something wrong with a knee, an arm, a hip, the spine, the neck, the head, anything and everything could be affected by this wretched disease. The smaller the child, the smaller the crutches, and these tiny children, already great sufferers, patiently going out in the sunshine on little crutches or sticks, bandaged, corseted, hopping on one foot, moving in a twisted and unnatural way, formed a pathetic procession of little cripples; a Dantesque apparition. In all the years I stayed there I could never pass such a group without tears in my eyes.

After years of constant movement, running, crawling, hiding, my daughter, ever-uncomplaining, was now incarcerated in a bed in a ward, with no prospect of knowing when, or if, she might ever walk again.

But despite this, we supported each other, gave strength to each other, deepening a loving relationship between mother and daughter.

We had overcome the past. We would overcome the future.

CHAPTER 45

The Matron

The matron at The Bluebells was a soft-spoken, hard-hearted, strange woman. An ex-TB case herself, she was rather good-looking, musical, but full of complexes and unfulfilled desires. She was always clad in a grey dress. She had grey hair, a grey face, a grey mind.

The older girls were the matron's chief concern. It was their souls which interested her, and not at all their physical condition which, she thought, did not need any special attention. But not so their minds, their religious outlook, their mystic life. Life was sin, men were beasts, bad instincts had to be rooted out, girls had to take nuns and pure, religious maiden old ladies as their examples. To achieve this, girls had to be taught all about the beauty of purity and simplicity.

Everything had to be simple. Food, for instance, was frugal. The evening meal would consist of a little porridge and an apple. The girls were literally starving and I had to bring Irène sandwiches, meat, fruit, anything, but I could not feed fifteen girls, although I would have loved to. So I brought a few sweets to distribute; this was not easy as I had very little money, and had to count every penny.

To soothe the hungry girls, there was music in the evening. Matron and the nurses would gather in the big girls' ward, seat themselves and sing long, lugubrious church psalms to the accompaniment of a guitar played by the matron. The guitar was adorned with gaily-coloured ribbons, and made an incongruous contrast to the long, sad psalms. The concert usually took place towards twilight, when the girls felt lonely and homesick, when life was difficult, when pains were greatest, and pangs of hunger strongest. I was invited once to assist at this musical performance and never in my life have I felt more forlorn, unhappy and depressed as during that moment.

There was a certain unwholesome current of adoration in the clinic in which the matron revelled. A couple of nurses were in constant adoration of her, and, in the evenings, would sit at her feet on little stools next to her armchair in her study, and look up at her with adoring eyes. If someone came into the room this would not stop, they were not ashamed of their feelings. It was somewhat similar to the adoration of the Virgin. Matron felt it deeply and played the role of the Queen Bee in a hive.

There was no normal sex life in the clinic. Nurses were not allowed to date young men. Sex was banned once and forever. The male simply did not exist. The Kingdom was of women, women only. This suppression of normal feelings and desires made the house into a sort of false nunnery. Feelings ran high, with everything centred on the matron. There was jealousy, there was adoration, there was exaggerated love, and there was the matron herself, receiving this adoration with a condescending smile of unearthly beatitude.

CHAPTER 46

Miss Hantler

Miss Hantler was matron's deputy. She started life as a maid, had come here as one, but her devotion to the matron was so tremendous, so outstanding and so exaggerated that in a short while she was promoted to the high position of matron's deputy. As such she was left in sole charge of the clinic when the matron was called away to a sick relative. This, naturally, provoked jealousy among other members of the staff. Why had she been promoted and not someone else?

Two young nurses, who particularly resented this injustice, decided to play a trick on her. Every night, when Miss Hantler retired to her apartment, they would come close to her door and whisper terrible things through the keyhole about rape, burglary, and all sorts of gruesome events that were going to take place in the clinic.

The whispers were so insinuating and persistent that Miss Hantler got extremely frightened. The whole house was her responsibility, as were the girls up to the age of sixteen, and here were bandits getting ready to rape the whole clinic. Who would not be frightened? She never dared to open the door to see who was whispering. How could she? The bandits were there, behind the door, ready to rape, perhaps even her, although she had long passed the age of desirability.

New regulations were issued. At eight o'clock in the evening, all doors and windows had to be closed, and all shutters put up. The patients in this resort lived outdoors, in the fresh air, on the balconies with open windows all the year round. Air, fresh air, is the principal, the only cure. No medicines are given, no special food is prepared, nothing is done, because the air does the trick. The air, the fresh mountain air, is supposed to cure everything – especially TB.

And there, all of a sudden, from one day to the next, fourteen girls had to be shut inside their overcrowded ward at eight o'clock each evening. The sun was still shining, the patients were on the balcony. Nevertheless, all the beds were taken indoors, the windows were hermetically sealed, the light turned out – the result, darkness, stillness, stench.

These were the new regulations, but that was not enough. In the resort lived an exotic Prince, in the last stages of TB. He was so ill that it was no longer necessary for him to stay in a clinic; he could not be cured. He lived in a room in the village. The room was paid for by the community as the Prince did not have a penny to his name.

In return, the community expected him to make himself useful. Miss Hantler summoned the Prince to come to 'The Bluebells' every evening, where he was to sit in an armchair in the matron's study and wait for the bandits. He was probably the only person in the place who possessed a revolver; there is nothing to shoot in a TB resort except, perhaps, microbes!

Whether this revolver was real or fake, nobody knew, as nothing ever occurred to make him use it.

So there he was, poor man, every evening at eight – pale, perspiring, desperately ill, sitting in an overcoat, shivering from illness and lack of sleep, guarding the purity of fourteen girls and several nurses between the ages of fifteen and seventy-five. In one hand he held the revolver, in the other, he held the crutches. There he sat, night after night, helping the matron's deputy save the honour of her wards.

The two nurses were going about whispering, the girls were choking in the foul air, the house was barricaded and shut. The Prince sat there, while the two nurses continued to whisper in front of the door: 'Rape, bandits, murder, defloration, rape, rape, rape.' It went so far that the matron's deputy began to show signs of abnormality. She gradually drifted into a state of mental chaos.

It was only when the children became much more ill and the

poor Prince felt so bad that he could no longer walk and had to stay in bed, that the doctors decided to call the matron back. Back she came, the good lady, by the next train. Back she came to open the windows, take away the padlocks, put up the shutters and let in the air.

The whole clinic, including even the very young children realised from the beginning that the whole thing must be a hoax, knew who the whisperers were and why they did it. The only person who never knew was Miss Hantler, who probably never stopped believing that she saved, at the peril of her own life, the honour of fourteen virgins. The gallant Prince was spared the knowledge of the ridicule of his unnecessary nightly vigil. He never knew the real facts and nobody told him the truth. Everyone was too sorry for him.

CHAPTER 47

Christmas

Christmas in a clinic is a depressing time, both for patients and staff. Everybody thinks of home, of fathers and mothers, aunts and uncles, Christmas trees, log fires, joy and happiness. It is a difficult time. Yet children must have a Christmas and arrangements were made so that the Yuletide did not pass unnoticed. What could be done, was done.

There could be no element of surprise in the preparations, as the ward was always full and the girls always watching. A Christmas tree was put up in the girls' ward. There was no tree in the babies' ward as the matron did not believe babies understood such things. All the girls wore clean nightdresses and new ribbons in their hair. The beds were put even closer together so as to get as many children as possible into the room, and there were more beds in the narrow passage between the two rows of beds on either side.

The programme of festivities consisted of a speech by a Catholic priest, a speech by the Protestant pastor and a concert by the matron and nurses. That particular year, the first speech was made by the pastor, who told the children a long and gruesome story about bears who were eating some children and how, at the last moment, when half a child was already swallowed, there was a miracle and the children fell out of the mouths of the bears and the bears died. The small children cried bitterly – they were sorry for the half-eaten children and for the bears, and they were frightened. My mind wandered back to the beautiful stories of Sholem Aleichem – they would have brought a smile to their eyes, instead of tears.

The priest made a much shorter and more cheerful speech. He told them about the little Egyptian children at the time of Moses, playing with their mechanical toys and electric trains! The children liked this speech, especially the part about the toys.

After this came the concert, with the nurses singing hymns,

accompanied by the matron on a guitar, decorated with long trailing ribbons. There was very little co-ordination between the guitar and the voices. Each did its own thing. The voices were untrained and each sang in her own style and tempo. The result was unusual, but not unpleasant to the ears of the children. After the programme, everybody received a little parcel containing a small present.

Pete, the unruly gamin of the clinic, was bored stiff. Being of the mature age of six, sophisticated and worldly-wise, he was not frightened of bears or of swallowed children, and found time dragging heavily. So he found an occupation. His bed was at right-angles to Irène's. By passing his hand through the railings of her bed he could tickle the heel of her foot, which was placed into position by special appliances so as to make her keep it quite still, each movement being agony. And there she was, experiencing this awful pain, being tickled by the small spidery hand of Pete throughout the solemn speech of the Protestant pastor.

CHAPTER 48

Yuri – and the Survivors

The TB resort consisted of a large number of clinics. To these clinics came Jews who had survived the horrors of the camps: boys, girls, young men and women in their teens, in their twenties, all TB sufferers, all brought to this resort by Jewish charitable organisations.

I remember them all, a rollcall of suffering, Eva, Anna, Edith, Helena, Laib, Izchok, Mordechai, Zipora, Max, Hershel, Leah, Rosa. Among them was Yuri.

He was an only son. There were four children in the family, but the other three were girls. Being the only boy, and being the youngest, he was spoiled and rather helpless. The war dispersed the family. Yuri went through hell, suffered terribly from cold and hunger, and finally passed two years in a concentration camp.

He was brought to the clinic by a relief organisation which paid his expenses. Things were all right for a long time but, suddenly, he had had enough of everything. He was not given to reading, had not received an education, and had no interest in life. There was nothing to occupy his mind.

The relief organisation provided him with a teacher to learn the language of the resort. He liked it to begin with but, as it became more difficult, involving grammar and suchlike, he gave it up. He might have been quite good at commerce, but there was no business to be done here and there was nothing else he could do. He started to let himself go. He became depressed, and deteriorated rapidly. He wanted to die. Something had to be done quickly to get him out of bed and out of the clinic, which was slowly killing him. The doctors decided on an operation.

Operations were performed at another clinic, a much more expensive one which had an operating theatre. Yuri talked about the luxury of the clinic he was going to, and the pleasure it would give him to lie in a bed which cost the relief organisation double. Whatever extras could be got out of the relief organisation were a great pleasure to him.

He used to buy all sorts of medicines – he ordered them by telephone – for the pleasure of putting them on the bill. This was stopped one day after he bought, and had taken, a medicine with a complicated, interesting-sounding name which turned out to be some drug to help women in their menopause, and which nearly poisoned him.

The great day of the operation came and went. As soon as Yuri regained consciousness, still dazed by the anaesthetic, he called the nurse and, notwithstanding the pain in his knee, asked for a steak and ripe, red cherries. Red cherries in January? How? And why? Yuri explained that it was because of all the blood he had lost during the operation. Naturally he needed underdone steaks and red cherries. Red cherries build red blood, he said, and he surely needed some.

The explanations of the nurses were of no avail. He explained that with the heavy money he paid for the room and attendance, he was entitled to get what he wanted, and red cherries should be provided. Yuri was not only physically scarred but also emotionally disturbed from his war-time horrors. He felt the relief organisation had an obligation to compensate him for his suffering. Whatever he could get, he took, poor boy.

As I looked around the clinic, I realised how much the terrible years of war had taken their toll of these young people. Malnutrition, terror, and the devastation of war had left them hopelessly confused in body and in spirit. I came to know all the patients – it became a way of life for me.

CHAPTER 49

Hopes and Fears, Parents and Children

I recall so many of the TB sufferers. Each had his or her own very special story. I learned from them their hopes, their fears. I tried my best to help them. Their parents suffered too, in a different way, and often reacted in a different way. So many of the cases were heartbreaking. Wherever hope and love existed, there was a future. For some there was no future, no hope.

Judith

Judith was a beautiful child. She was fair, fat and dimpled. She was cheerful and content. She enjoyed life and life enjoyed her. At the age of four, between smiles and sunshine, something went wrong with the child. She started to tire easily, did not want to play and cried frequently. She lost her appetite and was unhappy.

Her character changed. She stopped smiling and became capricious and difficult. A doctor was called in and diagnosed TB of the hip. The child had to be sent to this resort at once. Her parents were young and wealthy and she was their only child. Everything was done to make her comfortable. The clinic was a first-class establishment, her clothes were beautiful, she had every luxury. And so she started her new life.

Years went by, the war came. Cut off from her country, there was no more news from her parents, no more communication, no more money. A charity organisation took the child over. They put her in a cheaper clinic and looked after her in the way charities do. There was no more love, no more attention, just the bare necessities for her to exist and, if possible, be cured.

Her illness was a serious one. It struck her early in life, and violently. There was a great deal of destruction in the hip and, as she grew, her affected leg became shorter and shorter. She hobbled on one leg, on crutches, on tiny little crutches because she was tiny herself. She still had her beautiful blonde hair, she was still a very nice little girl. She started to love the nurses, the doctors, the matron. She needed love badly and ultimately she got love in return.

Years went by. By now she was fifteen. The war ended and there came news from her parents – she now had two more sisters and two more brothers. It was difficult for her parents to leave the family alone, but they would do their utmost to come and fetch her and would be arriving in under a year's time. Then things started to happen. Judith started feverishly to knit, to paint, to make little dolls and trinkets. She was busy the whole day, and even at night tried to knit and embroider so that the presents would be ready for the visit of her beloved unknown parents.

The whole clinic was excited. Quite a few girls had no parents at all. Some of them had either a mother or father, others had a remote uncle or some cousin. But to have father and mother was a rarity. And to have a home and to be able to be taken home was an unheard-of happiness. The war had passed through their homelands – many a village had been destroyed, many a family killed or dispersed, and here was a girl who was expecting her parents to come from far away to take her home. Happy Judith!

The day came at last, and the parents arrived, well-to-do, contented people. A table had been prepared for them with the little parcels. Each of them had been made with hope, with happiness, with utterly unselfish love.

The parents came. Judith was so excited that she could not speak. She was hobbling on her short leg, with the huge orthopaedic boot, with the difference in her legs of at least four inches. It was a sad sight. Her parents looked at her with despair and unhappiness. There was nothing, absolutely nothing of the beautiful, plump, dimpled little girl they had brought here eleven years ago. Here was a hideous cripple!

There was no more conversation about taking her home. How could they? What would the neighbours say? What would their friends and relatives say? A tubercular cripple? Probably runs in the family! What about the other children? Two beautiful girls of five and three, and two sons. When the time came, who would want to marry them? Surely this was no good – they simply could not bring Judith home. They simply did not want her. What was one to do with her?

Judith began to feel something was wrong. She clung to her mother, she kissed her father, but there was no response, and although her mother kissed her sometimes, the kisses were cold and unmotherly. Judith became very unhappy, not knowing and not understanding what she had done wrong and what was the fault, which surely was hers, which made her parents and herself so unhappy.

The parents asked my advice. What should they do with this girl? They were willing to pay for her, they were willing to send her somewhere, even if it was expensive, but they would never take her home. They would never show her to the other children. They were rich people, but they were ordinary people, and the word TB frightened them to death. They had to make a very great effort to kiss the girl. They were frightened for themselves, let alone for the small children they had at home.

I spoke to them and said that this was not Judith's fault, she had not chosen to be ill, and she had lived all these years for the moment when she was be able to go home to her parents. The parents showed me a photograph of their other children and one of Judith when she was four. 'That is what I gave them,' said the father, 'and this is what they give me back – the girl with the short leg, hobbling, crippled, terrifying. I have no use for that child.'

A boarding school was found for Judith, a kind of finishing school, in some remote place in the mountains, far away from everybody and everything. She could learn languages there, perhaps she could learn to play the piano. She could hobble for little walks. She had nice clothes, but she had no life. She was buried alive for the remainder of her days.

Zorrie

Zorrie was ugly. Zorrie was short. He had a funny body with a long upper part and very short legs. His head was square, his hair crinkly and he had almost no forehead. He was sixteen and had already passed ten years in the clinic. He was very ill, very sad and depressed.

He knew that he was ugly. Girls did not like him, neither did the boys, the nurses or the matron. He was unpopular and grumpy. He was alone in the world. No-one ever wrote to him, no-one ever asked about him, no-one ever visited him. His whole family had been killed in the war. The village from which he had come had been wiped out. He simply had nothing to live for, and the improvement in his health was very, very slow.

One winter morning, when the weather was bad, a gale blowing, the sky dark and tempers short, Zorrie received a letter. The whole ward was there to look at him. Who could write him a letter? It must have been a mistake. But there was no other boy with this unusual name, and the letter was for him. One of his sisters had been found in a concentration camp and liberated by the Americans. She had been taken to America and was writing to him from there, telling him how difficult it had been to find him, how glad she was that he was alive and how she was looking forward to meeting him.

Sunshine came to Zorrie's heart. There was no more despair, there was happiness and hope, there was gaiety and *joie de vivre*, there was everything to live for, to look forward to, to enjoy. Life was wonderful. It was worth living. Zorrie wanted to live.

His health improved miraculously. Every day was a new day of happiness and health. The doctors were amazed and pleased. The nurses started to like him. The boys and girls were interested in him. He became popular and enjoyed this new status immensely.

Days went by, weeks went my, months went by. The boy was almost cured and conversation began about his being discharged. Where could he go? To his sister, naturally! He had a home, he had a sister, everything was absolutely perfect.

But letters from his sister came less frequently. And letters, if any, were cold and impersonal. The sister had found a man in America and was going to be married. She was starting a new life and in this new life there was no room for that unhappy, ill, crippled brother of hers.

Then a time came when the letters stopped completely. There simply were no more letters. The boy did not give up hope at once. He was still cheerful and popular, he was still pleasant for quite a while. But then he understood that there would be no more letters, and his mood began to change.

He again started to hate everybody and everything. And everybody hated him, and the inevitable happened. He had a relapse. The illness came back. There was no more struggle, no more hope, there was no more need to live. Why should he live, and what for? He let himself go. Soon he was back in bed, unable to walk, unable to move.

The girls upstairs did not know he was so ill. They did not know and they did not believe that Zorrie could die – he was part of the house, like a fixture or a piece of furniture.

When they were told that he was desperately ill and sinking fast, Irène wrote a letter to him. It was a sweet and gentle letter. She told him that she liked him and that she wanted him to struggle and get well. She explained to him that life was worth living, that at seventeen one does not die, that he should strive to become a man and show that life was given to him to achieve something, and not to let himself die. It was a beautiful letter which was given to a nurse to bring down to Zorrie. But in the excitement of what was happening, the nurse forgot to give it to him.

Zorrie died on the first day of spring. The letter was put in his coffin together with a few crocuses, the first and last flowers he ever received.

Irène stayed at 'The Bluebells' for one year, during which time she managed to get mumps. The mumps were brought into the clinic by a kitchen-maid and dismissed by the doctor as 'a small cold'. When seventeen cases were well-advanced the doctor realized her mistake but, by that time, a lot of damage had been done.

Irène had outgrown her child's bed. The food was far from adequate. 'The Bluebells' did not cater for grown-ups, and, having reached the mature age of sixteen, Irène was now considered a 'grown-up'. A new clinic would have to be found. The other girls in the ward were very envious – fancy being sixteen, and too big for one's bed, and going to a clinic where one might even meet real, grown-up men!

CHAPTER 50

'The Laurels' – a New Clinic

The Laurels was a better clinic, more like a hotel than a hospital. Almost everybody had a private room, and both men and women were admitted. Instead of two doctors visiting the patients twice a week, there were three – two doctors and a specialist. There were more nurses and complete freedom. Unfortunately, the cost was double that of 'The Bluebells', but we had to go there as nowhere else was available. The rooms were nice and there was running water – hot and cold, a luxury which seemed quite unbelievable.

First impressions were pleasing. The clinic stood much higher up the mountain. There was a beautiful view from the balcony. Irène would share a room with a girl of her own age – Rosa, who was also bedridden. Rosa could not move at all and had been in bed for over two years. She was an orphan and had lost her entire family – father, mother, brothers and sisters – in the war.

I said goodnight to Irène that evening – there were no rules about visiting hours, and one could stay as long as one liked – and kissed her. As I did so, the girl in the next bed burst into tears. It took me some time to soothe her. I said that she too was like a daughter to me and there was no reason to resent my kissing Irène. I told her how I had lost my husband in the same war and that Irène had only me left. But Rosa could not stop sobbing and I went away broken-hearted, thinking and imagining what these two young girls would have to tell each other, of nothing but sorrow and pain, both physical and moral, and of how this would affect their health.

We soon found that it was not very easy to be in a room with Rosa. She was frantically religious and extremely intolerant of anyone who did not fully share her views. She was given to saying prayers and singing psalms in a loud voice all the day and part of the night. The prayers and psalms were always very sad. As the days went by, we could not help feeling more and more sad and depressed ourselves.

Like 'The Bluebells', this new clinic contained many sad cases. Yet I continually marvelled at how the will to live, to love, had such a powerful effect on a patient's recovery. Love and hope are two of the most potent medicines. Time and again in my life, in Russia, in France and here in the clinics, I had witnessed the positive effect of the love of one human being for another. I am reminded of one story from 'The Laurels'.

Klopok

Dolly was a wisp of a girl, curly-headed and sweet. Tom was in love with her. Tom was an officer in the Air Force, a nice, straightforward clean boy. He had done his duty in the war, and after three years in a prisoner-of-war camp paid the heavy price of TB. He stayed in a clinic not far from ours.

Tom was able to walk and would come and visit Dolly every day, stay with her the greater part of the day, as much as his condition and treatment would allow. He looked after her, cheered her up, brought her little presents of flowers, fruit and sweets. But the most important thing he brought was his affection, true understanding and love. He dreamt of marrying her after both of them were cured, of taking her back to his country, of starting a new and happy life.

Everything was so perfect, and could be even more perfect if only one little detail had not spoilt both their lives. Dolly liked Tom, liked him very much indeed, she admired him, but – she did not love him. And she could not marry without love. Tom left the resort half-cured and broken-hearted. Dolly saw him off. She was sad and lonely without his daily visits and missed him a lot, but she was pleased in a way that this impossible situation had come to an end.

In the next room to hers, a very ill young man struggled to live. He was a 'spine' and 'hip'. But the worst were his legs – they were completely paralysed. The doctors in his country and in the resort had made the mistake of telling him the truth about his condition –

that he would never be able to walk. Always bed, or perhaps, in time, a wheel-chair, if his condition could be cured, which was unlikely.

Klopok was very tall, so tall in fact that a special bed had to be provided for him. He was also very handsome, with a sunburnt face, beautiful hair and eyes. His hands were unusually small and delicate – too small and delicate, pathetic in their idleness. He had been in bed more than five years already and, knowing that nothing could be done to make him well, had decided to 'live his life' as much as was possible in his condition.

As he was handsome and witty and full of repartee, the girls loved him and showed interest and affection in all possible and impossible ways. But in moments of despair, and these were frequent, he took to drinking, excessive smoking, anything to change his ideas and, if possible, to hasten the inevitable fatal issue.

He would send invitations to parties to all the patients who could move, whether they were on crutches or sticks, to the nurses, the kitchen-maids, to everybody. These 'whoopies' were frequent and noisy. The manageress should have interfered, but drinks were served liberally and, because these drinks were expensive, his bills were high and he paid them, so there was no objection from the management.

Each night after a 'whoopie', and these became more and more frequent, Klopok came near to death. Doctors were called, nurses came running, injections were given, and after quite a night of it, he would slowly revive, only to start anew, to have another party so as not to think, not to suffer, to forget.

Drama was in that room. Everybody knew that this was a continuous attempt at suicide. Girls came and girls went. There was love, there was jealousy, girls falling in love and out of love. Girls were fighting among themselves for this cripple, this bedridden invalid, this hopeless and desperate man.

He was a virtuoso at the looking-glass game. By holding up small mirrors at various angles, one could see what was happening on the other balconies, and, if one was very good at it, one could also see what was going on in other rooms. He had achieved such expertise that no girl was safe from his mirror wherever she might be, in whatever corner she might hide – he could always see her.

One afternoon on the balcony, looking idly round and playing the looking-glass game, his gaze met another looking-glass reflecting a sweet curly head – Dolly's. Dolly was not interested in this man. She knew all about his illness, his despair, but also about his 'whoopies', the drinking and kissing parties – there were even dancing parties in which only the kitchen-maids could indulge. They would dance among themselves and the patients would look on, being too ill or too crippled to move, let alone dance.

Dolly found the 'whoopies' and the parties disgusting. She was also a very serious case, fighting for her life and lonely and unhappy, yet she could understand the impossible behaviour of this patient who was ruining the purpose of his stay here through drinking, smoking and other indulgences.

His expression in the looking-glass was, however, so appealing, so pleading, so humble in a way – he surely had a way with girls – that it struck a chord in her lonely heart. He smiled, and she smiled back. To speak was difficult, although their balconies were adjoining. They spoke different languages and neither could understand the other well. The smiles went on for quite a while, through the looking-glass, from balcony to balcony.

Dolly was able to get out of bed a little and one rainy day she went to pay him a visit. They had little knowledge of each other's language and spoke in broken words, but friendship, nevertheless, developed between them. They started to see each other more often. Interest in their respective illnesses, their suffering, their hopes, developed more and more. They started to learn each other's language. And finally, this grew into love. By now Dolly visited him every day, passed most of the day with him and part of the night. She literally lived in his room.

Gradually the 'whoopies' and parties stopped. Under the

influence of this wisp of a girl, Klopok stopped drinking and stopped his excessive smoking. The nights became calmer and there were no more doctors and injections at night. Klopok felt better and, wonder of wonders, regained hope of recovery. The doctors were amazed at his behaviour and at his progress. The idyll went on. Dolly started to speak about marriage, and among friends called herself by the surname of this man.

But the excitement was too much for the sick girl. She relapsed and became dangerously ill and had to be taken urgently to a hospital, where she underwent several major operations in an effort to save her life. She was so ill that the doctors called her only relative, an aunt who had brought her up. The aunt came from a distant country to say goodbye to her dying niece.

Klopok was desperate with grief. He insisted on seeing her and arranged, with great difficulty, to be taken on a stretcher by ambulance to the hospital. Each movement was for him an agony of pain, yet he achieved the impossible and was taken to her bedside. He lay on a stretcher next to her for about a quarter of an hour. The doctors could not let him stay longer. The girl could not speak but she put all her heart and love in her look.

The hospital was run by nuns, who were kind and understanding and wanted to help. Both patients were so desperately ill and so much in love. They felt the girl's pulse, they felt the boy's pulse. They gave him an injection when he fainted from sorrow, pain and exhaustion. The priest too wanted to help them and went to and fro, from clinic to hospital, bringing news and messages.

There came a day when the doctors gave her up. She was too ill to fight and was sinking rapidly. But she was so much in love, she simply could not and would not go away and leave her beloved alone. So she struggled desperately with all the odds against her. Her will to live was tremendous and she lived through the crisis and, miracle of miracles, began very slowly to recover.

The day when she was brought on a stretcher back to 'The Laurels' was a red-letter day for the whole clinic. Everybody was excited and happy, everybody wished them well. There were flowers in her room, and in his. Everyone wanted to see them and everyone who could walk or crawl went to see them, to congratulate them and bring more flowers.

Days went by, weeks went by, months went by, and one morning we got to know to our absolute amazement that the cripple, the paralysed, incurable young man was going to be lifted from his bed to be put in a special appliance to keep him upright and teach him to stand and perhaps, in time, in some remote future, to teach him to walk. Every attendant in the house, male and female, even the kitchen boys, all were there to assist him, to help him, to keep him upright.

There he was, the hopeless cripple, the desperate incurable case, condemned at the age of twenty-six to stay in bed for the rest of his life, standing erect on small, withered feet, excited and happy, almost fainting from the effort, deathly pale and perspiring, but standing and oh! how happy .... He was allowed to stand for one minute, but what had not happened in that one minute! Hope was restored to him, the strength to struggle, energy and willpower were given to him. All this for one minute of standing. Now the real struggle could begin.

When he left the clinic several years later, he was already up for half an hour a day, and on crutches. The triangular-shaped appliance in iron and steel, with wheels, handles and knobs, which kept the patient standing – this appliance which was generally known as the tricycle, and which he called his Cadillac, was no more. Love had created yet another miracle.

The power of love works in many strange ways. Not every case ended like Klopok's.

CHAPTER 51

Storm and Night

Years passed, life went on, always the same pattern – no medicines, rest, air, sun and bed, bed, bed. Irène started to get worse and her knee more painful. She also had stomach trouble and could not digest anything. No treatment was given for this. She was put on a 'white diet' which consisted of semolina or porridge three times a day, nothing else. She was left on this diet for weeks and months, but her stomach did not improve. She became thin and pale and suffered more and more pain in the knee.

While she was undernourished and weakened by this digestive trouble, there was an epidemic of chickenpox in the village. Many of the village children caught it, as did the schoolgirl daughter of our doctor. Whether he was the carrier or whether it was someone else we do not know – anyhow Irène caught chickenpox in an exceptionally violent form and was covered with large black boils. It is, alas, a well-known fact that in these TB resorts the doctors are interested in one thing only, TB. All other diseases are considered trifles, not worth bothering about.

I was abroad at that time, summoned by my sister who was seriously ill with cancer. I had had to leave at once, and, hoping that my daughter's treatment would be good in this better-class clinic, was away for about a month. Irène wrote to me regularly, her letters were gay and cheerful, full of hope and courage. They led me to believe that things were going satisfactorily.

Then I received a letter from friends who had been on vacation and had visited Irène. They wrote that Irène was very ill and urgently advised me to return to her at once. Irène had mentioned nothing about illness in her letters. On the contrary, in each and every one of her sweet, long letters she had tried to convince me that she was feeling 'immensely better' and that her morale was so good and so high that it was right up 'in the stratosphere'. So the news about her came as a shock.

By the same post came two letters from Irène. One was her usual kind of letter, full of hope and courage, assuring me that 'she was feeling fine'. The second was a pathetic little note begging me to come because 'she needed love and help very desperately' and was 'terribly sorry for causing me so much trouble'. The two letters had been written on the same day and sent off by the same post. What had happened?

Alarmed, I telephoned the clinic. It took a long time to get through. I sat next to the phone, cold, excited and miserable. At last it rang. The voice of my daughter was faint. She said she had 'a touch of chickenpox'. She said I should not worry, it was alright, but could I come at once? Then she asked me if I would still love her if she were no longer a good-looking little daughter.

I said I would come at once. She wanted to know how long it would take. She again said I should not worry and that she loved me very much. When I put down the receiver I felt ice-cold. There was an empty feeling in my stomach. What had she meant by a 'touch' of chickenpox? If it was a 'touch' why was she so anxious about the number of hours it would take me to come? What was the meaning of the cryptic phrase 'Will you still love me if I am no longer a good-looking little daughter?' I felt sick with worry.

I left my sister at once and arrived at the clinic in the evening. When I came into the hall, I was met by the manageress. She told me Irène was dangerously ill, and had had neither food nor drink for the past six days. I brushed her aside. I did not listen.

I ran upstairs to my child. There she lay, emaciated, a mere shadow of herself. Her face was completely covered with huge black boils, itchy and suppurating, her lips were swollen beyond recognition, tears of pain rolling down her poor little face. Her face was covered with some sort of cream which for some incomprehensible reason someone had put on. Every mother knows that chickenpox can only be treated with talcum powder, alcohol, anything which dries the boils, and not with oil or cream, which makes them worse.

I looked at her drawn face, and in a flash it came to me. I understood what had happened. What an ordeal, what pain and anguish my child had endured the past week, or was it perhaps even the past month, only to spare me the sorrow of seeing her so desperately ill. What love, what superhuman courage had inspired this child to write me gay and happy letters every day for the past month so that I would believe she was well and would not fret.

I looked at Irène and saw that to save her there was only one possibility – I had to stay with her in the clinic, in the same room, and look after her myself, comfort her, feed her. She surely could not eat or drink when her lips, tongue and throat were so dreadfully swollen and painful.

I took a medicine dropper and with it gave her a little orange juice. This was the first liquid she had had for several days. This was also the first time she smiled. There was now no question of my going back to my room. Seeing her pathetic face, her emaciated body, her unbearable pain, I knew that I had to take a serious decision on the spot.

At the unusual hour of seven in the evening, the doctor turned up. Doctors came in the morning, twice a week, and that was that. He must have been told that I was back and very upset about Irène's condition. I told him that I insisted on staying with my daughter in this room and asked him to tell the manageress about my wish.

The doctor got very excited and started to argue with me. He explained that it was extremely dangerous for me to stay with Irène while she had chickenpox. Had I ever had it? No, I did not think so, but I would stay with my daughter. The doctor said he thought such a thing quite impossible. I was sure to get it, and at my age, with my heart, which was not too good, it could well be fatal.

I was adamant and told the doctor that although he might be a great TB specialist, he could never be a mother. Therefore I wished to stay with my daughter who needed me and could not otherwise get the proper attention her state of health required. There was sufficient proof of this, sufficient proof that she had been neglected, when she had been left for six days without food or drink. If he did not intend to let me stay, I would do so all the same, even if I had to sleep on the floor.

The doctor went away, telling me that he wished to bear no responsibility for whatever might happen to me. He had done his duty and warned me. It was up to me to decide my fate. My decision was taken, and I stayed on and started my life in the clinic. I was to be in this room with Irène for years, looking after her, nursing her night and day, comforting her, teaching her, reading to her, doing what I could to enable her to stand her great ordeal.

The chickenpox was virulent and took well over a month to cure. Afterwards Irène had unbearable pain in her bad knee. I asked the doctors about it again and again, but this did not help. Rules were rules, X-rays were made every six months, never mind the state of illness and the pain of the patient. Irène suffered agony; the slightest movement of her bed, the slamming of a door, brought tears of pain into her eyes.

By this time she had been in bed, without movement, for three full years. When she first came to this village she had a swollen knee, but the bone itself was not affected and if there was any microbe, its presence was in the muscles, ligaments and soft parts of the knee. Now, after this chickenpox, the bone too must have become affected. According to Irène's description, the pain was like a violent toothache. She had had pain before, severe pain, but not the same kind. This was different.

Six months of this pain, six months of severe violent toothache-like pain, without being able to move, to shift one's position, six months of unbearable excruciating pain – I need hardly say how upset, how worried I was. But rules were rules, X-rays would be made in due course, then one could know how the patient progressed. There surely was nothing seriously wrong with her. She had stayed quietly in bed so long, following her treatment rigorously. There was nothing to worry about. The knee was most probably healing nicely, and after the next X-ray the patient would most probably be allowed to get up.

The pains? Oh, they must be pains of calcification, the healing process is always a little painful. Twice a week, every week, the same conversation took place and the same answers were given. Everything was perfect, the knee was so much better, almost healed really, and all these stories about unbearable pain were just imagination. Was the patient an only child? She was? Ah well, just a little spoiled, that was all.

Once even I began to wonder, and I talked to my little sufferer, and asked her if, perhaps, she was tired of being ill so long and perhaps losing patience and imagining that her pains were getting worse and worse. The reproachful look in her big tear-stained eyes told me enough, and I was bitterly sorry I had doubted my courageous little martyr.

At last the six months were over. The day came when the X-ray was due to be taken. That meant, of course, a journey to 'The Oaks', an expensive clinic which had an X-ray machine in-house. This was the only clinic in the resort which had an X-ray machine, and patients were taken there and back every six months.

A journey to 'The Oaks' meant transfer to a stretcher, the stretcher taken down on the lift and out of the garden to the car. At the other end, the same procedure again, out of the car, into the X-ray room, off the stretcher, onto the table. Then back again to 'The Laurels'. For the last three years the trip to 'The Oaks' had always been a treat, being considered as an outing. This time things were different.

It took over half an hour to move Irène from the bed to the stretcher. The suffering of the child was unbearable and impossible to watch. Perspiration was running down her face, her whole body, even her hair, was dripping wet. After half an hour of inhuman suffering, Irène was on the stretcher. In accordance with the policy of 'no drugs', nothing was given to her, not even an asprin.

Mothers were not allowed to accompany patients, so I stayed at the clinic and supervised the changing of the sheets and the turning of the mattress, a thing which, for the very ill patients, happened twice a year, when the patient was taken to be X-rayed. The upper sheet was changed every week, so were the pillow-cases. But the lower sheet could not be changed as the patient could not be moved.

Irène's leg was resting on special cushions piled high on a wooden appliance. There were eighteen of these cushions. There was also a special hard cushion with a hole in the middle which was placed under the patient's seat. To clean the bed with the ever-present lower sheet the nurses used a special brush. It was not very convenient, and disturbed the patient, especially in the case of Irène, where the slightest movement provoked impossible pain. But rules were rules, and the brush was used twice a day, pain or no pain.

The X-ray took an unusually long time. Irène was brought back hours later, exhausted, flushed, soaking wet, sobbing with pain. The nurse who had accompanied her said it had taken a full hour to get the patient on to the X-ray table. Nothing had been done to ease the pain.

It took three days to get the X-ray and report back to our clinic. On the fourth day the specialist came to see us. He said that he had wanted personally to announce the good news to Irène and her mother, that after three long years in bed the moment had come at last to start to get up and gradually to learn to walk again. Irène and I, smiling and hopeful, were waiting for the X-ray, still in a closed envelope, to be brought for the specialist's inspection.

I was standing behind the specialist so as to be able to see the X-ray when he looked at it, so that I too could see the progress. At last the X-ray picture was taken out of its envelope and the specialist held it up to the light.

We both gave out a cry – this could not be the right picture, there must be a mistake, it was impossible, it was awful, whose X-rays were these anyhow? And who had made the mistake? We both looked again at the name on the X-ray, and the specialist started slowly to read the report.

I could not read this report at the time, it was strictly confidential – but in a day or two I got hold of it through somebody's kindness. The report did not spare its words – it said in simple terms that this was a criminal case of neglect, that there was no possibility of finding an excuse for what had been done to this poor child, that there simply was no more knee, the bone was completely eaten up. It was impossible to imagine, continued the report, how this poor child could stand the unbearable pain the destruction must have given her. Never had one seen such unheard-of neglect and cruelty.

The specialist finished reading the report. His face got red. He folded the report and looked again at the X-ray. Now his face was pale. He had to talk to the patient and her mother.

'Well, my child,' he said, 'contrary to expectations, the X-ray is not good. I now understand your complaint about pains, which are justified. I am sorry to say that there seems to be a serious evolution of the illness, which has now become extremely virulent. One cannot tell how far it will go.'

Irène, pale, almost blue in the face, her eyes shining with fever and tears, asked in a husky but firm voice what was going to happen now. Nothing much could be done, said the specialist, but bed and sun and patience. For how long?

Oh, at least another two years in bed, then one would see. Could the knee be saved? There was nothing much to save, as there was no more knee. One would try to save the leg but, of course, one could not promise anything. It really had developed in a tragic manner, things had taken a very bad turn and nothing definite could be said as yet. Goodbye, and try to be courageous, all one's courage was needed now. The specialist left.

We two stayed behind, but then an idea passed through my mind. I ran out into the corridor and stopped the specialist just when he was leaving. I asked if it was possible to take out my knee and transplant it into my daughter's leg. I explained that I was welling to sign a paper that I had proposed this operation myself and that I was prepared to risk the consequences of such an operation. I explained that my daughter, at eighteen, needed a knee more than I did and that I would be happy to give her mine.

The specialist looked at me and his look was somewhat softer and kinder. 'You are an exceptional mother, aren't you?' he said. I assured him that I was not, that I was merely trying to save my child, that my own life was of little interest to me and that being crippled at my age would not matter. I had to save my daughter, and begged him to consider my proposition seriously.

The specialist thought for a moment, then explained that the illness was now so virulent that such an operation could not succeed. As it was, he could not promise to save her whole leg, he was not sure that the illness had not spread. In fact, there might be no hope of saving Irène at all. He was sorry, but nothing could be done.

Things had taken a terrible turn. It was, of course, a pity that no-one had believed in her complaints about pain when something might have been done. But really, her courage was unheard-of, and it was impossible to understand how anybody was able to stand such unbearable pain for six months and complain so little. If Irène did survive the crisis, then there remained only one course – to operate and stiffen the knee. But this could not be done before the illness quietened down again, and this would take a year or two. He could not tell.

All these long years, all these terrible years, I had been fighting desperately to save Irène's knee from being stiffened. Leaving my own country to come here had been a difficult decision because it had also meant forfeiting the financial help from our insurance, which would have paid almost 80 per cent of the cost of hospitals and treatments. And funds were low, very low. My husband had been killed in the war, our home ransacked, our fortune taken away.

But in our own country there was no real cure for this disease and nothing could be done except that drastic and major operation – removing a portion of the bone, taking out the knee and stiffening the knee. Or else there was the second alternative – plaster. Lying in plaster for years, sometimes for life, in plaster corsets, in hard, rigid iron appliances. Whatever came out of these plasters, if ever, was always a terrible, frightening cripple.

It may be that the operation back home would have been a better plan – less suffering, fewer years lost. But Irène was then fifteen and still growing. An operation would have halted the growth of the leg and this, in time, would have crippled her even more.

So, after thorough consideration of all these problems, I had brought my child to this clinic, where there were no plasters and no operations. I was even more pleased that I had taken this decision when, upon my arrival, the specialist had said that he found the bone had not been affected and that the illness was concentrated in the muscles and soft parts of the knee, and that it would not take long for Irène to be quite well again. A few months in bed, a year at most – trifles in this place.

And yet here I stood, all hopes vanished, everything I had struggled for, gone. Nothing could be done to save the knee, there was nothing left of it. The question now was about the leg as a whole, about Irène's life.

This was a difficult period to go through, it was difficult to get used to the idea that nothing could be done and still more difficult to find words to make Irène believe that nothing was lost, that miracles happen, that young as she was she might grow a new piece of bone, she might even get back all of her knee.

I helped her as much as I could. I helped her not to lose hope, not to become neurasthenic, not to stop struggling, not to become desperate but to keep cheerful as much as her terrible pains would allow. I helped her to want to live, to think of the future, to think of a normal life to come, prepare for it, hope for it. And, of course, the future, in my description, was all rosy and beautiful. Everything could only be joy, happiness and delight, life was worth living, worth struggling for, life was beautiful, and the more one had to suffer at present the more one had to prepare for the happy, happy future.

That was my daily dose for her – the only medicine my daughter ever had in this clinic. Sometimes it was difficult to convince a poor little girl, wriggling with pain and despair, to believe in the absolutely unbelievable – health and happiness. But I achieved it somehow, although I sometimes had to leave my darling in the middle of my cheerful conversation to go out of the room and have a good long cry. Dark sunglasses, which everybody wore, helped to conceal my red eyes, and to continue the cheerful conversation.

What didn't I say! What didn't I picture! The happiness, the beauty, the health, the wonderful unusual life we were going to live, the absolute certainty of happy marriage, and love and bliss ever after. I still do not know where I got this power of constantly inventing, over a number of years, happy, pleasant stories, always a happy ending, always cheerful and amusing. A mother wanting to save her child, fighting with all the odds against her, cannot afford to lose hope.

A mother finds superhuman strength to struggle and make desperate efforts to cure an almost incurable child. When the specialist said that he did not think Irène would pull through, that she was sinking rapidly and that there was little hope, if any, it only gave me more force to struggle, more determination to do the impossible, to induce my daughter to fight more and more, to the very last possibility of human endurance.

The Almighty was good to us and helped Irène to pull through, but oh, the struggle, the courage, the suffering, the patience, the unbearable pain, the sublime efforts to hope, hope again, every day, every hour, every moment.

CHAPTER 52

The Healer

In my despair I decided to approach the healers. There was a small area of the country where healers were authorised to practice without restriction. I went to a town in that area and contacted several healers. One, an old woman, asked me for a lock of Irène's hair, held it in her hands for some time and stated, 'Your child has a very serious illness in her left knee and is in great danger. She needs immediate help.'

A cold shiver went down my back. I had not given the woman any details about the nature or location of Irène's illness. She just knew, in some strange and mysterious way.

The old woman taught me how to apply a special herbal poultice made with cabbage leaves. This she said would have to be put on the knee each night for many, many months. It would, she said, drain all the poisons of the disease out through the pores. It sounded preposterous, but I had little choice. I did it.

Every night for eleven months I applied the poultice. This had to be done without either the doctor or the nurses knowing anything about it – they would have stopped me at once. I would apply it when the nurse left in the evening, take it off at dawn, and later in the day bury it somewhere outdoors.

Every morning the bandages covering the poultice were soaked. The 'poisons', as she had referred to the matter in the knee, were indeed being drawn out through the pores of the skin. The swelling went down. The hot, red swollen knee gradually became cool and comfortable. It was, to me, the nearest thing to a miracle. Every day the dressings were soaked with an evil liquid substance.

The doctors watched Irène's progress with amazement. Still I did not dare to tell them what I was doing. The knee healed. Irène was allowed out of bed. The first day she was allowed out for one minute. The next day for two minutes and so it went on until she was able to be up for half an hour.

But she still could not walk. The destruction in the knee had been too great. The bones were ragged and uneven, with fragments sticking painfully into her flesh. It would be necessary to carry out an operation to remove these jagged pieces of bone.

There was, said the surgeon, absolutely no other way of Irène being able to walk without agonising pain. The operation would have a second great advantage. By removing the destroyed section of bone, all the traces of disease would be removed with it. Irène would be able to go through life without even the slightest vestige of tuberculosis in her. It was, the surgeon explained, as radical as removing an appendix. Nothing was left behind. She would, however, have a stiff left knee for life. The idea of this broke my heart, but there simply was no alternative.

In the years to come, Irène overcame this handicap in a remarkable way. She taught herself to walk in a certain way, using the hip joints instead of the knee to give the necessary mobility and balance to her walk. She practised this walk for hours, perfecting every move until she got it to a fine art and achieved the impossible – the ability to walk with a totally stiff left knee with nothing more noticeable than a slight, a very slight, limp.

As the years went by, she learn to walk for hours at a time, she learned to dance, and she danced beautifully, but I was not to know this at the time, and my heart ached for what I believed would be my crippled child.

To this day, however, the doctors are unaware of the real cause of Irène's improvement, and I blessed the healer for her help.

CHAPTER 53

The Final Operation

I was sitting in Room 22 at 'The Oaks', waiting. 'The Oaks' was the clinic where operations were performed. Irène had just been taken to the operating theatre. My beloved daughter, my hope and happiness in life, my reason for living, was lying on the operating table waiting for the doctors to start their work.

Smiling and courageous, Irène went to her ordeal. While we waited together for the nurses to fetch her she was still trying to give me courage and to raise my morale. She explained again and again how good it was that she was to have this operation. Our lips were smiling bravely but our hearts could not help but be aware of the fact that this operation would make Irène into a handicapped person. Never again would she be able to run, or to walk without a limp, never again would she be able to do her beloved ballet.

Outside the weather was awful. A tempestuous storm raged with lashing, icy rain. The partitions on the balconies were creaking. The storm dislodged the partition between our balcony and the next and it was beating against the wall with an eerie sound.

During the weeks preceding the operation, other 'knees' had been telling us of their experiences after undergoing this operation. All had suffered agonising pain for some time. Irène listened, sometimes quite pale, but at once comforting me, telling me how glad we must be to have it done.

The day before the operation, as I washed her, I could not help noticing how cool and white and healthy the knee now looked – no trace of inflammation or of swelling. Was this crippling operation really necessary? I was full of doubts. Sensing my distress, Irène immediately demonstrated how badly she walked, every step causing agony. She tried to reassure me once again.

The operation began at 2.30 pm. By 3.15 there was still no news.

What were they doing to her? What stage had it reached? It was the rest hour after lunch when the patients sleep. The house was quiet, no sound whatever, just the storm, the rain, the rain and the storm. I read over and over again the loving letters Irène wrote to me the day before. She handed me the envelope marked 'to be read during the operation' just before she was taken to the operating theatre. They were full of courage, hope and love.

Three-twenty – still no news. I tried to read but could not. Three-twenty-five – how slowly time went! I walked around a little in the room. The house was waking up – the hour of rest was over. There were sounds of voices, the clatter of teacups. Three-thirty – still no news. They had said it would take no longer than one hour.

Three-thirty-five. I was cold in the room. The wind blew in under the balcony door. I felt lonely, lost, unhappy. I worried, worried so much.

Three-forty. Still no news. What were they doing? What had they found in the knee? How much had they taken out? How badly would she limp? Three-forty-five. I prayed, I walked, my anxiety increasing with every minute. Three-fifty. Still no news. They had said an hour at the most. Perhaps they had not included the time it would take to put on the plaster. I prayed that this was the reason for the delay. Three-fifty-five. No news. How was my child and what was happening? Why did it take so long? I was frantic with worry.

Four o'clock. She was back! The nurses wheeled her bed in. Irène was still unconscious, her leg from hip to toe in heavy plaster, the bed a mountain of cushions, one leg high up. The nurse and I held her chin to prevent her biting her tongue when she woke up. Irène awoke an hour later. Still very groggy, she smiled, asked me to give her a hug, and thanked me profusely for being there. She said many endearing things.

As the anaesthetic wore off, the pain began. As always, Irène voiced no complaint, but by the way she repeatedly clenched her hands and bit her lip I knew the pain was fierce. My poor child, subjected to this after so many years of pain and suffering.

At nine o'clock she was given a pain-killing injection and the night nurse asked me to leave. Rules were rules, they were sorry, but they would not allow me to spend the night sitting by her bed. This was the first separation we had had for years. It could not have come at a worse moment. The nurse explained that Irène was now drugged from the injection, and would not realise that I was not beside her.

With sorrow in my heart I left the clinic. The storm still raged and a thin coat of snow covered the ice. The road was like an ice-rink and, as I emerged into the darkness, the wind nearly threw me over. I wore rubber overshoes and slipped and slithered on the ice. I fell countless times, and the track back to our clinic took me hours as I battled along, inch by inch, in the darkness and the storm.

CHAPTER 54

Farewell to the Clinic

On 16 September 1951, Irène said goodbye to the resort. It was a day of liberation, a kind of VE Day. She had lain on her back for almost as long as the Second World War had lasted.

Goodbye to 'bones', nurses, maids, proprietor, manageress, goodbye to doctors. Goodbye to years of abnormal existence, to bed-pans, special beds, position cushions, cures, sun, air, oil on the body, nakedness, sunburnt backs, foreign doctors. Goodbye to the manageress, who could not understand why I had fretted so much during Irène's operation. 'It's not your leg they are operating on, so why are you in such a state?' Goodbye to owing money to the clinic, the impossiblity of paying it, the signing of papers, interminable talks with the proprietor, his demands and threats, softened by the soothing voice of Irène, her charm making the demands less strong and immediate.

Another chapter began for a mother and daughter who had been through so much together. A new life faced us. We had no money, no apartment, no home, nothing, even a small room in a third-rate hotel was too expensive. I had nowhere to take her, nothing to give her, nothing to make life more pleasant after all these terrible years.

Five years of war in the mountains of France – fear, danger, Gestapo, Wehrmacht, Resistance. Nights in the snow and days of fright expecting torture and death. All this by the age of eleven. Then six years of illness, four of them lying on her back without being able to move, to turn, her life full of sores and pain.

In between the pain and suffering, there had been learning. Studying languages, general knowledge, music, symphonies on the radio and from records. Studies – Spanish, Russian, Italian. Trying to earn a few pennies making leather purses at a farthing a piece for a purse manufacturer. Anything to forget, to get away from the present, to think of the future, anything different, anything new.

Sometimes, to give Irène a change from the dreary clinic food, I cooked her some *kotelety* (Russian meat balls). We had a tiny spirit stove, about the size of half a hand, and a minute frying pan. It took ages to make one small meat ball. The smell of the spirit was appalling. But how delicious they were! To us these *kotelety* were symbolic. They represented home cooking and freedom. We dreamt of *kotelety* made on a real stove in a real kitchen of our own and eaten at 4 o'clock in the morning. That was an unusual time to cook meat balls, but it struck us as daring, exciting and bold. We dreamt of these *kotelety* for four years.

How I longed to spoil Irène, to buy her a new dress, some shoes, to show her that life was still nice and full of pleasant things! But how to do it?

I found a small furnished room in a town not far from the clinic. Irène was not well enough to return to the city. Anyway, there was no home there either. Our home was taken by the Germans during the war, when we were in the Maquis, and there was nothing left of it.

Dead tired, worn out and miserable, I somehow found the strength to go to the clinic and take Irène from her place of ordeal, from that unearthly place of suffering and sorrow and deliver her at last from the sights of suffering humanity, to bring her to our shabby little hotel room, to our unsettled life, our insecure future. Physically and mentally I was worn out. I needed rest after those terrible eleven years, but my daughter needed life, love, happiness and normal surroundings.

CHAPTER 55

Geneva - City of Opportunity

Over the years I acted as teacher to my daughter. During the war, when regular schooling was not possible, I taught her the usual school subjects – history, geography, arithmetic and so on. But I made a point of incorporating the history, geography and literature of the countries whose languages she spoke, so that by the age of fifteen Irène had a culture embracing at least four countries – England, France, Germany and Switzerland.

I continued teaching throughout her bed-ridden years at the clinic. First I added the culture of the countries whose languages she was learning, Spanish, Russian, Italian. Then we passed on to 'higher education'. I had studied medicine before finding myself unable to cope with the more gory aspects of a medical training, and switched to law. I also had a degree in music. I coached her in all these subjects.

My husband and I had travelled widely and I was able to describe to Irène the countries we had visited. Most important of all, I taught Irène life. This I did by describing the theatres she would visit when she was well again, concerts she would attend, restaurants, balls. I gave a demonstration of what took place at a ball, standing next to her bed pretending to be a young man asking her to dance. I would mimic the whole scene, buttoning my jacket and bowing politely. I described in lyrical detail the wonderful life she would lead when she was well again.

Irène had a vivid imagination. She could visualise the scene as I talked and see in her mind's eye all the things I described. Over the years we 'travelled the world' together whilst never leaving her room at the clinic. I found an Italian lady who had a sick child. I gave English lessons to the child, and the mother gave Irène Italian lessons. The lady came from Florence and her accent was exquisite.

Irène acquired a perfect knowledge of Italian, so once again we 'travelled', to Italy, in our own way, visiting Venice, Florence, Rome and many other cities, admiring the priceless works of art the country had to offer. I then discovered a Spanish student, also a patient in a clinic, so I gave him English lessons and he taught Irène Spanish.

During Irène's four years in bed at the clinics she studied intensively, from morning to night. She was, she said, preparing our future. She described to me in detail exactly what she intended to do when she got well, and how she would work and strive to build up a decent existence for us both. This was part of her vow of being the 'man in the family' which she had made at the age of twelve.

Her bravery was extraordinary. In all the years of illness I did not once hear a word of complaint. Sometimes my heart would break when I saw the bright smile whilst reading in her eyes pain and anguish. In every cloud she would find a silver lining and describe that silver lining to me in detail.

Over the years, quietly, systematically, she planned and prepared our future. Her plan was to acquire as much knowledge of foreign languages and cultures as she possibly could, then to apply for a scholarship at Geneva University. This university had a world-famous Interpreters' college. When she qualified, she hoped to obtain a post as a linguist with the United Nations whose Economics Section was situated in Geneva.

And so, over the years, with a single-minded determination, she prepared herself. Laying flat on her back, writing was not easy, especially as she insisted on using ink and not a pencil. Normal people would write with ink, she said, and so would she. This resulted frequently in a blue nose, where the ink had dribbled. Smiling mischievously, Irène would refer to her 'aristocratic blue-blood' nose!

We had come to know a chaplain who visited the patients from time to time. He was a cultured man and greatly impressed with Irène's erudition. They had long talks together. He had given Irène a letter of introduction to the head of the Ecole d'Interprètes (Interpreters School), one of the faculties at Geneva University, and suggested that she apply for a scholarship. She obtained an interview, and on the great day we made our way to Geneva, a short train journey from when we were staying.

We had decided that this vital interview was something that Irène would have to tackle on her own. It would never do for the 'man of the family' to arrive for the interview accompanied by her mother! So, we decided that I would wait for her in a small café next to the University. My heart went with her as I watched her painfully making her way towards the building of the University. She looked so frail and so vulnerable, limping along with her two sticks.

What, I wondered, would be the outcome of the interview? So many years of hope, work and preparation had culminated in this moment. I could not bear the thought of her being disappointed. How I wished that I had the financial means to send her to the University myself.

I waited, I prayed. I stared at a large ticking clock on the wall facing me. I did not expect the interview to last very long, half an hour at the most, as the Dean was a busy man. The clock ticked on, and on. An hour. An hour and a half. Two hours. What had happened? Had her weak ankles given way once again? Had she fallen? I was sick with worry.

At last I saw her approach in the distance, hobbling as fast as she could. It is very difficult to swagger while on two sticks, but swagger she did. Beaming with pleasure, she hugged me and said, 'Come at once, he wants to meet you.' On the way she explained what had happened. It appeared that the Dean could not quite understand how so young a girl had so wide a culture. So Irène told him all about our university-in-bed at the clinic, and how I had coached her over the years.

We entered his office. 'Here is my teacher,' Irène proudly said. The outcome of this interview was that not only did Irène get her scholarship, but the Head of the Ecole d'Interprètes gave me a scholarship too! This child, as he put it, was still very frail and would continue to need all my help for a while. Realising our financial predicament, this wonderful man also offered us the possibility of staying in a small spare room at the administrative offices of the Ecole d'Interprètes for a nominal rent. We both went wild with joy, and, on our way to the station, stopped at the little café and celebrated in a totally spendthrift way – we had *two* cups of coffee and *two* pieces of cake each!

Our shattered world was beginning to come together again. Dared I hope that, after all I had been through, Communists, Nazis, the Resistance, the TB clinic, at last some kind of normal existence might be ahead of me, together with my beloved daughter?

CHAPTER 56

Once Again an Accident

And so began our new life in Geneva.

The administrative office of the Ecole d'Interprètes was situated away from the University building, in an ancient, dilapidated house in the Old Town. It consisted of a flat, where the rooms had been turned into offices. The flat had a bathroom, a kitchen and also a small spare room not being used at the time. This was the room which had kindly been let to us, with use of the kitchen and bathroom.

The furniture consisted of an old divan, and a couple of rickety chairs. Our room was separated from the bathroom and kitchen by a large entrance hall, in which were rows of chairs on which students sat whilst waiting to be interviewed. We had to cross this hall to get to the bathroom or the kitchen, so there was little privacy. As the students sat chatting to one another, it was also frequently noisy. But we were away from the clinic, its dramas, its set routine, its smells, its pall of doom and bursts of gaiety, its total abnormality. So, to us, our small flat was sheer heaven.

Money was desperately short. We had our scholarships, but had to find money to pay for the room and a minimum of food. The Head once again came to our rescue by channelling some translation work our way. We became two happy students, mother and daughter. We went to the University together, and loved every moment of it. There was little time for sleep, as the translations we did between classes were not enough to keep body and soul together, and we had to continue working at them at night. We were tired, very tired, but happy. Food was short, but we managed once in a while to have the meat balls, the *kotelety*, we had dreamt about at the clinic.

Alas, our happiness was not to last. After six weeks, while I was out one afternoon delivering a completed translation, Irène decided to give me a surprise and spring-clean our room. She attempted to stand on a chair to reach a high and dusty shelf. Her weak ankles gave way and she fell heavily. Upon my return, I found her on the floor, unable to move, and in agonising pain.

A doctor was called and we were told that after four years in bed Irène's muscles were completely wasted and that she should never have been allowed to leave the clinic without a lengthy course of physiotherapy. There were no such facilities at the clinic.

It is true the doctor at the clinic had told us that Irène needed rest and rehabilition after her ordeal, but by then lack of funds had made this impossible. Also, Irène had carefully hidden from me how weak her limbs were and how exhausted she felt. In any case, said the doctor, she would have to be taken to hospital as she had dislocated her right hip and this would have to be set under general anaesthetic. He would make arrangements for her to be admitted immediately.

We had to explain that this was not possible, as we could not pay the hospital fees and had to raise funds. We had no medical insurance cover, and the hospital fees were prohibitive. The doctor left, saying Irène could not wait long as the pain was quite appalling, and to get in touch with him again as soon as possible.

I made Irène as comfortable as I could on the floor, with cushions and blankets – she could not be moved – kissed her and set forth to try and organise some money. Irène tried to convince me that the pain was not nearly as bad as the doctor made out, but the pinched look in her face and the sad eyes behind the bright smile convinced me of the contrary.

Our 'travelling brooch' was still at the pawnbrokers and could not help us this time. This brooch was my only remaining piece of jewellery, as everything else had been sold to pay for the clinic and nobody had liked it sufficiently to buy it. So it went in and out of the pawnbrokers, and was known in our household as 'the travelling brooch'.

The Head gave me an introduction to a charitable organisation where he knew the principal. This organisation was run by a group of society ladies – a similar set-up to the one I had been leading in Paris. Unfortunately, these kind ladies, who had had no training in social welfare, did not possess a great deal of natural tact and had a tendency to think of the poor more as 'cases' rather than as people with feelings and emotions.

They came to our room to assess the case, and at the end of the interview Irène and I felt like crawling away into a hole. I could not help remembering the length to which I had gone to make my 'cases' in Paris feel at ease and get them to accept my help without loss to their dignity and self-respect.

An ambulance was called, and Irène was taken to hospital.

CHAPTER 57

Hospital Again

Irène was taken to the operating theatre, and the hip was put back into position under anaesthetic. The Consultant explained to me that Irène would have to remain in bed for some time and then undergo a complete rehabilitation programme at the hospital before she was able to tackle normal life. The muscles in the whole of her body were so wasted and so atrophied that he could not understand how she had managed to walk at all.

I, however, understood. Irène had once again hidden the true situation and somehow, some way, coped, as she had done many times before.

I went back to the charity organisation. This time I was received more cordially. Perhaps having spoken to me, the ladies had come to the conclusion that my background was similar to theirs, and that I was 'one of them' after all, although impoverished! There was a charity scheme at the hospital known as 'the Third Class' which was for the very poor, and they had succeeded in getting Irène accepted.

There was, however, no spare bed at the time for a 'Third Class' patient in any of the surgical wards, but a bed was available in the geriatric ward, so that is where she went.

It was a large ward, with peeling walls, badly in need of redecoration. The entire hospital was old, and crumbling, and has since been completely rebuilt. The ward was dark and dingy, with an atmosphere of death and decay. It was crowded and cold, the available heating being insufficient to heat a room of this size with such high ceilings.

After her brief spell of freedom, Irène faced again a hospital routine. At 5 am, the night nurse came to wake her. Time for washing. The lady two beds away then began her morning monologue. She had a powerful voice. A farmer's wife, she was used to getting up at dawn, and always sounded as if she was calling the cattle. Dawn invariably broke to the sound of Mme M's booming voice. She also had an odd way of repeating every sentence three, four, five times. Since her conversation was dull anyway, repetition made it duller still.

As at the clinics, each patient in the ward was a world unto himself. I mention but two cases described to me by Irène, one lively, the other incredibly sad.

The bed opposite Irène was occupied by 'the lady in mauve', an ex-chorus girl in her seventies wearing a heavily embroidered mauve négligée with lots of little mauve ribbons. She was in for a heart condition and was on a strict salt-free diet. Pale and frail, she spent the day in bed, quietly resting. At night, however, she came to life and during an interval between the night nurse's rounds gave the sleepy ward a nightly performance of the French Cancan, kicking her legs high into the air. She then collapsed onto the bed, panting and exhausted.

This was followed later by a midnight supper of salami, sausage and pickles, smuggled in during the visiting hour by Gonzales, her elderly Spanish lover. The sleeping ward was thus wakened again by much noisy crackling of grease-proof paper and loud mutterings about starving to death long ago had it not been for Gonzales.

Completely different was the occupant of the bed next to Irène. This was an elderly widow in her eighties who told Irène that, having no children, relatives or even friends, she was so desperately lonely that at Christmas she faked illness to get herself admitted to hospital where it was a bit warmer and there was company. The poor lady stoically suffered all the painful medical tests and investigations, but these were less of an ordeal to her than yet another Christmas spent alone in a cold and lonely flat.

Poor Irène. Back once again to the ward and its 'characters'.

CHAPTER 58

The Ordeal

The consultant and his entourage of students spent quite a while by Irène's bedside. It was decided she would have to stay in bed for some time while her damaged hip recovered and treatment was given for her wasted muscles. Little did we know that she would have to remain in bed for a full nine months. It was also decided that a complete check-up would be carried out. The consultant said that the hip looked serious. The students all nodded in agreement, all thirty of them, and Irène's heart sank a little further.

For the check-up, Irène was trundled around on a trolley from department to department. In the ear, nose and throat department a young doctor told her to open her mouth, looked in and remarked that her tonsils were not very nice. 'But,' he added after a moment's thought, 'it won't help your hip if we yank them out, so we'll forget about it for the moment.' Greatly relieved, Irène and her tonsils were taken back to the ward.

Irène went through all the departments but one, and that one we felt she would certainly not be taken to, as it was the *Maternité* (Obstetrics and Gynaecology).

We were mistaken. Routine was routine, and the routine in this hospital was that everyone passing 'through the Department' had to have a check-up at the *Maternité*.

On the way there, the male nurse who was pushing her trolley did his best to comfort her. She should not be unhappy, motherhood was a marvellous thing, he had three children of his own, all grown-up now, and he remembered how they were born at the very same Maternité. He really tried so hard to comfort her, but Irène did not have the heart to disillusion him. Anyhow, she was too shy to do so.

They brought her to a large theatre full of frightening objects. Row upon row of gleaming knives and forceps, steel basins and weird appliances. She was greeted by a young house doctor and several smiling young students. Perhaps they were not students, but doctors too. I do not know. But they were certainly men. Desperately, Irène begged the doctor to spare her this ordeal, trying to explain that she was still a virgin and that there was nothing to look at, and anyhow she was here for a dislocated hip. Her explanations did not seem to register.

'Ever been pregnant?' asked the doctor in a matter-of-fact voice, 'if so, how many times? Any abortions?' Blushing crimson, Irène proceeded once more to explain the position. She begged, sobbed and pleaded. Nothing helped. Irène was put on a gynaecological table, half chair, half bed, and the ordeal began.

The doctor said that she should tell him if it hurt, and if it did he would not insist. It hurt very much and after a while Irène told him so. The doctor turned to the other young men, saying 'Impossible, can't even get the instrument in properly, take her away.' Sobbing, Irène was taken away. Oh, doctors! why don't you listen?

Passing the crowded waiting-room, a woman nudged her neighbour, pointed at her and whispered loudly: 'Look at her, so young, abortion I bet you. Youth today ....'

Why, why, why try to examine what as yet cannot be examined? Why submit one to this unnecessary ordeal of embarrassment and pain? Irène could never forget the horror, the shame, and those watching young men.

Years later a gynaecologist, to whom Irène related this experience, expressed a sense of horror at the insensitivity and cruelty shown by the young doctors.

CHAPTER 59

New Year at the Hospital

It was many years later, on the eve of the Jewish New Year. I was remembering the past, and comparing the old times with the new. I was dwelling at length on the happy times of my youth in Russia, surrounded by family and friends, and describing the family meal on the New Year, the cheerful atmosphere, the people, the laughter. But now there were just the two of us. As I spoke, I became more and more despondent and depressed. Irène was always able to cheer me up. On this occasion she did not succeed and I sank deeper and deeper into a feeling of misery.

She gave me a long searching look, got up from the table, rummaged for a while in some drawers, and quietly put into my hands a small black notebook. This, she said, was something she had kept hidden from me for many years. Now I had to read it. I opened the notebook. The first page was headed 'Geneva Hospital. 31 December. Midnight.' I began to read, and this is what it said:

'The New Year has just begun. All the bells of the city are ringing, ringing to welcome the New Year. I am sitting in bed, crying my eyes out. The ward is dark, but for a small lamp with a dull green shade. The old women are asleep. Some are snoring, some are moaning. The dim green light envelops everything in a desolate green sheen – the bleak, peeling walls, the hospital beds, the sleeping old women.

'I awoke with a start a little while ago, having had a nightmare. I was struggling in a cold ocean. I could not swim. In the distance there was a sinking ship. I heard a tocsin ringing. Gradually it dawned on me – there was no ocean, there was just me in bed, covered in a cold sweat and shivering.

'There was no tocsin, just the bells of the town churches welcoming the New Year and people giving each other the traditional kiss under the mistletoe. With it too comes the picture of the cold and gloomy little room where my darling mother is alone, this New Year's Eve, sobbing her heart out I am sure.

'In the ward there are the old women snoring and moaning. In the corridor there is the night-nurse doing her rounds, going from one ward to the next, coughing. The night-nurse has whooping-cough but the hospital is short-staffed and there is no one to replace her, so she roams the corridors and wards as usual, coughing, coughing, coughing. The acoustics in these huge high corridors are tremendous. They simply amplify the sound of her coughing and it reverberates, eerie and frightening.

'I have the feeling of utter loneliness, a desperate longing for the presence of my mother, for some warmth, some happiness. I long and ache to be away from this ward, close to her again. I long to comfort her. I feel her every tear, her every sob, her every sigh. But what can I do, prisoner that I am, in this lonely and desolate ward, unable to walk, unable to move, with nothing but the feeling of my own breaking heart.

'I reach out to the night table and get hold of a small mirror, I look at my dishevelled hair and tear-stained face, and I resolve that I am going to give myself a talk, a courage-giving talk of the kind I have so often given to mother. So I look at the mirror and I begin.

'The situation, I say to myself, is appalling. One cannot sink much further than this – a charity case in a charity ward. Therefore, the only direction one can go now is upwards, provided that is, one does something towards it. Lying here wallowing in grief is not going to help change the situation. The only person who can actually *do* something is me. There really is no-one else. Therefore, I must begin. The doctors have told me that it is going to take many months before I can leave my bed. Something has to be done to speed this up, and it is going to need more than doctors and medicines.

'It is going to need force, sheer force of will. I *must* have this force of will. I *must* fight my illness myself, with every ounce of strength that I can muster. I *will* fight, and I will fight with the energy of despair. I *must* get us out of this dreary, difficult and hopeless existence. After all I am the self-appointed 'man of the family' and this is up to me.

'I have a strange kind of tiredness these days. I am so tired that the slightest effort exhausts me. Even reading is an effort. My mind goes blank. The doctors call it 'total exhaustion'. I shall therefore have to call upon my mind to overcome the weakness of my body.

'I must begin to study again, to prepare for our future. The tiredness has been so overwhelming that I have not studied since coming into the hospital. I have lost over ten days of study time. This must not be allowed to continue. I have read that Darwin, who was a sick man, could at one point of his life study no more than fifteen minutes a day. But he did not give up. I shall do likewise. When I try to read my mind goes blank after about five minutes. So, I am going to utilise those five minutes, then stop, and start again later. Five minutes are nothing, but several periods of five minutes amount to time.

'And so, I make my New Year's resolution. To struggle, to fight, to overcome. I pray for strength. May the Almighty help me to create a warm and happy home for my darling mother, and may we be there next year, celebrating New Year's Eve joyfully and thankfully.'

I closed the little black notebook. I took Irène in my arms. I hugged her, and asked the Almighty to forgive me for my ingratitude.

In the spring, Irène was transferred to a small room in the loft of the hospital, which she shared with another girl of her age. To get to this room one had to go up a narrow staircase and walk though a large loft which was used as a store room for old furniture. I thought with horror of what could happen if there was ever a fire in that loft full of old, tinder-dry wood. There was no means of escape. During the time Irène spent in that room I lay awake at night trembling with fright every time I heard the sound of a fire engine in the town.

Irène was delighted with her new room. It was quiet and peaceful. There was light and sunshine, none of which she had had in the dismal, dark ward on the ground floor. Through the little window she could see the sky.

Juliette, her room-mate, had a gastric condition. She also suffered from deep depression, and spent most of her time sobbing. We did all we could to help and comfort her.

For the next nine months Irène was to remain in bed in that little room while doctors and physiotherapists proceeded to rehabilitate her poor, wasted body. The hospital may have been old and dilapidated, but the care was excellent and the doctors and nurses kind and helpful. We remember their help with gratitude.

The Head of the Ecole d'Interprètes was helpful too. He lent me many books for Irène so that she could continue to study. Irène helped me with the translations so that we could pay the rent for our room at the University offices. The translation work was hard because so much of it had to be done at night. The work done during the day simply did not produce enough money to meet the bills.

After eight months of nightwork, I collapsed and I too was taken into hospital. They very kindly put me in Irène's room – Juliette having left by then, and I was with Irène for some three weeks. The diagnosis was complete exhaustion and malnutrition. Once again the Head helped, and waived the rent during my hospital stay.

As I think back on my life, I recall the selfishness of some and the kindness of others. How often were we at our lowest ebb, and how often, as with the Head, were we saved by acts of warm generosity.

CHAPTER 60

Students Again

We left the hospital and returned to our room at the University.

Irène was much better, but still not able to walk properly. We were given an introduction to Dr Illi, a skilled chiropractor and founder of the Institute for Human Static and Dynamic in Geneva. It was Dr Illi who enabled Irène to walk free from pain. He measured her on some intricate-looking machines, and worked out to the millimetre the difference in the length of her legs. The sole of one shoe was slightly raised, and the heel of the other, and Irène was filmed on a special machine which X-rayed patients while they were walking.

With infinite patience Illi worked on Irène, and once he had established her static profile, he taught her how to walk, using the joints in her hips and ankles to replace the mobility of the missing joint in her knee. His fees were normally very high, but he was extremely generous and allowed us to settle his modest bill by instalments. We have a deep debt of gratitude to this wonderful man.

The new walk had to be learned and practised. It took months of intensive effort before Irène could walk reasonably well. She would do the exercises early in the morning before leaving for the University.

During the vacation Irène spent some time at a convalescent home in the mountains run by nuns, where she taught languages.

The short spell at the convalescent home turned out to be a blessing for both of us. I had been feeling unwell for some time. I felt sick, giddy and ill. There was always a slight smell of gas in the flat, but the gas board, when we called them in, assured us that there was no leakage of gas. I visited a doctor and was told that I may well have cancer of the colon and that a thorough investigation was necessary. I thought about this, as I did not have the financial means for any sort of medical investigation, let alone a thorough one.

Irène returned from the convalescent home. As soon as she arrived in the flat, she began to vomit and passed out. Her symptoms were identical to mine, but much more violent. She also mentioned the strong smell of gas in the flat. The gas board had been the previous day and had once again reassured us that all was well.

I got in touch with the fire brigade and they arrived at once, checked out the flat and found an enormous leak from a gas pipe in the kitchen cupboard where we kept our food. It was leaking directly into our bread bin! Irène, they said, had acute gas poisoning because she had been away for some time. I, who had been in this atmosphere regularly, had a chronic form of poisoning which accounted for all the sickness and giddiness I had suffered from for some time.

The entire gas installation would need replacing as the whole system was ancient and leaking and, as the main did not function properly, it could not be cut off. The flat, they said, was not fit for human habitation and we would have to vacate it at once. They told us that we could not stay for even another night. They left. Whenever things began to look better, fate took a hand and another blow fell.

Where to go? It was conference time in Geneva. There was not a room to be had anywhere. Not that that made much difference. I had been so ill that I had not been able to complete the last translation and there was very little money.

We spent the night huddled on two chairs next to an open window. Once again the Head came to our rescue. He gave us an introduction to a lady who had a spare room she was prepared to let for a nominal rent. So we moved in and resumed our studies.

CHAPTER 61

The Shattered Dream

Another crisis loomed. My body was weakened by the chronic gas poisoning and lack of proper food and sleep. I had resumed my war-time tactics of telling Irène that I had no appetite and had been giving her part of my rations. We slept less and less, trying to keep up with the translation work. I had vague pains in my chest, and one night I collapsed. The doctor was called. It was not a heart attack, he said, but total exhaustion and heart strain. Unless I changed my way of life immediately, a proper heart attack would follow. I was to stay in bed and any form of work was forbidden.

For the next couple of days Irène was quiet and thoughtful. She left the house for long periods and returned looking tired and strained, her red beret firmly planted on her head. She gave no details, just said that she had much to do at the University. On the third day she returned home, hugged and kissed me and flung the red beret into the air with a gesture of gay abandon. 'That's it,' she said, 'everything is taken care of, now you can get well.' She proceeded to explain.

She had asked for an appointment with the Head and had told him about my collapse. This meant that two-thirds of our income had immediately vanished. We had hardly been able to make ends meet before. Now it was simply not possible for Irène to continue her studies. She would have to find work immediately; would he help with an introduction?

I was broken-hearted. I knew what this degree had meant to Irène. I thought of all the years of work and preparation. It was her life's dream. She was a brilliant student and now all this was to be shattered because of me. I sobbed uncontrollably.

'Stop sobbing,' she said, 'I've got news.'

She told me that the Head had given her a letter of introduction to a friend of his, a professor who was the head of the Institute of Graduate International Studies in Geneva. The professor knew many people at the United Nations as his graduates frequently obtained posts in their organisation. There had been a repetition of what took place once before. Irène's knowledge of half a dozen languages and familiarity with half a dozen cultures made an impression on the professor, who spoke with her for a couple of hours and gave her a letter of recommendation to the head of a Department at the UN where he knew there was a vacant post. Irène had passed the interview with flying colours. She had, she told me, got a job.

'But what about the degree?' I asked, still in tears. For a brief second her features clouded over, then she shook her head and explained to me that obviously this was not meant to be. Had it been God's will that she should have a degree, He no doubt would have made it possible. She smiled brightly, but I could see sadness in her eyes. This degree which she had planned and prepared for all these years was not to be. I knew how much pain and disappointment she was feeling.

'Let's celebrate,' she said, and with a flourish presented me with a paper bag. On the bag was drawn a picture of the Two Musketeers! These two musketeers had for many years symbolised to us our struggles and our achievements. They first appeared on the loving notes she used to write to me at the clinic. I opened the bag. In it were two pieces of cake. Once again, a celebration!

CHAPTER 62

The Job

So Irène began work. Money came in regularly, enabling us to rent a flat near the UN so that Irène could walk to work. She still had difficulty in getting onto a bus. Although she walked quite well, there remained a weakness in her ankles which made steps difficult for her.

The other problem was the large marble foyer she had to cross to get to her office. It was slippery and here again her weak ankles caused her difficulty. She should, of course, have used her stick, but felt that it was better not to, having given the medical officer at the UN a glowing report about her excellent health. Irène was not given to white lies, but decided that my welfare warranted this little one and had explained her limp as 'an old ski-ing accident'.

Apart from the ankles, there were other health problems, but these she carefully kept to herself.

Irène had suffered from stomach trouble throughout the war and during her years at the clinic. The cause of the trouble, as we were to discover years later, was an allergy to various foods, but neither we nor the doctors realised it at the time. Her main allergy was wheat, and everything containing wheat. The doctors at the clinic had put her on a special diet, and, as this consisted mainly of rusks and semolina – both wheat – her condition deteriorated more and more. During our student life we had existed on bread and buns as these were cheap and filling – wheat again. By the time Irène started work, she suffered from colitis, as well as hypoglycaemia, which caused sudden attacks of extreme weakness.

On her return home every evening her face was pinched and drawn. She had a severe form of colitis and was pale and thin as a result. We consulted many doctors, and got nowhere. Nothing helped. Poor Irène ended up something of a physical wreck, riddled with colitis and rattling with pills.

But she worked on stoically with never a word of complaint. She also suffered dreadfully from toothache. Her teeth had not been attended to properly for many years. The years of war had prevented her from seeing a dentist – there were no dentists in the Maquis! Then the years in bed had made dental care impossible once again.

Irène said nothing to me about this, and quietly took herself to a dentist to ascertain the extent of the damage. The estimate the dentist gave her was prohibitive – everything had to be done; her teeth were in a dreadful state. The cost was way beyond our means. So Irène yet again quietly decided that the 'man in the family' had to wait until circumstances made it financially possible to have the necessary treatment. She said nothing, and bore the pain with courage for some two years.

Through her weak ankles, she had little confidence in walking. She decided that to get this confidence she would attempt the impossible and master it. She would learn ballroom dancing. She said nothing to me and quietly took herself to Mr Kritz's ballroom dancing school, explaining to him what she intended to do. The lessons began. With infinite patience, Mr Kritz half-carried Irène around the floor. She was frightened to death, but persisted and achieved the impossible.

Over the years my daughter became a very good dancer, stiff knee and all. One night, years later, at the Palace Hotel in Saint Moritz, she stopped the show as everyone applauded the wild samba she performed. I watched her on that occasion, and remembered how, years before, I had demonstrated at the clinic what would happen at a ball. We had well and truly achieved the impossible. I thanked the Almighty, and swallowed hard to get rid of the lump in my throat.

CHAPTER 63

Singing

In Geneva we met a delightful lady who was a famous singing teacher. She discovered that Irène had a fine soprano voice which, in her opinion, was eminently suitable for coloratura. She became enthusiastic about Irène's voice and offered to train her free of charge.

Irène was delighted. She had never got over the loss of her beloved ballet and here once again was an opportunity to express herself in art.

The lessons began. Irène was a brilliant pupil and reached the highest notes with astonishing facility. Alas, in her enthusiasm the teacher went too fast, and gave Irène, a beginner, the 'Bells of Lakmé' as an exercise. Irène's voice cracked.

Later, when we lived in London, Maestro di Veroli, the wonderful *Bel Canto* teacher, mended it a little, but it had lost all its sparkle and brilliance.

The Maestro lived in a mews and to reach his studio one had to climb some very narrow and very steep stairs. Irène often collided with interesting people on those narrow stairs. She particularly remembers Harry Secombe who always had the most wonderful warm and friendly smile.

However, Irène learned some folk songs in various languages and provided the entertainment at a few charity balls. But, being a perfectionist, she was not content with 'second best' and did not persist. With sorrow in her heart she gave up singing and never sang again.

CHAPTER 64

Irène the Healer

During Irène's annual leave we went to Vienna to visit a specialist who had been recommended to us. It was as if fate had led us there, for this doctor worked in partnership with a healer – an unusual combination in those days. When given a healing, Irène went into a deep sleep, and it was only later that we understood that this was a state of trance, not of sleep. When she came to, the healer was bending over her saying, 'You are one of us. You do not belong in the commercial world. You have other work to do.'

We stayed with the healer during the whole of Irène's holiday. She lent us many books, rare and wonderful books, and allowed Irène to make as many notes as she wished. Irène spent days and nights writing things down into a series of exercise books. Thus were our eyes opened to the real meaning of healing, and we were introduced to a new and wonderful world. Soon Irène had made up her mind – she was determined to become a healer. But having a scientific mind, she wanted to combine her healing gifts with medical knowledge.

Healing has a long and interesting history. Known since the dawn of ages, it has been practised by every civilisation on earth. How many people are aware that Elisha of the Old Testament was one of the earliest healers and that the Baal Shem Tov, the great Jewish *Tzaddik* (holy man) of the eighteenth century practised the art of healing? A learned rabbi told us that Maimonides, the philosopher, also known as the Jewish Hippocrates, possessed the gift of healing, which he used when he was court physician to the Sultan of Egypt in the twelfthth century.

The healer is a channel through which the Life Force flows into the patient. We can actually feel these energies. When we give healing we become aware of a pulsating current of energy flowing through our hands and there is a vibration in the right hand. Healing is, however, more than just the laying on of hands. It is a deep, loving concern for every living thing. As in everything, there are degrees, but the spiritually-developed healer experiences an overwhelming feeling of care and compassion towards every sufferer who comes his or her way, along with a deep desire to help.

Many years later, when she had become a fully-fledged healer, Irène understood that everything she had suffered was part of the 'apprenticeship' the healer in France had spoken about years before. Her destiny was healing, and to achieve it her artistic career, be it ballet, films or music, had to be sacrificed.

CHAPTER 65

Irène - Researcher

I had travelled a long road since my childhood in Latvia at the end of the last century. A large and lively family then had grown smaller and smaller, and was now largely concentrated in one person, my daughter.

The year after we had been in Vienna, we spent Irène's annual leave together in England visiting such few relatives as were left. While in London, Irène started going out with a young man who had been introduced to her. We did not return to Geneva. Irène got married and settled in London. To my infinite regret this marriage turned out to be a very unhappy one, and some years later Irène divorced her husband.

It had been a whirlwind romance. The young people had not allowed enough time to get to know each other sufficiently. Had they done so, they would no doubt have realised that they were not at all compatible. Irène emerged from this unhappy experience deeply shattered.

Our health continued to deteriorate. We were both suffering from colitis, cystitis and hypoglycaemia, and no amount of medical treatments had been able to help us. Irène decided that she would attempt to find the answer to our problems herself.

It was at this time that she read a book which made a great impression on her. It was about Michael Faraday, the pioneer of electricity. Here was the story of a man with a brilliant mind, too poor to afford colleges and universities. He studied on his own, and became a brilliant inventor and a world-famous scientist. Irène decided that she would follow his example and acquire sufficient medical knowledge herself to enable her to carry out research into our conditions.

And so began her long quest for more knowledge, an

extraordinary way of life which was to go on for twenty years. This was the time it took before Irène felt that she had acquired the knowledge she needed.

After her divorce, she set up her own business. She saved money, took a course, studied, passed examinations, qualified, went back into business for a while in order to earn more money, and then took the next course.

She bought books and more books, and read and read and read. She has thousands of books, lining the walls of her home and stored all over the house. Even the bathroom has books. Irène may have had ill-health, but she had a great determination and ultimately she achieved her goal.

Over the years, as Irène explored every possible avenue, she gradually became convinced that some kind of intolerance to certain foods was at the back of our problem. In due course she studied a number of American medical books, and discovered that she was not alone in her assumption. In America, the theory that a masked allergy to a substance in food or in the environment could adversely affect every organ in the body was already well established, and an increasing number of doctors were carrying out research in this field. This new approach was known as Clinical Ecology or Environmental Medicine.

Clinical Ecology was brought to England by Dr Richard Mackarness, whose books, *Not All in the Mind and Chemical Victims*, were aimed at the general public and made a great impact. It is estimated that one person in seven suffers from some kind of masked allergy, due to the enormous amount of chemical substances and additives in our food. The human body was not designed for this chemical invasion, and protests.

There are over three thousand permitted chemical additives in our food. A simple slice of white bread contains a whole collection. Chemical fertilisers and pesticides, some of them possessing a high degree of toxicity, are used on the land. Chemical substances and hormones are injected into our cattle and many allergenic substances are used in the manufacture of cosmetics.

Various factors in the environment will affect sensitive individuals in many different ways, causing symptoms ranging from simple irritability and fatigue to a whole range of complaints. Asthma and migraine, colitis and cystitis, angina and hypertension can all be symptoms of allergy, and so can certain forms of arthritis and, of course, eczema.

One of the most interesting manifestations of wrong diet is hypoglycaemia (low blood sugar) which in itself can be responsible for some forty symptoms including psychological ones ranging from depression to suicide attempts. Marilyn Light of the Hypoglycaemia Research Foundation in the USA has written a fascinating booklet on this subject.

Irène cured me of both my colitis and my cystitis, and succeeded in stabilising her own condition by following a strict allergen-free diet.

I recovered my health. As well as being the second guinea pig for Irène's early research into allergy, I was also the guinea pig for her research into ageing. She developed methods of counteracting the effects of ageing and tried them out on me. They certainly worked. At a very advanced age, in my nineties, and after all the traumatic experiences I have endured, I remain in possession of all my faculties, spend long periods of the day at the piano, playing and composing, and write in the various languages I speak.

CHAPTER 66

Speaking in Many Tongues

Irène established herself as an international negotiator and formed a company providing services to British, French, German and Swiss firms. By combining her skill in multilingual simultaneous interpreting with her knowledge of foreign cultures and mentalities, she created a new concept in the use of language in export negotiations, which she called Commercial Diplomacy.

The British businessman is generally not eager to learn another country's language, and this barrier alone proves a difficult hurdle in his attempts to sell abroad.

Irène believed that language was not the only problem in foreign business negotiations. Differences between the foreign businessman of one country and another extend to the way each thinks and reacts. Overcoming not only the language problem but also the stumbling block of differences in background and temperament could, she felt, lead to a greater measure of success in business relations and negotiations.

To get her services known, she called on Chambers of Commerce, banks and embassies both in Britain and abroad. Equipped with letters of introduction from banks and Chambers of Commerce in the UK, she visited the equivalent organisations abroad, making her services known. She designed all her own sales literature, which she left with these organisations. She became an MIL (Member of the Institute of Linguists).

As time went on, a great many of these organisations wrote about her services in their journals, which led to steadily increasing business. She took a stand at an Export exhibition, which she manned alone for four days. Again, this helped to make her services known and resulted in publicity in the business sections of newspapers and magazines.

Irène put her heart and soul into every assignment she took on. First, she would spend a good deal of time studying the product. As she had little time during the day, she used to do this at night and at the weekend. When the product was technical, she would put together a small notebook of the technical terms, which she would study.

It is widely thought that all that is needed to make a good interpeter is 'a good knowledge of languages'. And of course it is one essential requirement, just as it is necessary to have a violin before one can play it. However, just as the possession of a violin does not make someone a violinist, this knowledge of languages is only an instrument in the hands of the interpreter. A fully qualified interpreter will often spend several years at the appropriate university, even after he or she has completely mastered the language in which they intend to specialise.

At these universities, one in Geneva and one in Heidelberg, the curriculum covers all the techniques of interpreting. There are two essential qualities for an interpeter, first the gift of being 'passively' receptive, to absorb quickly and without reaction the ideas which the speaker is expressing, and secondly an active mind in order to play what may be termed a game of very fast mental tennis. Each of these qualities is fairly common, but they are rarely found in one person. That is the reason why there are so few good interpreters.

The interpreter must have a first-class memory. This memory has to store two kinds of data; first of all a permanent store of an extensive vocabulary which must be immediately accessible to provide the desired expression at once, and then a faithful and detailed image of what has been said.

The interpreter must have a thorough knowledge of the languages from which he is translating. In order to know a language it is not enough to know its grammar and to have a good vocabulary. It is also necessary to be steeped in the spirit and traditions of the language, its sources and its evolution from the beginning to the present time, to be familiar with the literature which has influenced it, to appreciate the native humour, to know the outstanding names in its history, to be familiar with its euphemisms, delicate shades of meaning and clichés.

However, it is not enough merely to know all that pertains to the language. It is also necessary to be in the closest possible touch with the speaker's country and to know and understand the mentality of its inhabitants.

Interpreting depends very considerably upon a knowledge of the subject. For this reason, it is essential, before a meeting begins, to familiarise oneself by studying not only the reports and memoranda to be discussed, but also some earlier documents and standard works on the subject. Before the meeting the interpreter must get together as complete a file as possible in all the languages from which and into which they will have to work. This is an essential part of their preparation for a job.

A first-class interpreter should not be satisfied with even a thorough knowledge of the subject dealt with at the conference. He or she also needs a considerable cultural background at any time. No matter what the subject in hand may be, a speaker may bring some completely unexpected matter into the discussion.

Like journalists, diplomats and politicians, the first-class interpreter must be able to join in a discussion on any subject. Unlike the others, however, he has had no warning and cannot look it up if he is in difficulties, and he does not have the right to hold back until he can find out. The perfect interpreter would be a complete walking encyclopaedia, always kept up to date with what is being done and said in every field everywhere. Obviously this is an unattainable ideal, but a conscientious interpreter must never cease trying to approach it. The qualified interpreter is strictly bound by professional ethics of secrecy in the same way as a doctor or a lawyer.

The very far-reaching culture Irène had acquired during her years at the clinics proved invaluable in her work. To these requirements she added one more. She strove to take over the personality of the client for whom she was interpreting, putting herself, as it were, into that person's shoes.

At the beginning of the meeting she would study the different personalities and their mannerisms intently, and soon would 'become' that person, using the same tone of voice, the same inflections, the same facial expressions, the same mannerisms. Her clients used to remark that they were not aware of an interpreter being present. They felt as if they were conducting the conversation themselves. She became extraordinarily skilled at this, and the way in which she would blot out her own personality and take on that of her client was at times quite uncanny.

Irène was good at negotiating, which turned out to be useful to her as time went on. Little by little, her clients began to leave the negotiations to her, remaining in their own countries and instructing her by telephone about what had to be done, where and with whom. Thus she gradually built up a career as negotiator in her own right. This enabled her to charge higher fees, and to establish herself in her own office in the West End of London.

Among her clients were some of the very big names of industry, as well as many medium-sized and smaller firms. None of her clients knew of Irène's health problem. To keep her allergies under control, she had to follow an incredibly severe diet and was completely unable to eat out in a restaurant.

This, of course, would normally have precluded a business career. Irène overcame the problem by carrying a lunch-box and a supply of bottled water (she was allergic to the chemicals in tap water) in her briefcase. Before the meal she would go to 'wash her hands' and take a little sustenance. Irène had lunch in a vast number of ladies' cloakrooms in Britain and abroad. There was no other way.

The question of the glass of wine at the meal – she could not drink at all – she would explain away as 'having to keep a clear head for the negotiations'. She developed a technique of cutting her food up in pieces and compacting it into a small heap which she would hide under the knife and fork. She took the idea from the practice of compacting worn-out cars, transforming them into a little heap of metal. It worked very well, and only rarely would a client remark that she had not eaten much, to which she would reply with a bright smile that the negotiations were so interesting that she was too busy talking.

Irène certainly did not have the health to lead this exhausting life. She carefully hid her pains and her fatigue from everyone and also from me. But her tired face told me the truth and I worried incessantly.

In my opinion, it would have been better and easier for her to have become the 'right hand' of an industrialist rather than to have all the responsibilities and anxieties of running her own business. I felt that her fluency in languages, coupled with her insight into foreign mentalities and her organising abilities, would have enabled her to make a brilliant career with an established concern, and provide her with a far more secure future. I voiced this opinion again and again as the years went by. In fact, not a week passed without my mentioning it. I am not given to nagging, but in this one instance I did!

Still, I was proud of my daughter and of all she had achieved, overcoming so many obstacles in such a determined manner.

CHAPTER 67

The Practice

Her company was doing well, but Irène was not fulfilled. The words of the healer in Vienna, 'You do not belong to the commercial world. You have other work to do' – kept on going through her mind. She felt instinctively that until such time as she gave her intense urge to heal and to help a free rein, she would not find true contentment.

Having solved the problem of our allergies, Irène felt that she would like to put this experience to use, and to help others who shared her predicament. She therefore decided to retire from her business and open a complementary medicine and healing practice specialising in clinical ecology.

She decided to leave London and set up her practice in a quieter place, where there was less traffic and the air was pure. After much consideration she chose Hove, in Sussex, which she felt had the advantages she wanted and yet was still accessible for any future London patients. Little did she know that patients would flock to her not only from London, but from such distant places as Scotland, Ireland, Wales, Guernsey and Spain!

Irène closed her London office and off we set for what was to become yet another facet our unusual life, another stage of our long, winding road.

In the course of her research Irène discovered that, in order to maintain her improvement in health, it was necessary to continue to follow a strict diet of non-allergenic and preferably organic food throughout life. This proved to be a great stumbling block in the practice.

The patients followed their diet, making spectacular recoveries. The majority, however, did not possess the necessary willpower. They would try it for a while and then give up, sliding back into old habits. They felt that they would rather put up with their condition than face a life of dietary restriction. Irène found this enormously frustrating.

Combining as she did the scientific with the esoteric, Irène found her radiesthetic faculty a useful tool in her research. She first discovered that she possessed this faculty in the early 1950s and developed it in Geneva under the guidance of a skilled radiesthesist, and later studied radionics in England. She is a member of the British Society of Dowsers.

The word radiesthesia means perception of radiation. Radiesthesia, also known as dowsing, has been known since antiquity. It is believed that Moses possessed this faculty, and it was used both in ancient Egypt and China.

The radiesthesist uses a rod, if he applies his skill to water-divining, and a pendulum for other types of research. The medical uses of radiesthesia were pioneered in France in the early part of the twentieth century by a number of French priests, of whom the Abbé Mermet was the most well-known. His book on radiesthesia has become a classic and has been translated into English under the title *Principles and Practice of Radiesthesia.*

Members of the medical profession in France became interested in the subject, and Dr Albert Leprince, who himself possessed the radiesthetic faculty, wrote a fascinating book about it with the title *Application of the Skill of Water Divining to Human Medicine.* This has not, however, been translated into English.

In England the first book on radiesthesia appeared in 1638. In the 1920s there was a great revival of interest in the subject, and several doctors took it up. Dr Guyon Richards, author of *The Chain of Life,* founded the Society for the Study of Radiesthesia in 1939. In due course, Dr Aubrey Westlake wrote extensively about the subject. Dr George Lawrence founded the Psionic Medical Society. Today there are radiesthesists all over the world, quietly working away, but it is a subject not known to the general public.

Parallel to her other studies, Irène studied and researched the field of healing. She became a registered healer and is registered with the WFH (World Federation of Healing), the NFSH (National Federation of Spiritual Healers), the SHA (Sussex Healers' Association) and JASH (Jewish Association of Spiritual Healers). The registered healer undergoes a lengthy probationary period before being accepted as a healer member. He has to have training and also must produce testimonials from four patients that he has been able to help. The registered healer is allowed into hospitals on presentation of his membership card.

As time went on, Irène developed her gift, becoming more and more skilled. This ability seemed to run in the family. My brother Buba was an excellent water-diviner and had practised this as a hobby throughout his life. So at least I had managed to pass on something valuable from my family background.

CHAPTER 68

The Healing Gift

Irène has always maintained that the laying on of hands is only part of healing. Healing to her encompasses the physical and spiritual. The soul, she feels, often needs healing as much as the body. And this force of healing can be given with words, a look, a smile, with love and compassion. To Irène there are a thousand different ways of healing.

Perhaps the best example of her concept of healing is the story of Anna. Anna was a patient in the children's clinic at the Swiss resort. She was a little Polish girl aged eleven. She had TB of the spine and was horribly deformed, with a huge hunchback and tiny withered legs. Her back was so deformed that she could not lie in bed without being held in place by a multitude of small sand-filled cushions. The infection had by now broken through the skin in appalling fistules which had to be dressed daily. She was a small, unhappy wreck of a child.

She had obviously been stricken very young in life and had been dragged along with her parents to a concentration camp, where, for some mysterious reason, she had not been killed. She was not Jewish. Perhaps she had been earmarked for medical research – who can tell? In any case, she was still alive when the camp was liberated, now a small, crippled orphan.

Anna did not speak the language of the resort well, although she seemed to understand quite a lot. She lay in bed all day, silent. She never spoke. At night, she sobbed quietly into her pillow, hour after hour.

Irène asked the nurse to put her bed next to Anna's bed. The nurse was happy to do so. No-one else wanted to have Anna as a neighbour. One could not chat with her and the sores were quite revolting. The poor child looked as if she were rotting alive. The dressings used to take so long that breakfast was invariably brought in before she was ready and the view was enough to turn anybody's stomach.

On the first night, when the lights were out, Irène began to speak to Anna. She spoke very softly, in a whisper so as not to wake the other girls. She spoke to her lovingly, with gentle words. No-one had ever spoken to Anna in this way before. She was so sullen and so unco-operative with the other girls and with the nurses that the girls tended to feel impatient with her.

Irène went on speaking. Gentle, tender words poured from her lips. And slowly, it happened – a little smile appeared on Anna's face. This was the first time Irène had ever seen an expression on this silent, sullen face. She went on. The next night she did this again. The smile was a fraction bigger. And so Irène went on, for weeks and months. Bit by bit, Anna began to respond, to speak to Irène.

It was spring, and Irène and I were celebrating Passover in our own very modest way. The celebration consisted of eating a piece of traditional matzah, unleavened bread, which had been brought to all the Jewish patients at the resort by a charity committee of Jewish women. This committee used to turn up on Jewish holy days and bring the patients a little token of celebration, and say a prayer with them.

When Anna would not emerge from under the blanket, Irène asked her what was the matter. A terrified and muffled voice came from under the blankets. 'I am afraid of you. It is the Jewish Passover, and you will have to kill me,' said Anna.

'I will have to *what?*' said Irène, aghast. So Anna, still from under her blankets, explained that in the little Polish village she came from everybody knew that the Jews would have to murder a Christian child on Passover night in order to drink its blood as part of the Passover ritual.

It took Irène quite some time to explain to Anna the absurdity of her beliefs. I think what calmed the child most was when Irène burst out laughing and said, 'And how do you expect me to murder you when I can't even get out of bed? And what should the murder weapon be? A thermometer?'

Anna emerged from the blanket, and in no time at all was happily tucking into a bit of the unleavened bread, which she found delicious.

The crying sessions, however, still went on. Irène's gentle probing was always met with the answer, 'I have a terrible secret which I can tell to no-one.'

Months passed. One night the barrier was broken down and Anna told Irène her secret.

She was not a child of eleven as everyone believed. She was a young woman of twenty. When the camp was liberated, the sick children were put into separate groups and told that they would be taken to clinics in Switzerland by a charity committee. So Anna quietly went and stood with the children's group. She was so tiny and so deformed that no-one ever guessed that she was not a child. She made Irène swear to keep the secret, and Irène kept her promise.

Anna had been treated like a child, and she was not a child. Her mind ached for some intelligent conversation, an opportunity to learn something, so Irène began to teach Anna many things. She told her many stories about the world outside, about art and culture and history and Anna absorbed it all like a dried-out piece of earth absorbs a spring rain.

All this had a salutary effect on her health. Slowly but surely Anna began to improve. The sores healed, the bones calcified. Anna was able to get up. When Anna left the clinic, some two years before Irène, she threw her withered little arms around Irène's neck and whispered into her ear, 'It is you who have healed me. It is you,' and it was, although there had never been a laying-on of hands. There could not have been – Irène was immobilised in her bed.

Irène's research into medical matters and her psychic development as a healer progressed on parallel lines. She worked equally hard to perfect herself in both fields. She believed that it was possible to combine the two and in this felt greatly encouraged by the fact that there were in England several doctors who had the gift of healing and openly used it.

The love and compassion in healing is something tangible. Many of the patients who visited Irène would sense it and, along with the description of their pains, they would open their hearts and tell her their innermost worries and problems. Irène's healing room became a haven where people would unburden their souls, in the knowledge that what they told her would go no further. And unburden their souls they did. So much was achieved in that room in addition to the easing of physical conditions. Marriages were mended, estranged children were brought back to their parents – not a day passed without someone being comforted and helped.

As Irène developed her gift of healing, her attunement with animals and plants grew even greater. Whether it was a sickly wilted potted plant, or suffering pets, Irène would lay her hands on them, talk to them tenderly – and heal them.

One day, as she lay in her bath, a small spider fell into the water. Irène fished it out and put it on the rim of the bath. It lay there, stiff, rigid and lifeless. But not to my Irène. There she was, sitting in her bath, projecting absent healing to the little creature. It took quite a while, the bath water became colder and colder, and Irène become more and more uncomfortable, but she could not stop. And, in due course, there was a tiny little movement in the spider. And then a little more movement. And then it began to walk along the edge of the bath quite happily. Out jumped my daughter, put a towel around herself – and tenderly carried the little spider to the garden.

'Saved a life today,' she informed me, 'it was a rather lovely experience.'

There were many other cases of the healing of animals, among them Fabergé our dachshund, and Delius the rabbit. The healing of Fabergé was a joint effort. My daughter and I worked equally hard to bring the little dog back to health. But Irène also helped me.

In my late eighties I was involved in a car crash. I went through the windscreen, cutting my face and breaking ten of my teeth. I lost consciousness and woke up in hospital. Irène was at my bedside. They had been very good to her at the hospital and accepted the fact that as a registered healer she could give me some comfort.

They allowed her to stay while they X-rayed and treated me – I had twenty-seven stitches – and they allowed her to remain at my bedside throughout the night. This was the longest healing Irène had ever given. She began in the evening, her gentle hands easing my pain, and stood beside my bed healing until the morning. She felt that in this way I would receive a continuous recharging of energies and that this would help me to recover.

She asked the doctors to allow her to take me home and look after me herself under the supervision of my doctor. This would enable her to give me the allergen-free diet I was used to, which for an allergic person like myself was an important point. She explained that she was familiar with all the routines of nursing, having cared for me so many times before. They agreed to her request and an ambulance took me home.

Irène nursed me night and day. I could not eat normally because of my broken teeth. The doctor felt that I was too weak to have the necessary dental bridging work done immediately, and so Irène fed me nourishing liquids. I was unable to open my mouth properly, so she used a medicine dropper and, with infinite patience, fed me countless times a day.

She did not leave my bedside for four months, the little sleep she got she took sleeping on the floor beside my bed. She gave me healing several times in the day and several times at night and, wonder of wonders, my face healed without a single scar.

CHAPTER 69

Last Steps

Having reached my mid-nineties as I write, I have so many happy reflections and so many sad ones, but mine has been such an interesting life, also such a restless life. One day Irène and I worked out how many times in our lives we had been forced to pack our belongings and move. We jotted down the numbers and the various addresses. The total came to fifty-three moves for me and forty-two for Irène!

In the course of her life Irène married more than once, and she too has known some moments of joy and many of sorrow. Nothing has ever been easy or simple in the life of my child. These are things I have not written about because they involve the personal emotions of others. I feel that a good mother should provide a comforting shoulder in times of stress and trauma and have the ability not to meddle and to be discreet.

I keep my mind occupied, which is important, for I have no wish for it to go rusty. I have an orderly day, which I think is necessary, even at my age.

Sometimes at night a new musical composition flows into my mind and I jot it down at once. I always keep pencil and paper by my bedside. I still compose a great deal and practice the piano daily. Music means very much to me. It is, after all, a universal language and I like the harmony connected with it . Music is something we can all understand and enjoy.

I continue to read avidly, in four languages, also at night, and my bed often looks like a cross between a bookshop and a public library. Irène and I converse together in English, Russian and French, so life is not at all boring.

A great part of my day is devoted to absent healing, healing at a distance, and at night I do some as well. I have many patients in different parts of the country, and I also help Irène. And then, of course, there are my animal patients.

It has been a long hard road, but it may be that all the pain and all the suffering were a necessary part of it. Before steel becomes usable it has to be put through fire. It could be that before being given the ability to understand the pain and suffering of others, the healer has to go through all this himself. God has been good to us, for He spared us and we came through darkness into the light.

Although I live in secluded surroundings, this does not mean that the world passes me by. On the contrary, I am well aware of the horrors in the world today. But there is also beauty. When I look at my daughter, I thank God for the many blessings that sprang forth from the darkness. There is always hope to be found, and a light at the end of the tunnel.

Now, at the age of ninety-four, I keep up with current events. Again we are witnessing unrest in the world – war, famine, poverty and the tragic shift of refugees hounded from country to country. Yet, in spite of all this, I hope for peace, for, in the end, I believe that love will triumph over hate, and will wind its way, however slowly, down the long, long road of life.

APPENDIX

1 **Memories of Vera** (by Irène Noah)
2 **The Jews of Latvia**
3 **The Jews of France**
4 **List of Places in Which Vera Lived, 1891-1985**
5 **Vera and Irène** (by Aubrey Rose)
6 **Glossary of Names and Terms**

INTRODUCTORY NOTE

The story of Vera Chesno ranges over not only most of the twentieth century, but also across many cultures, languages and lands.

The historical backcloth to her life included pre-First World War Latvia and Russia, the First World War itself, the October Revolution of 1917, inter-war France, the Second World War, post-war Switzerland and finally England.

Her life too reflected the development of Jewish life in recent centuries. These include her distinguished rabbinical and intellectual forebears, celebrated Jewish writers, philosophers, musicians and philanthropists, as well as leaders of the modern Zionist movement involved in the Return to Zion.

The breadth of her involvement in so many aspects of life, based on her academic and practical achievements, touched on legal and medical worlds, and political, social and spiritual spheres.

She not only wrote this autobiography in her nineties, a rare enough achievement in itself, but also a variety of other articles and comments. We therefore thought it helpful to include here, at the end of the book, some of her comments and observations, as well as a few factual items felt to be of interest, and some comments of our own.

Among Vera's papers were found her notes on French-Jewish notables. These we have included, alongside details of her family as well as a note of the many towns in which she lived during her long life.

We were tempted to include a lecture given by Vera on the Dreyfus case, which indicates her mastery of detail and clarity of mind and expression, but felt there have been enough studies and books on that affair, reflecting the deep divisions and prejudices in French society.

Finally, we have included a short Glossary of names and terms, familiar to some, though not to all, which we hope readers may find of use.

Aubrey Rose and Irène Noah

APPENDIX 1

Memories of Vera
by Irène Noah

The interrogation went on night after night.

'Your name?'
'Jeanne Chesnot.'
'Date of birth?'
(The new date in the false papers.)
'Where were you born?'
'Laval, France.'
'Your father's name?'
'André Jamin.'
'Mother's name?'
'Madeleine Pelletier.'
'Are you Jewish?'
'No.'
'Have you any Jewish blood?'
'No.'

The routine never varied as I, a twelve year-old, questioned and was questioned nightly by my mother, until every answer was given automatically, without hesitation.

The year was 1942. There was a new profession in Paris, that of *passeur*, someone who, for money, smuggled Jews into Vichy France and provided them with sets of false papers. Our *passeur* had been arranged by father who was in hiding. Mother rubbed the papers against a wall to make them look well-used, as advised by the *passeur*.

Thus Vera and I took on new identities. My grandfather Zalman Hindin became André Jamin, and grandmother Rebecca Hindin became Madeleine Pelletier. Every evening before we went to bed we fired questions at each other, questions that would be put to us during a Gestapo interrogation.

As I grew up, I was filled with admiration for mother's wisdom. She had been so right – a child of twelve could easily have hesitated or even forgotten her new name during the absolute panic of an interrogation.

The rehearsals did have one unforeseen consequence. My brain had become so programmed, like a computer, that, well after the end of the war, I would still find myself answering automatically when asked 'Are you Jewish?' 'No - I mean yes.' 'No' used to shoot out before I had a chance to say 'yes'.

My father, Senia, rose splendidly to the occasion when war came. He found us the *passeur*, and thus saved our lives. He deposited carpets, silver and articles of value with a friend, which came to light after 1945, and helped to pay my expenses at the TB resort in Switzerland. What would we have done but for father's foresight?

The crisis of the war brought out the best in him. I remember so well his fiftieth birthday. I decorated our wartime room with paper garlands. Mother – bless her – was trying to cook a meal. She was no cook. She didn't know how to boil an egg. When she was young, grandmother never allowed her near the kitchen. 'You, my child,' she would say, 'you are a pianist. You will have staff to do everything for you as long as you live.' Little did grandma know.

On this occasion, mother's attempt at cooking was hilarious, but, being Vera, she rolled up her sleeves and began, surrounded by cookery books. The roast beef was like chewing gum, the spinach disappeared into nothing, and the pancakes landed on the floor!

But, meal or no meal, that fiftieth birthday was one of the happiest days in our lives. Even though in hiding, we laughed, we joked, we sang, we celebrated, and the flat seemed like a palace of joy and happiness.

Two weeks later father was deported to Auschwitz. We never saw him again. To this day, his picture stands in the gallery of my loved ones.

During the next three years, while the Germans hunted Jews, we moved from town to city, village to cottage. We remembered the roast beef, however badly cooked it had been. Our food situation, as the war went on, became critical. The best food was sent to Germany. Erzatz substitute food was our lot.

Bread contained lucerne, a grass normally fed to cattle. Coffee was made from walnut shells, butter from a kind of candle grease. Milk was pale blue in colour. Meat there was none. Toilet paper did not exist, and the tiny piece of soap available was like pumice-stone and tore the skin. We were always hungry, while the German troops were always well fed.

The world for me was a nightmare. But for Vera's love and strength I could not have survived. She had seen to it that my early years had been happy and secure. I had had French, English and German governesses, and by the time I was six could speak all three languages. Whatever Vera's cooking may have been like – she excelled in one dish, *kotelety* or meat balls – she did have a wonderful sense of style in most things, not least in clothes.

In the 1920s and 1930s she wore beautiful 'couture' clothes. Her taste was exquisite. When, after the war, seven trunks appeared – again father's foresight – there came to light the clothes of past years. These included beautiful silk and lace garments for me as a child (and my favourite doll, thoughtfully packed by father), but also mother's 1930s dresses, which proved a blessing for me in the 1950s.

I remember grand balls I attended then, and also charity balls in London where I sang folk songs in seven languages. I wore mother's clothes, which needed no alteration, as we were the same size. The compliments I had! 'Must be French,' said one lady. 'Oh yes,' said I. 'Paris.' It was Paris, but of the 1930s, not 1950s.

'Ah, yes,' said the lady. 'It shows.'

How often did mother's musical gifts help us in our wartime predicament, exchanging musical lessons for food, especially when we had practically nothing to eat. After all, she had been a *Wunderkind*, giving her first piano concert at the age of twelve. She had been friends with the world's greatest performers, who respected her musical ability. Vera would have loved to follow a musical career, but her mother had made her give her word of honour that she would never 'disgrace' the family by going onto the stage as a concert pianist. Vera promised, but regretted it always.

Her other regret was not to have left for America in 1939. When war broke out in September of that year, we were on the point of leaving for the United States, where a film contract was waiting for me. How often did mother say to me, 'If only I taken you to America, you would have been spared the terror, the hunger, the penury, the pain, and the crippled knee,' and how often did I reply, 'Mamotchka, how do you know that I would have found happiness there, or how I might have finished up.'

Memories, there are so many of them, too many to relate. I will never forget one afternoon we spent with Sir Isaiah Berlin, a relative whom we knew as 'Shaya'. He told us how hard he had worked behind the scenes to rally support for the establishment of the state of Israel. I sat absolutely fascinated by his stories, his knowledge, his eloquence. But, of course, memories of Vera, my mother, remain uppermost in my mind.

Can I ever repay her for her care for me during my 'TB years' in the Swiss clinic? We had survived the war – just. What agonies Vera must have gone through. No wonder her health collapsed at intervals in the post-war period. But during those four years, while I lay on my back, she was a tower of strength. Would I ever have been admitted as a student to Geneva University, as I was in 1950, or later obtained a post with the United Nations, had Vera not taught me, day after day, languages, cultures, history, geography? She was a veritable university in herself.

Throughout that period she kept hope alive. She painted for me pictures of dances, balls, marriage, happiness to come. When eventually I could walk again, albeit with a slight limp, I was determined to surprise her and, despite having a surgically stiffened left knee, I learned from a ballroom dancer and a fashion model how to use my hips and ankles to such effect that my disability would barely be noticed. She was amazed at the foxtrots, tangos and sambas I was able to perform as a result of my lessons.

To perfect my walk I consulted a chorus girl, who taught me a special kind of walk, full of 'bumps' and 'grinds', using especially my hips to good effect. I used to undulate around the room behind curvaceous, peroxide-haired Maisie, swivelling my stiff hips to the sound of sambas. I practised 'the walk' for months. Eventually I displayed my newly-found athleticism to mother. She was fascinated. 'Wonderful,' she said, 'but don't ever use that walk in *shul* (synagogue)!' How right she was. It was not a walk befitting a descendant of Rabbi Schneur Zalman of Lyady!

This famous rabbi, my esteemed ancestor, a major figure in modern Jewish religious history, was part of a remarkable movement. It believed in joy, laughter and the power of the spirit as opposed to formal legalism. It also believed that the spirit of those who had departed could influence those of us here in our material world, something which I later experienced.

Vera lived into her nineties, overcoming accidents, ill-health and the effects of many years of stress, hunger and danger. A car accident did not help. After the accident I nursed her for four months, sleeping on the floor next to her bed. In the still hours of the night we both had pains, she from her injuries, me from my bad back. We would give each other healing. I remember so well sitting on the edge of her bed and the warm and soothing feeling of her hands on my aching lower back, gentle and loving hands that would ease and comfort me.

She was so very dear to me but, as with us all, there is a time when the body wears out and just cannot continue. And so it was with Vera in 1985.

My cherished and adored mother left this world in her ninety-fourth year, after an illness borne with courage and fortitude. She had kidney failure and uraemia. The doctor explained that nothing could save her life, for she was too old and too frail to stand dialysis.

Frantically I called in doctors, specialists and natural medicine practitioners. The verdict was unanimous. I was told she would gradually sink into a deep coma and would be taken to hospital from which she would not return alive. I begged the doctors to allow me to nurse her myself at home, as I had always done, and they granted me my wish.

And so began the heart-breaking vigil. I put her bed in the living-room, close to her beloved piano, now closed and silent. And I began to nurse and to heal. As a healer, I knew that while I would be able to soothe, ease and comfort, I would not be able to restore the function of those old and worn-out kidneys.

I nursed and healed through the days and the nights. Sleep no longer mattered to me. A nurse came in for a little while in the morning to help turn her over and change the soiled linen – I am handicapped and turning presented a great difficulty. In the later stage there was another such call at 2 am. Then there was Stella, our dear, wonderful nurse Stella who used to drop in for a few moments after her rounds to comfort and help.

The rest of the time I sat by her bed. Between nursing and changing linen I kept my hands on her body, now so thin and pathetic, hour after hour after hour. I forgot about sleep, I forgot about food. Neither mattered to me any more. The weeks went by as I watched with despair my brilliant, my exuberant, my wonderful mother, decline into a still, small, pathetic bundle of flesh. From the age of eleven I had prayed to God, morning and night, asking that when the time came I would be taken with her, in the same way as my grandmother Hindin had accompanied my grandfather Hindin on the day of his death. But it was not to be.

Her last night will forever remain with me. Mother could neither see nor hear me as I stood by her bed, pouring all my love into her with my hands, which lay gently on her body throughout the night. How I begged and prayed to be allowed to leave this world with her! I knew that I must not attempt this release myself, however much I might long to do so. My mother had made me swear to her that I would never attempt such a thing, and I knew that I could not break a promise made to her.

Slowly her limbs became cold. It began with her feet which I had been frantically warming with my hands. The icy feeling of cold gradually crept higher and higher and I knew that the end was drawing near. The doctor had told me the previous day that twenty-four hours were the most he could foresee for her. Her breathing became increasingly laboured and difficult. At five o'clock her body gave a sudden jerk – the first movement I had seen in her for weeks, her lips twisted into what seemed almost like a little smile, and life left her.

I was overwhelmed with grief. I did not want to live. All I wished for was oblivion. And then it happened. On the day after her death I became aware of something which I can only describe as a bolt of energy which came through my body and made me shake like a leaf. With it, an overwhelming feeling of her presence, a gentle, loving presence. As if in a dream, I found myself going towards her writing desk at the end of the room. I never went to her desk. I opened it. In a prominent position stood an envelope, addressed 'To my darling Irène'. I read the following words:

To my darling Irène, with all my love and gratitude to the Almighty for the perfect, charming, lovely and loveable daughter He gave me. I implore you with all my heart to live happily, to enjoy life to the full, to continue your career, and I shall look upon you, from wherever I shall be, and feel happy and content. My soul will follow you, bless you, and give you all the happiness you so rightly deserve.

Yours with love,
Mother.'

It was dated twenty years before her death.

Things began to happen in rapid succession, one stranger than the next. The feeling of her presence continued. First there were the dreams. I would see her in a dream and she would speak to me.

One night in a dream I saw her standing by my bed. She looked at me, smiled, and said, 'Touch me, pass your hands over my body, and you will see that I am still with you.' I did so, and her body felt as it had always done, warm and real. 'You see?' she added, 'I'm still here.' I awoke with a start.

On another occasion she said to me, 'I do not want you to visit the cemetery. I'm not there. I'm at home with you, and that is where I want you to be. Not at the cemetery.'

One winter evening in the garden, emptying vegetable peelings on to the compost heap, I felt her presence vividly, so I lingered for a while. Then I heard her peremptory voice saying, 'Go indoors. It's cold.'

There was the time when I had a chance meeting with a person who was mediumistic. I had not met that person before, and he did not know me. Suddenly I heard him say, 'I want to talk to you about my book. You will have many problems with it, but persist. It will be a success. And also I want you to know that the pain in my right knee has gone.' As mentioned before, this person had never seen me before, did not know who I was, and certainly knew nothing about the existence of a book or about my mother's arthritic right knee. He was as surprised as I was.

I bought a large number of books about life after death and began to read. From these books I discovered that my experiences were not uncommon.

I knew that our religion did not allow us to seek contact with the departed, but I had not attempted this. Contact had been made with me. I thanked the Almighty for having answered my prayers after all, even though, in His wisdom, not in the way I had hoped and expected. We were not to be separated after all.

One of mother's musical compositions is called 'Healing Theme'. I often listen to this tape when I give healing, and I then feel her presence so strongly that I am certain she is helping me.

Mother was a brilliant pianist, and at the age of ninety-four could play the most complicated pieces of music, entirely from memory.

She loved composing and would spend many happy hours at the piano. Oh, how I missed the sound of that piano, which had permeated my home and my life for so many years!

One day I had an impulse to go and sit at my mother's grand piano which is in my living room. As I cannot play the piano at all, I glanced at the keys and just sat there, looking at a large photograph of her which stood on the piano. As I was doing so, I suddenly felt my hands move on their own accord and to my absolute astonishment there emerged a tune, a beautiful tune, gentle and very loving, in her own style of composition. As I looked at my hands, everything stopped. So I looked at the photograph once more and again my hands began to move and again there was a tune, a. piece of music, then another, and another.

This has become a daily routine. Each day I sit for a few moments at mother's piano, looking at her photograph, and the eyes in that photograph seemed to sparkle and the lips seem to smile. It is as if I were a channel, enabling her to continue to compose. The tunes just flow and there is never a wrong note. But if I look at my hands, everything stops, and all I can produce are the discordant sounds of someone who cannot play the piano.

Mother's presence is around me at all times. It is a gentle and very loving presence and I am very conscious of it. This is by no means unique. Many people have had similar experiences.

For fifteen years I have been in daily contact with Vera telepathically. She has continued to guide and help me, not least over the content and form of this book. Her personality is the same as it always was, vibrant, definite, loving. People don't immediately change all that much on death. In this way the partnership we had for so many years continues, despite physical separation. For me, she remains a continual inspiration.

Just as I studied languages, and had careers in interpreting and clinical ecology, so, in a scientific and systematic manner, I have studied the extraordinary truth of the survival of human consciousness and the continued link and dialogue between the two worlds.

I have read many beautiful words about the nature of passing from our world to our next abode, but to my mind the best description remains that of Vernon Scott Holland, with which I conclude memories of my mother.

'Death is nothing at all ... I have only slipped away into the next room. I am I and you are you .... Whatever we were to each other we are still. Call me by my familiar name, speak to me in the same way as you always used to. Put no suffering into your voice. Wear no air of sorrow. Laugh as we have always laughed at the little jokes we shared together. Play, smile, think of me, pray for me. Let my name be ever the household word that it has always been. Let it be spoken without effort, without the ghost of a shadow on it. Life means all it ever meant. It is the same as it ever was; there is absolutely unbroken continuity. What is this death but a negligible accident? Why should I be out of mind because I am out of sight? I am waiting for you for an interval, somewhere very near, just around the corner. All is well.'

APPENDIX 2

The Jews of Latvia

Jews have lived in Latvia for many centuries, especially in the separate provinces of Kurland, Livonia and Latgale. Each group had its own characteristics and, whilst influenced by German and Russian culture, remained until 1940 intensely Jewish in spirit and aspiration.

Latvian Jews played a prominent role in the Zionist movement, with Hovevei Zion (Lovers of Zion) groups in Riga and elsewhere in the 1880s, and in following decades were represented at Zionist conferences, including the attendance of Meir Berlin, a relative of Vera, at a conference in Helsinki in 1906.

The formation of an independent Latvian state in 1918 resulted in increased communal activity, though this was affected seriously by a right-wing coup d'état in 1934. Many Jews emigrated to Israel, to the United States and other lands. They were the fortunate ones, as the Nazis in the Second World War slaughtered at least 24,000 Jews in Riga alone, the place which had been the scene of Vera's upbringing and her cherished family home. Today there are a few thousand Jews left in the country.

The community had numbered about 90,000 before 1939, and over the years had produced scholars, lawyers and Jewish leaders of note, among them Rabbi Abraham Kook, later a Chief Rabbi in Israel, as well as prominent members of Israel's Knesset and judiciary, and academics of distinction.

As Vera has already noted, many Latvian Jews were well versed in both Yiddish and Hebrew. It was not unusual for business transactions to be conducted in both languages.

It is of interest to look a little more closely at the personal stories of some of Vera's relatives, as they throw a revealing light on the individuals and their times.

Jacob Hindin – Vera's grandfather

He came from the town of Velizh in the Vitebsk Government District, owned forests in the Pskov District and an alcohol factory until the introduction of the Russian government monopoly. One of his sons, named Zalman, Vera's father, was a shareholder in ships that sailed on the Dvina, together with Lipman Rachmilevitch. A second marriage made him the brother-in-law of Rabbi Samuel Mohilever, who persuaded him to take an interest in the resettlement of Eretz Israel (land of Israel). He purchased the Hedera lands, referred to in Vera's account of her family, for his son-in-law Shneur Zvi Schneerson of Dvinsk, who was one of the first settlers in Hedera and whose descendants lived there for many years.

An indication of the pride and independence of this group, who lived in magnificent dwellings in the town before moving to Riga, and who often had the local authorities at their service, can be judged by the following story, told by Jacob Hindin's grandson, J L Schneerson of Hedera, in his reminiscences *Mipi Rishonim* (Tel Aviv, 1964).

'Some years before the War, my grandfather Jacob Hindin came to Eretz Israel to visit us. While he was in Hedera, Baron Edmond de Rothschild also visited the country. The Hedera settlers decided to send a delegation to him and selected two men for the purpose: Shakter and my grandfather Hindin.

'The Baron spoke to them in Alsatian German. He was accustomed to having people come to him for help, and naturally asked them at once what they needed. But they answered him that they did not need any help at all and had merely come to pay him a courtesy visit on behalf of the settlement. Baron Edmond then said that he was a Baron and could help them. To which Hindin answered: "We ourselves are little Barons and do not need any help."

'"Heraus!" (Get out!) cried Baron Edmond, and sent them away.

'The Baron was very angry indeed and nobody dared to mention the name of Hedera in his presence for a long time .... Only after years had passed, and thanks to the efforts of Dr Hillel Yaffe and Rabbi Zadoc-Kahn of Paris, did he finally agree to help in draining the Hedera swamps ....'

J.L. Schneerson goes on to tell how Jacob Hindin transferred 267 dunams (about 66 acres) of swamp from his own private estate to the Baron. In due course, a forest was planted there. He also gave 50 dunams (12 acres) of his property for planting a citrus grove in the name of his brother-in-law, Rabbi Samuel Mohilever. This was the site of the kibbutz Gan Shmuel. In his will Jacob Hindin left 120,000 roubles for charity and other purposes, to be expended at the discretion of Baron Edmond de Rothschild.

The Brothers Isaiah and Shlomo Zalman Berlin

They also came from Velizh and were among the best-known timber merchants and manufacturers in Riga. The forest they owned, the sawmills they established, the numbers of their employees and the scale of their exports made them leading figures.

Isaiah Berlin was married to the daughter of Menahem Nahum Schneerson of Niezin, a great-granddaughter of Rabbi Schneur Zalman, the founder of Habad Hassidism. The leading officials employed by the Berlin brothers were well-known house-holders in Riga. They were all Hassidim and in close touch with the Hassidic Rabbi of the Schneerson stock. Such were Alexander Zisskind Berlin, Vera's grandfather, Zalman Isaac Volshonok, his brother Avigdor Volshonok, who was Chairman of the Riga Agudat Israel in independent Latvia, and others.

A fund of 300,000 roubles in the name of Isaiah Berlin was created – a very great amount at the time – in order to build a hospital in Riga. However, most of the money was expended to support war refugees during the First World War.

Isaiah Berlin had no children, so he adopted the Zuckerman family, who were also of the Rabbi's kin. Mendel Berlin, the son of the adopted son, Dov, was a partner in the Berlin and Luria factory, one of the largest timber export enterprises in the city.

The son of Mendel Berlin was Professor Sir Isaiah Berlin, the famous English historian and scholar.

Shlomo Shalit

He came from the small town of Ula in the province of Vitebsk and had six sons and four daughters. Three sons established the firm of Emolip, the name being derived from the initials of their own names, Elijah, Mordechai and Lipman. The latter married Vera's sister Raissa. This was one of the largest enterprises engaged in bringing timber from the heart of Russia and exporting it abroad. At their saw-mills in Riga and the vicinity they employed Jews from the Pale of Settlement, who had no right of residence in the city. The police knew of this and turned it into a regular source of income by arresting the 'illegals' every Sabbath.

Another son, Zalman Shalit, set up the Berlin-Shalit partnership together with Meir Berlin, son of Alexander Zisskind, for wood-sawing and export. They were both Zionists, and generous too, and established a special fund to support householders who had lost their money, rabbis who needed medical attention, etc.

Zalman Shalit, his brother-in-law Dr M Pines (who wrote a history of Yiddish literature in French) and his partner Meir Berlin helped to established the paper *Die Yiddishe Stimme* (The Jewish Voice) in Riga. This paper was organised on the initiative of the Hebrew writer, Yehuda Leib Kantor, who was serving as Crown Rabbi of Riga in the year 1910. The Shalit family also contributed the ground for the erection of The Jewish Club at the corner of Dzirnava and Skoliaya Streets.

Elijah Shalit took part in the Kovno Conference of 1909, and was a member of the Relief Committee established in 1915 in aid of the Kurland refugees who were expelled to Inner Russia by the Russian army.

Vera therefore emerged from a rich background, materially, spiritually and educationally. It was also a background of enterprise and creativity. The Riga community has long since disappeared, but the qualities that distinguished it were only too evident in the story Vera tells of her life. Vera's 'Long Road' stretched to many countries for herself, but even further afield for members of her family.

Her story, remarkable though it is, is but part of the extraordinary Jewish story of the twentieth century.

Note: The book, *The Jews in Latvia*, published in 1971 by the Association of Latvian and Estonian Jews in Israel, is acknowledged as a most helpful source for the above information.

APPENDIX 3

The Jews of France

Vera spent many years in France, twenty years in peacetime and five years during the Second World War. In some ways those twenty years were among the happiest periods of her life. She had put behind her the drama of the escape from Bolshevik Russia. She could not foresee the even greater, and more tragic, drama that lay ahead. So, in the inter-war years, she enjoyed life, she travelled, she entertained, and, with pride, watched her daughter grow and develop.

Jews had been in France since Roman times. There had been some periods of peace, when great Talmudists like Rashi flourished, but generally the authoritarian church, especially from the time of the medieval Crusades, bore down heavily on the Jewish populace.

It took 1500 years, until 1791, for the Jews of France to be officially accorded equality as human beings, but the curse of anti-Semitism lived on, exploding publicly in racist decrees directed against them in Napoleonic times, and in the Dreyfus affair at the end of the nineteenth century.

Yet, despite all this, the Jews of France managed to make a contribution of note to their country in many fields. There were musicians and composers such as Jacques Offenbach, Halévy, Paul Dukas. Camille Pissaro shone as a painter, whilst the School of Paris included Soutine, Chagall, Mané Katz and many others.

A host of writers adorned the French literary scene: André Maurois, Edmund Fleg, as well as philosophers such as Henri Bergson and Nobel prize-winners including scientist Gabriel Lippman.

Vera's own notes refer to several prominent statesmen, but there were also such leading figures as Adolphe Crémieux, a President of the Alliance Israélite Universelle, especially noted as Minister of Justice, who worked for the abolition of slavery.

Another great public figure was René Cassin who did so much for the cause of human rights. Isaac Pereire was especially prominent in the fields of finance and banking, as were the ubiquitous Rothschilds. The list of prominent Jews who adorned the French scene is long and distinguished.

'People lived in harmony,' Vera once wrote. 'Many Jewish people, prominent in politics, in government, in the Army, in industry, and many other fields of French life, were accepted and honoured, notwithstanding their religion or creed.' Reproduced here are Vera's own assessments of some of these figures.

Bernhardt, Sarah (Rosine Bernard) (1844–1923)

World-famous actress. Although converted to Catholicism at the age of ten, and brought up in a convent, she never denied her Jewish background, was proud of it, and brought it out whenever possible. After a serious accident, and fitted with an artificial leg, she played the title role in *Hamlet* and the Duke of Reichstdt, Napoleon's son, aged twenty-one, at the age of fifty-five. I saw her in both these roles.

Blum, Léon (1872–1950)

Member of an Alsatian Jewish family, a brilliant scholar, he became leader of the Socialist party in 1899. On 4 June 1936, he became the first Socialist Prime Minister of France. He introduced the 40-hour week, nationalised the war industries, and strengthened the country's defences. He strove desperately to keep pace with German re-armament, but French industrialists refused to co-operate with his government. In October 1940, Blum was indicted by the Pétain regime on charges of war crimes, and was brought to trial on 19 February 1942. He was arrested and put into a concentration camp in Italy. He survived the Holocaust only because of Marshal Pétain, who personally stood up for him, probably the only case when Marshal Pétain saved a Jew! Blum was liberated from the concentration camp by American troops.

Citroën, André Gustave (1878-1935)

Of Polish Jewish origin. Engineer and industrialist. Born and educated in Paris. His talent and organisational gifts manifested themselves in successful enterprises related to the automobile industry. During the First World War he was instrumental in increasing French ammunition production. After the war he concentrated on his favourite project, the production of low-priced cars. He organised the traffic lights in Paris, and in return secured the use of the Eiffel Tower for advertising Citroën cars. He sponsored the first Trans-Asian and also the Trans-African automobile crossing of the Sahara in 1920.

Dassault, Marcel (1892–1986)

French engineer, achieved prominence as designer of aircraft, including the Mystère and Mirage, which were used by the Israel Air force. Survived the Buchenwald Concentration Camp where he had been interned by the Nazis. Was made a Senator in 1957.

Mendès-France, Pierre (1907–1982)

One of the leading financial experts. The youngest member of the French Parliament, the Assemblée Nationale. An advocate of resistance to the Nazis, even before the Second World War. He was imprisoned by the Pétain government. After the war, in 1945, he was Minister of Economic Affairs. In 1954 he became Prime Minister with a huge majority.

His prestige rose considerably when he ended the war in Indochina, and introduced the plan for a Western European Defence Community, with a British military commitment to the defence of Europe. He remained an important figure in French politics, and frequently opposed de Gaulle's policies. Mendès-France was a consistent supporter of Zionism, and outspoken in his championship of the cause of Israel. His books are widely read and translated into many languages.

Munk, Elie, Chief Rabbi (1900-1978)
Father of Lady Jacobovits, the former British Chief Rabbi's wife. Rabbi and writer. Published *The World of Prayer* in English, the translation of Rashi's Pentateuch Commentary into French and several other books.

Rothschild (family)
The French branch were very interested in Zionism and Israel.

Rubinstein, Ida
Ballerina, who brought many new ideas to the French ballet.

Veil (family)
A member of this family, Simone Veil, was President of the European Parliament. She was five years a Minister of Health. She survived a year in Auschwitz, her family's only survivor.

Many synagogues, of which the La Victoire is known throughout the world.

All the Jewish societies – WIZO, B'nei B'ris, Ort, Ose - functioned very well in France.

The Jewish theatre, Habima, from Moscow presented the Dybbuk by Ansky, and had a great success with the Jewish and non-Jewish public. The outstanding talent of its chief artist, Michoelis (Solomon Mikhoels), was praised and admired. Unfortunately, upon his return to Russia after his triumph in Paris, he was brutally killed on Stalin's orders.

The list of well-known Jewish personalities is too long to mention them all, not forgetting Marcel Proust (*A la recherche du temps perdu*).

These are Vera's own comments on some French Jewish personalities. They touch briefly on a few features of some individuals, but are included as they highlight the individuals whom Vera either knew personally, or had seen, or whom she admired. Her lively interest in people, past or present, never abated, from earliest childhood to her very last years.

APPENDIX 4

List of Places in Which Vera Lived, 1891-1985

Towns, cities and countries in which Vera Chesno lived or stayed for long or short periods between the years:

1891-1919

RUSSIA
Riga
St Petersburg
Dubbeln
KislovodYalta
Odessa
Staray Russa
Vitebsk
Dwinsk
Kichinew
Kiev
Kharkov
Kremenchug
Novorossisk
Essentuki
Rostov

GERMANY
Berlin
Munich
Leipzig
Mainz
Frankfurt-am-Main
Baden-Baden

CZECHOSLOVAKIA
Prague
Karlsbad
Marienbad
Franzensbad

AUSTRIA
Vienna
Salzburg
Italy
Venice

TURKEY
Constantinople (Istanbul)
Switzerland
Lausanne

ENGLAND
London

FRANCE
Paris
Nice
St Raphaël
Cannes
Royat
Vichy

1919-1939

FRANCE
Paris
Nice
St Raphaël
Cannes
Menton
Marseille
Vichy
Royat
Evian
Deauville
Trouville
Le Touquet

AUSTRIA
Vienna
Salzburg
Bad Gastein

CZECHOSLOVAKIA
Karlsbad
Franzensbad
Marienbad
Prague

SWITZERLAND
Zürich
Bern
Geneva
Lausanne
Vevey
St Moritz
Bürgenstock
Lucerne
Montreux
Territet

GERMANY
Berlin
Munich
Leipzig
Wiesbaden
Mainz
Baden-Baden
Kissingen
Schwarzwald
Rippolds Au

ITALY
Venice
Abano
Padua
Florence

ISRAEL
Jerusalem
Tel Aviv
Haifa

HUNGARY
Budapest
Egypt
Cairo
Luxor

MONACO
Monte Carlo

ENGLAND
London
Harrogate

BELGIUM
Brussels
Ostend

1939-1945	1954-1985
FRANCE	**ENGLAND**
Paris	London
Le Touquet	Brighton
Hossegor	
Dax	**SWITZERLAND**
Marseille	Bad Ragaz
Perpignan	St Moritz
Lyon	Zürich
Pontaneveau	Wengen
Grenoble	
Alpe d'Huez	**AUSTRIA**
Autrans	Vienna
Meudon	Bad Gastein
Font Romeu	Salzburg
1946-1951	**FRANCE**
	Paris
SWITZERLAND	Bagnoles-de-l'Orne
Leysin	
	ITALY
1951-1954	Florence
	Abano
SWITZERLAND	Montecatini
Clarens	
Geneva (3 addresses)	**ISRAEL**
	Jerusalem
AUSTRIA	Tel Aviv
Vienna	Haifa
GERMANY	
Munich	

APPENDIX 5

Vera and Irène
by Aubrey Rose

At the request of Irène, following her reading of my book *Journey into Immortality* about my late son David, I have been involved in this presentation of Vera's book. The more I have been so concerned, the more have I realised that these two women were in fact an extension of each other. In many ways they lived for each other, helped each other to survive. And survival is at the heart of their joint lives.

Who could have imagined, reading of Vera's escape from the Bolsheviks, and later from the Nazis, that she would die peacefully in her own bed at the age of ninety-four, that she would be playing the piano and receiving the attentions of male admirers in her nineties? Hers is therefore a story worth telling, expecially in her own graphic words.

And those words reveal her character, her qualities. Born and raised in great luxury - a distinctly unusual feature of Jewish life in Eastern Europe - then a perilous escape from the Bolsheviks in 1918, on to a pampered inter-war life in France, only to be immersed during the Second World War, not merely in poverty but also in constant peril for her life. These circumstances reveal a woman made of stern stuff, determined, enterprising, brave.

What emerges from her story is a multi-faceted personality. She spoke many languages, like her daughter; she was by all accounts a brilliant pianist – her daughter loved ballet; she was vivacious, full of self-confidence, immensely strong-minded. Yet she was also down-to-earth and practical, with an eye for detail, a quality that saved both their lives many times, as did her obvious attraction to the opposite sex. So often does she relate how an enraptured male assisted in her escape from death.

Her husband Senia played but a shadowy role throughout. Indeed, her account of life in the Paris of the 1930s makes little mention of him. Clearly, apart from his invaluable help in 1940, they had drifted apart.

Once Irène was born in 1929, her daughter became the centre of Vera's life. All the energy and enterprise, which she had shown in her escape from Russia in 1918, she threw into her hopes for her child. Vera had been one of six children, but due to medical reasons had only one child herself, to her regret. That child, affected by a series of illnesses, mainly allergies, as well as tuberculosis of the left knee, became Vera's premier concern.

She exulted in Irène's knowledge of languages, indeed taught her several of them, strove to advance the young girl's ambitions as a potential ballerina, even encouraged her film career, which, but for the outbreak of war in 1939, might have blossomed into something notable.

Vera's motherly dedication is exemplified in her constant devoted care for Irène whilst the latter lay on her back for four years in a Swiss clinic. During that time Vera gave Irène an education of a kind a young person rarely receives. After all, Vera had studied at the Universities of St Petersburg and the Sorbonne. Vera has written extensively of life in the Swiss clinic, its strange characters, its medical uncertainties.

Emerging eventually into a more normal life in the 1950s, both mother and daughter were accepted at Geneva University, possibly unique in itself, Irène as a *membre regulier* (full student), Vera as a *membre auditeur* (allowed to attend all lectures) in the Faculté de Lettres.

Vera's story thereafter merges with that of Irène's, both histories punctuated by bouts of ill-health, the results of hardships suffered during the war. Both were indeed Nazi victims, like the millions who perished, and also the millions who survived, though permanently scarred.

As one reads the account of wartime German bestiality in Grenoble to the Resistance, to innocent villagers, one wonders to what depths human beings can descend. But the overwhelming love and devotion that passed between mother and daughter is a redeeming gleam of light amidst the dark night of appalling atrocities.

The last decades of Vera's life, before her death in 1985, were relatively peaceful. She had had excitement enough. She played the piano, enjoyed a game of bridge, lived anew through the achievements of her daughter. For Irène possessed that same determination to survive, to succeed, to overcome, that had guided her mother to safety. Indeed, there seems to have been some life-preserving guide hovering over Vera that saved her, time and again, when all seemed lost. There were just too many coincidences, too many strokes of luck.

Irène, with Vera-like vitality, despite her afflictions, threw herself into career after career, gathering several husbands en route. Again the men, with one exception, seemed almost like background scenery along the way. Vera was fascinated with languages, so was Irène, but the daughter used her gifts to further her income. Just as the mother had supported the daughter economically, so the daughter, by her business efforts, supported the mother.

Having studied at the Ecole d'Interprètes in Geneva, where languages were studied in-depth, particularly in the art of simultaneous interpretation, Irène became a skilled linguist, proficient in six languages. She travelled widely in Europe as the mouthpiece of businessmen of various countries, who could communicate only through her.

She became more that an interpreter. She studied the psychology and mentality of each of her clients, and those not her clients, so that her words could be spoken with the same character as the original speaker. This involved an acting ability, a chameleon-like quality rare in interpreters. Her work prospered. She set up her own business, exhibited at a national exhibition, and became a member of the Institute of Linguists.

Irène had another interest that grew in importance. She was among the first practitioners – for that is what she became – to understand the growing medical perception of allergies and their effects. She gradually wound down her interpreting business, partly due to chest problems brought on by the haze of businessmen's smoke-filled rooms.

The more she studied, again with Vera's intensity and mental agility, the more she realised that the high carbohydrate diet, based on wheat, given to her during her TB years in the Swiss clinic was the worst possible food for her, as she was allergic to wheat. The war had affected Vera, but she had grown up in Riga free from stress and famine. However, Irène's formative years were lived against the background of the Nazi war with its perennial fear and endless malnutrition, so that her immune system suffered profoundly.

A number of allergies, potential from childhood, erupted in later years, leading on to MCS (Multiple Chemical Sensitivity syndrome). Irène became allergic to a vast range of chemicals, making it dangerous to leave her house, or to be treated by normal medicaments. She required special food and a home that, as far as possible, was free from the many chemicals that float in our atmosphere.

As a result of her own experience and her wish to help others, Irène became one of the first of the few practitioners involved in the field of clinical ecology in Britain, accepted as such by professional bodies. From 1971 to 1987 she practised this skill, helping afflicted people, and also animals, even having patients recommended to her by conventional physicians. Her studies in this field intensified and continue today.

I have seen letters from grateful patients ('You have given me back my soul,' wrote one grateful woman) that testify to her signal achievements. Once, unbelievably, she cured a pedigree goat of its allergies, whilst she explored allergies such as the one that causes dogs to bark continually. Animals were, and remain, very important in Irène's life.

Yet, between these two women, sharing abundant gifts, encouraging and supporting each other, living through each other, there developed a further and less material side to their lives. There was obviously something about Vera that had charmed and captivated people, whether famous statesmen and musicians, or ordinary workers and clerks. Likewise there emanated from Irène a quality that overcame adversity and seemed to impress itself on both humans and animals. Both women suffered terribly, and suffering is often said either to destroy hope or to encourage and enliven perception and sensitivity.

With Vera and Irène, the latter was the case. They developed spiritual insights which advanced their healing gifts. Together they healed an animal simply by covering it with their hands. What we today call spiritual healing has been part of man's entire recorded history, yet only more widely acknowledged from the twentieth century. Alongside this, Irène developed mediumistic qualities which enabled her to keep in touch with Vera, and with others, long after the latter's death, in what Judaism calls the world-to-come, but which is really nothing more that the world next to ours.

We can trace these gifts back to ancestors of Vera, the Hassidic masters of the eighteenth century to whom the development of the spirit was of supreme importance. Many believe that the gifts of a healer and a medium are inherited. If so, it is not surprising that both are evident in the Vera-Irène entity. In fact, everything both Irène and I have endeavoured to do in presenting this version of the book has been influenced by Vera's wishes through her constant contact with her daughter.

The lives of these two women encompass much of modern Jewish history, elsewhere recorded in detail by noted historians. Yet historians do not have the personal experiences Vera describes, the bursts of luxury, rare amidst the grinding poverty of the Jewish masses, the endless pogroms and persecutions, invariably based on centuries of church indoctrination, the birth of modern Zionism with its revival of the ancient Hebrew tongue, the many gifted Jewish artists and musicians, religious orthodoxy and secular enlightenment, the gleaming hopes of democracy and the restoration of Jewish self-respect amidst the dark nights of Nazi and Communist ideology.

And the lives of these two women illustrate so forcibly the triumph of hope over despair, of love over hate, of life over death

APPENDIX 6

Glossary of Names and Terms referred to by Vera Chesno

LIST A: PEOPLE

Achad Ha'am (literally 'one of the people') (1856-1927)
Pen-name of Asher Ginzberg, essayist and philosopher. Born in Ukraine, moved to Odessa, lived later in London, before settling in Tel Aviv in 1922. Believed in a spiritual and cultural Zionism, based on Judaism, to underpin the physical return to the land of Israel.

Aleichem, Sholem (literally 'peace be unto you') (1859-1916)
Pseudonym of Shalom Rabinovitch. Celebrated and much-loved Yiddish novelist and humorist. Born in Ukraine, died in United States. Best known for creating character of Tevye the Dairyman, basis of the popular musical *Fiddler on the Roof,* and for his humorous portrayal of Jewish life in the East European *steitl* (village).

Bakst, Léon (1866-1924)
Jewish artist from Russia, noted for his theatre decors, especially those executed for Diaghilev's Russian ballet in Paris. He revolutionised the application of decorative arts for the theatre.

Balfour, Arthur James (Lord) (1848-1930)
British statesman and philosopher. Negotiated with Herzl,
1902-3. Impressed by Chaim Weizmann's personality and Zionist philosophy. In 1917, as Foreign Secretary, issued the Balfour Declaration. In 1925, he opened the Hebrew University in Jerusalem.

Bar-Ilan (Berlin), Meir, Rabbi (1880-1949)
Prominent in Mizrahi, a religious Orthodox Zionist movement. President of Mizrahi for many years. In 1926 he settled in Jerusalem. Wrote autobiography, *From Volozhin to Jerusalem.* Bar-Ilan University near Ramat Gan was named after him. An uncle of Vera Chesno.

Benois, Alexandre (1870-1960)
Russian painter, art historian, and designer. Born in St Petersburg, moved to Paris in 1926. Worked with Diaghilev's Ballets Russes as artistic director alongside Leon Bakst. Designed sets and costumes. Noted for his work on *Petroushka* (1911). Also designed for Paris Opera and La Scala, Milan.

Berlin, Isaiah, Sir (1909-1998)
Outstanding scholar. British political scientist. Professor of social and political theory at Oxford University. Author of works on philosophy, Russian history, literature and political thought. Born in Riga. Awarded Order of Merit by Queen Elizabeth II. A relative of Vera Chesno.

Chaliapin, Feodor Ivanovitch (1873-1938)
Russian opera singer, born in Kazan. Became leading interpreter of bass role in Russian and Italian opera, particularly as Boris Godunov and Ivan the Terrible. World-famous, he toured extensively in many countries.

Cocteau, Jean (1889-1963)
French playwright, novelist, poet, film director and writer. Wrote *Les Enfants Terribles* (1929), and modern versions of Classic Greek stories. Collaborated with Picasso, Stravinsky and others in works for the stage.

Coué, Emile (1857-1926)
French psychotherapist. Was chemist, then studied hypnotism and auto-suggestion which became part of his treatment of patients to overcome illness, effecting organic changes. His famous formula, 'Every day, and in every way, I am becoming better and better', is proverbial.

Diaghilev, Sergei (1872-1929)
Famous Russian ballet impresario. Led celebrated company known as Diaghilev Ballet Russes. Organised concerts and performances in Paris and many countries. His original ideas revolutionised

choreography. Produced celebrated productions of *Petroushka, Three-Corned Hat* and many others.

Dizengoff, Meir (1861-1936)
Born in Bessarabia. Helped found city of Tel Aviv, of which he became distinguished mayor for over 12 years. Played a leading role in the city, founding economic and cultural concerns, including museum. Main square in the city is named after him.

Fernandel (1903-1971)
Actor. Born Fernand Joseph Désiré Contandin in Marseilles. Noted for his horsey jaw, tombstone teeth and huge grin. Awarded Légion d'Honneur for his comic acting. Appeared in many films, several for Sacha Guitry and Marcel Pagnol. Famous for his Don Camillo roles.

Glazounov, Alexander (1865-1936)
Russian composer, born in St Petersburg. Studied with Rimsky-Korsakov. Composed symphony at age of sixteen. Conducted his own works in London and Paris. Became Professor at St Petersburg Conservatoire and later its Director.

Heifetz, Jasha (1901-1987)
Famous violinist. Born in Vilna. Appeared in concerts from age of five. After 1917 Revolution in Russia, he settled in United States. In 1924 he donated a concert hall to Tel Aviv. Transcribed many works for the violin and wrote original compositions.

Horowitz, Vladimir (1904-1989)
Celebrated pianist. Born in Kiev, Russia. Toured widely in Europe and United States where he settled. Married daughter of Toscanini, the famous conductor. Noted for his great technical fluency.

Jabotinsky, Vladimir (1880-1940)
Born in Odessa. Zionist leader, journalist, writer, orator. Prominent in Jewish self-defence. Helped form Zion Mule Corps and Jewish Battalion in which he served in 1918. Leader of Zionist Revisionists, activist. Gifted linguist and translator. Buried on Mt Herzl, Jerusalem.

Kerensky, Alexander (1881-1970)
Russian political leader. Prominent as defence lawyer. After February 1917 Revolution became Minister and later Prime Minister. Fled from St Petersburg after October Revolution. Lived in Paris and later United States.

Lenin, Vladimir Ilyich Ulyanov (1870-1924)
Founder and guiding spirit of October Revolution of 1917, the Soviet Union and the Communist International. Attended St Petersburg University, became lawyer but devoted his life to overthrow of capitalist system, as leader of Bolshevik party. Died in 1924 after a series of strokes.

Lloyd George, David (1863-1945)
British statesman of Welsh origin. As young lawyer represented Zionist organisation. Was Prime Minister at time of issue of Balfour Declaration. Noted for role as Chancellor of Exchequer in 1909-10 and as War Premier from 1916 and peacetime Prime Minister. Outstanding orator and Parliamentarian.

Michoelis (Mikhoels), Solomon (1890-1948)
Born in Russia. Well-known actor and director of the Jewish State Theatre in Moscow which presented literary plays in Yiddish, including those of Sholem Aleichem, Shakespeare, Pushkin and Gorky. Executed in purge by Soviet dictator Stalin.

Milstein, Nathan (1904-1992)
Celebrated violinist. Born in Russia. Left there in 1925. Appeared with major orchestras throughout Europe. Settled in United States in 1928.

Mohilever, Samuel, Rabbi (1824-1898)
Born in Lithuania. Leading orthodox Rabbi in many communities, including Radom and Bialystok. Devoted himself from 1880s to Hovevei Zion (Lovers of Zion) movement and Jewish settlement in land of Israel, which led later to the work of Herzl and the Zionist movement.

Nijinsky, Vaslav (1890-1950)
Born in Kiev. Considered one of greatest ballet dancers of all time. After début with Imperial Russian Ballet, he joined Diaghilev's company as dancer and choreographer. Ceased dancing in 1918 due to illness. Died in London.

Pavlova, Anna (1885-1931)
Born in St Petersburg, joined Imperial Ballet School, became prima ballerina. Appeared worldwide, and in Diaghilev's company in Paris. Most famous ballerina of her generation, noted for performances in *The Dying Swan, Les Sylphides* and *Coppélia*. Lived for a period in London.

Piatigorsky, Gregor (1903-1976)
Famous cellist. Born in Russia. Performed with leading orchestras throughout the world. Settled in United States in 1929.

Rasputin, Grigori Yefimovich (1872-1916)
Russian monk, born in Siberia. Gained reputation as a 'holy man'. Many believed he exerted harmful influence on the last Russian Tsar and Tsarina due to their belief in his healing powers. A group of noblemen feared such influence and he was murdered by Prince Yusupov in 1916.

Rothschild family
Famous family of financiers and philanthropists founded by Meyer Amschel Rothschild (1743-1812). His five sons established branches in many European cities. Lionel Rothschild was first Jewish MP. His son Nathaniel was first Jewish peer. Edmond (1845-1934) greatly helped Zionist enterprises and agricultural settlements in land of Israel. Co-operated with Weizmann and Sokolov and Jewish Agency.

Schneerson family
Hasidic dynasty founded by Rabbi Schneur Zalman of Lyady. Centred originally in Russian village of Lubavich, now headquarters are in New York with branches worldwide. The seventh Rebbe was Menachem Mendel Schneerson who died in 1994.

Sokolov, Nahum (1860-1936)
Zionist leader and Hebrew journalist. Born in Poland. Established Hebrew newspapers, *Ha-Tzephireh* and *Ha-Olam*. Key figure in negotiations for Balfour Declaration. Became President of World Zionist Organisation and Jewish Agency. Wrote many books including *History of Zionism* and *Hibbath Zion*.

Temple, Shirley (1928-)
Famous as a child performer in films in 1930s. Made début at age of three. Later became a United States Ambassador. Born in California.

Trotsky, Leon (1879-1940)
Born Lev Bronstein in Ukraine. Played leading role with Lenin in 1917 October Revolution and founding of Soviet Union. Organised the Red Army. Negotiated Brest-Litovsk Treaty with Germany. Exiled in 1927 and assassinated by Stalin's agents in Mexico in 1940.

Yusupov, Prince Felix (1887-1967)
One of a small group of highly-placed Russian noblemen who were determined to end influence of the monk Rasputin over the Russian monarchy. As a result, Yusupov both poisoned and shot Rasputin dead. After the 1917 Bolshevik Revolution Yusupov lived in Paris.

Weizmann, Chaim (1874-1952)
Chemist, Zionist leader, first President of the State of Israel. Born in Russian Pale of Settlement. Moved to England in 1904. Helped British war effort 1914-1918 as scientist. Played leading role in issue of Balfour Declaration in 1917. President of World Zionist Organisation for many years. Retired to Rehovot in Israel to work at Weizmann Institute, where he is buried. Man of vision and deep Jewish knowledge and feeling.

Zalman, Shneur ben Baruch of Lyady (1747-1813)
One of the great figures of the Hassidic movement of the eighteenth century. Founded Habad Hassidim based on knowledge, wisdom and understanding. Emphasised study and contemplation. Noted for the Tanya, his interpretation of Kabbalah. Among his descendents were the Lubavicher Rebbes and Vera Chesno.

LIST B: ORGANISATIONS

BNEI BRIS (B'nai B'rith)
Worldwide fraternal body founded in New York in 1843, includes women's chapters. Based on principles of benevolence and brotherly love, its objectives are moral, social, philanthropic and educational.

ORT
Major worldwide Jewish body, founded in Russia in 1880, for the promotion and development by vocational training of skilled trades and agriculture among Jews. World ORT Union after 1945 undertook massive training programme in Israel and over 52 countries. Over 3,500,000 people have benefited from ORT schools and technical training.

OSE
Worldwide body, founded in 1912, for child care, health and hygiene among Jews, assisting mother and child, fighting epedemic diseases, disseminating knowledge about public health. Accredited to UNESCO, UNICEF and the WHO.

WIZO
Women's International Zionist Organisation. Major world body founded in 1920, involved in vast variety of welfare activities in Israel. Branches in many countries.

LIST C: RELIGIOUS BOOKS

Talmud
Great body of Jewish teaching incorporated in Palestinian Talmud and Babylonian Talmud compiled in first 500 years of the Current Era. Comprises 63 books, over 3,000,000 words, on an immense range of subjects. Major source of Judaism and Jewish learning.

Torah
The first five books of the Bible. The term is also used to cover a wider range of Jewish religious teaching.